STECK-VAUGHN
PRE GED® TEST PREPARATION

SCIENCE

- Instruction at manageable reading levels and practice of basic skills aligned to the 2014 GED® Test content areas

- Emphasis on science practices and critical thinking skills

- Pretest and posttest assessments identify strengths and weaknesses

- Complete answers and explanations

**Houghton
Mifflin
Harcourt**

CONTENTS

CONTENTS

How to Use This Book

The purpose of this book is to help you develop the foundation you need to pass the GED® Science test. In this book, you will be introduced to different areas of life science, physical science, and Earth and space science. Throughout the book, you will learn a variety of thinking and reading skills. You will also learn graphic skills, such as interpreting diagrams and drawing conclusions from graphs, that are necessary for success on the GED® Science test.

Units

Unit 1: Life Science Life science is the study of living things, where they live, and how they affect each other. In this unit, you will develop such thinking skills as making inferences and predictions, distinguishing fact from opinion, and comparing and contrasting. The graphic illustrations in this unit also provide practice in skills such as interpreting diagrams and reading maps, timelines, and graphs. You will read articles about the human body, plants, animals, the environment, ecosystems, and evolution.

Unit 2: Earth and Space Science Earth and space science is the study of Earth and the universe. This unit covers skills such as drawing conclusions and reading tables and weather maps. You will read articles about Earth's geologic history, weather, the greenhouse effect, water resources, the planets, and the universe.

Unit 3: Physical Science Physical science includes the subjects of chemistry and physics. Chemistry is the study of matter and how it changes. Physics is the study of energy and forces, and how they affect matter. This unit includes skills such as understanding chemical formulas, reading line graphs, and making predictions. You will read articles about the chemistry of household chemicals and cooking, mixtures, solutions, combustion, machines, momentum, energy, and forces.

Pretest and Posttest

The Pretest is a self-check of what you already know and what you need to study. After you complete all of the items on the Pretest, check your work in the Answers and Explanations section at the back of the book. Then fill out the Pretest Evaluation Chart. This chart tells you where each skill is taught in this book. When you have completed the book, you will take a Posttest. Compare your Posttest score to your Pretest score to see your progress.

Lessons

Each unit is divided into lessons. Each lesson is based on the Active Reading Process. *Active reading* means doing something before reading, during reading, and after reading. By reading actively, you will improve your reading comprehension skills.

The first page of each lesson has three sections to help prepare you for what you are about to read. First, you will read some background information about the passage presented in the lesson. This is followed by the Relate to the Topic section, which includes a brief exercise designed to help you relate the topic of the reading to your life. Finally, Reading Strategies will provide you with a pre-reading strategy that will help you to understand what you read and a brief exercise that will allow you to practice using that strategy. These are activities you do before reading. Vocabulary words important to the lesson are listed down the left-hand side of the page.

The articles you will read are about interesting topics in science. As you read each article, you will see Skills Mini-Lessons. Here you learn a reading, science, or graphic skill, and you do a short activity. After completing the activity, continue reading the article. Two Skills Mini-Lessons appear in every article. These are the activities you do during reading.

After reading the article, you answer fill-in-the-blank, short-answer, and multiple-choice questions in the section called Thinking About the Article. Answering these questions will help you decide how well you understood what you just read. The final question in this section relates information from the article to your own real-life experiences.

Science Practice Focus

Each lesson is followed by Science Practice Focus pages that provide additional work with science practice skills. These scientific reasoning skills include drawing conclusions from data, making predictions based on evidence, and applying scientific models and theories.

Science at Work

Science at Work is a two-page feature at the end of each unit. Each Science at Work feature introduces a specific job, describes the science skills the job requires, and includes a related activity. It also gives information about other jobs in the same career area.

Unit Reviews and Mini-Tests

Unit Reviews tell you how well you have learned the skills in each unit. Mini-Tests follow each Unit Review. These timed practice tests allow you to practice your skills with the kinds of questions that you will see on the actual GED® Tests.

Answers and Explanations

Answers and explanations to every exercise question are at the back of this book, beginning on page 246. The explanation for multiple-choice questions tells why one answer choice is correct.

Use this Pretest before you begin Unit 1. Don't worry if you can't answer all the questions. The Pretest will help you find out in which science areas you are strong in and which you need to practice. Read each article, study any graphics, and answer the questions that follow. Check your answers on pages 246–248. Then enter your scores in the chart on page 11.

The Plant Cell

All living things are made of cells, the working units of the body. Plant cells differ from animal cells. Plant cells have a cell wall for strength. They also have a chemical called chlorophyll for making food. The food gives the plant cell energy and substances needed for growth. The diagram shows the structures of a plant cell and describes the function of each structure.

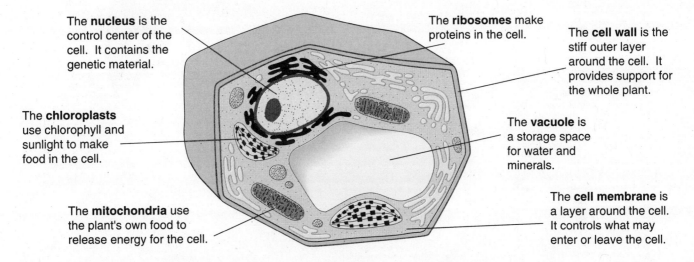

The **nucleus** is the control center of the cell. It contains the genetic material.

The **ribosomes** make proteins in the cell.

The **cell wall** is the stiff outer layer around the cell. It provides support for the whole plant.

The **chloroplasts** use chlorophyll and sunlight to make food in the cell.

The **vacuole** is a storage space for water and minerals.

The **mitochondria** use the plant's own food to release energy for the cell.

The **cell membrane** is a layer around the cell. It controls what may enter or leave the cell.

▶ Fill in the blank with the word or words that best complete each statement.

1. The control center of a cell is its _____ .

2. The _____ makes the plant cell stiff.

▶ Circle the letter of the best answer.

3. You can predict that a plant likely will need water when its

    A.   mitochondria are empty

    B.   chloroplasts are empty

    C.   vacuole is empty

    D.   ribosomes are empty

The Muscles of the Arm

Pick up a cup of coffee. You bend your elbow and raise your lower arm. This action is caused by a muscle in the upper arm. Now put down the cup of coffee. You straighten your elbow and move your lower arm down. This action is caused by another muscle in the upper arm.

Muscles work in pairs. The biceps muscle bends the elbow joint. The triceps muscle straightens the elbow joint. Why does it take two muscles to operate one joint? Muscles pull, but they cannot push. A muscle works by contracting, or shortening. When the biceps contracts, it pulls on the bones of the lower arm. The elbow joint bends. When the triceps contracts, it pulls on the same bones but in the opposite direction. When one muscle is contracting, its partner is relaxing.

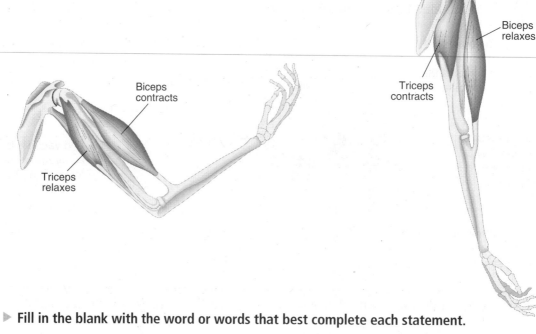

▶ **Fill in the blank with the word or words that best complete each statement.**

4. When a muscle _____, it gets shorter.

5. When one muscle in a pair is contracting, the other muscle is

_____.

▶ **Circle the letter of the best answer.**

6. The large muscles at the back of the thigh bend the knee joint. Where are the muscles that straighten the knee joint?

    A.   at the back of the thigh

    B.   at the front of the thigh

    C.   at the front of the lower leg

    D.   at the back of the lower leg

Bacteria

Bacteria are simple one-celled organisms. They can be found just about anywhere. The action of bacteria can be good for people, or it can be harmful. The bacteria that turn milk into cheese or yogurt are useful. These same bacteria also turn the milk in your refrigerator sour. Then they are not so useful.

If sour milk and yogurt are made by the same bacteria, why does sour milk taste so bad? The difference is in how the bacteria are controlled. When yogurt is made, the bacteria are killed before they make the product too sour. In your refrigerator, the bacteria keep on going. The result is that the milk gets much too sour. The bacteria that make milk sour use the sugar in the milk for energy. Their waste product, lactic acid, is the sour substance you taste in the spoiled milk.

The activity of bacteria depends on the temperature. People are often surprised when they find that food has gone bad in the refrigerator. Keeping food cool does slow down the bacteria. However, it does not stop their action. Freezing food does stop the action of bacteria. But it does not necessarily kill the bacteria. So food that has been in the freezer can spoil after it has been defrosted.

Bacteria can be killed by high temperatures. Milk and other dairy products are pasteurized. In this process, the milk is heated to a high temperature, then quickly cooled. The heat kills the bacteria. But once you take the milk home and open it, new bacteria may get in. Then the spoiling process begins.

▶ **Fill in the blank with the word or words that best complete each statement.**

7. _____ , which is a waste product of bacteria, makes spoiled milk taste sour.

8. Milk is turned into yogurt by the action of _____ .

▶ **Circle the letter of the best answer.**

9. Alex and Lila have samples of the same milk. They follow the same procedure to pasteurize the samples. Then they place drops of their pasteurized milk under similar microscopes and examine them. Alex observes active bacteria in the milk but Lila does not. Which of the following statements best explains their different findings?

   A. The activity of bacteria depends on the temperature.

   B. Bacteria can be killed by high temperatures.

   C. Freezing food stops the action of bacteria, but it does not necessarily kill them.

   D. Once you open the milk after pasteurizing, new bacteria may get in.

Go on to the next page.

The Flower

The reproductive organ of a plant is the **flower.** Flowers come in many shapes and sizes. Some are large and bright. Others are so small, you might not notice them.

Flowers make pollen. The pollen contains sperm, which is made in the anthers of the flower. The pollen is carried from one flower to another by insects, birds, or the wind. When pollen from one flower reaches another flower of the same kind, the sperm in the pollen joins with the egg, which is made in the ovary of the flower. The fertilized egg becomes a seed. The seed begins the next generation.

Flowers that are pollinated by insects such as bees often are bright in color. They have large petals, which give the bees a place to land. Many of these flowers also make nectar. This sweet juice attracts bees to the flower. When the bees drink the nectar, some of the sticky pollen gets on their bodies. This pollen rubs off when the bees get to the next flower.

The flowers of many trees and grasses are pollinated by the wind. These flowers usually have tiny petals. Some have no petals at all. The pollen is dry and dusty. These features make it easy for the pollen to blow from one plant to another.

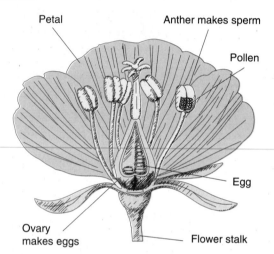

Petal | Anther makes sperm | Pollen | Egg | Ovary makes eggs | Flower stalk

▶ Write *insects* or *wind* in the space provided to identify each of the following as a characteristic of a plant that is pollinated by insects or by the wind.

10. Sticky pollen _____

11. Sweet nectar _____

12. Very small petals _____

13. Dry pollen _____

▶ Circle the letter of the best answer.

14. A student is designing a scientific investigation in which she will collect and compare only the parts of flowers that are necessary for reproduction. Which of the following should be a step in her investigation?

    A.   Collect anthers only.

    B.   Collect ovaries only.

    C.   Collect petals and anthers.

    D.   Collect anthers and ovaries.

Heat Transfer

Heat transfer is the flow of heat through a substance or from one substance to another. Some substances transfer heat better than others. A substance that transfers heat well is called a **conductor.** Most metals let heat flow through them easily, so they are considered to be good conductors. Most conductors of heat are also conductors of electricity. An **insulator** is a substance that does not transfer heat well. Many insulators block the flow of both heat and electricity. Most solid substances that are not metals are insulators.

Conductors and insulators have many commercial uses. For example, insulators like fiberglass insulation and wool coats help prevent heat from escaping from your warm house or body on a cold day.

Conductors and Insulators of Heat					
Conductors			**Insulators**		
Steel	Gold	Iron	Wood	Rubber	Glass
Aluminum	Copper	Brass	Most plastics	Most cloth	
Silver					

▶ **Fill in the blank with the word or words that best complete each statement.**

15. Straw is a substance that does not transfers heat well, which makes it an example of

a(n) _____ .

16. Platinum is a metal that transfers heat well, so it is an example of a substance called

a(n) _____ .

▶ **Circle the letter of the best answer.**

17. A student is designing a new thermos to keep beverages hot in cold weather. Which of the following materials would be the least effective for this purpose?

A.   plastic   C.   glass

B.   aluminum   D.   rubber

18. A hypothesis is a statement that explains something related to a problem or question. Scientists conduct experiments to test whether a hypothesis is correct. Ray and Sandra are planning an experiment. Ray wants to test the hypothesis that cardboard blocks the flow of electricity better than copper. Sandra wants to test the hypothesis that copper blocks the flow of electricity better than cardboard. Which of the following statements best explains what they should do?

A.   test Ray's hypothesis, because cardboard is more likely to be the better insulator

B.   test Ray's hypothesis, because cardboard is more likely to be the better conductor

C.   test Sandra's hypothesis, because copper is more likely to be the better insulator

D.   state a new hypothesis, because copper and cardboard are both likely to be good insulators.

The Water Cycle

When you are caught in a rainstorm, you are experiencing one step in the water cycle. The **water cycle** is the circulation of water on Earth and in its atmosphere.

Water covers more than half of the planet. This surface water is found in oceans, lakes, and rivers. Surface water is constantly both evaporating and condensing. Water in the atmosphere is also constantly evaporating and condensing. Where there is more water condensing in the atmosphere than evaporating, clouds form. When water droplets in a cloud join together, they may fall as precipitation. Rain, snow, and sleet are forms of precipitation. When it rains, some water soaks into the ground and some moves along the land to rivers and lakes.

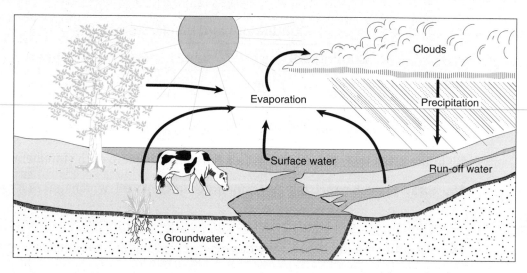

▶ **Match the part of the water cycle with its description. Write the letter of the part of the cycle in the blank at the left.**

Description	Part of the Water Cycle
_____ **19.** rain and snow	A. surface water
_____ **20.** lakes and oceans	B. groundwater
_____ **21.** water that soaks into the soil	C. precipitation
_____ **22.** water flowing over the top of the soil	D. run-off water

▶ **Circle the letter of the best answer.**

23. Suppose you randomly drop a pin on a map of Earth. The probability that the pin will land on a part of the map that represents water is

A. 50 percent

B. less than 50 percent

C. more than 50 percent

D. 100 percent

Rocks

Have you ever washed your hands with gritty soap? The soap probably had ground pumice in it. Pumice is a kind of rock. This rock forms when lava from a volcano cools and hardens. **Igneous rocks,** such as pumice and granite, form when melted rock hardens. Some buildings are made of granite.

Over a long period of time, wind and water can wear down rocks. Small pieces of the rocks are blown or washed away. These pieces may settle slowly and form layers. Such particles are called sediment. Slowly the layers harden, forming **sedimentary rocks**. Sandstone, limestone, and shale are sedimentary rocks. Sedimentary rocks are not as hard as igneous rocks. Sandstone and limestone wear away much faster than granite.

Igneous and sedimentary rocks can be changed into new forms. This is caused by high temperatures or great pressure. Rocks formed in this way are called **metamorphic rocks**. Marble is a metamorphic rock. You may have seen statues made of marble.

▶ **Fill in the blank with the word or words that best complete each statement.**

24. Rocks that form from the cooling and hardening of melted rock are called

_____ .

25. Rocks that form under high temperatures or great pressure are called

_____ .

▶ **Circle the letter of the best answer.**

26. A student observes and then classifies an unknown rock as a sedimentary rock. Which observation recorded by the student would best provide evidence to support her finding?

   A.   The rock contains layers of small pieces of granite.

   B.   The rock is the same color as known samples of shale.

   C.   The rock feels gritty like known samples of pumice.

   D.   The rock occurs near other layers of limestone.

27. An area where many igneous rocks are found may once have had

   A.   many rivers

   B.   large amounts of sediment

   C.   high pressure

   D.   volcanoes

Go on to the next page.

The Atom

All matter is made up of atoms. An **atom** is made up of three types of particles. **Protons** are particles with a positive electrical charge. **Neutrons** have no charge. Protons and neutrons are found in the **nucleus,** or center, of an atom. All atoms of a particular element have the same number of protons. The number of neutrons can vary.

Orbiting around the nucleus are **electrons,** particles with a negative electrical charge. The number of electrons in an atom is equal to the number of protons. That means the amount of positive and negative electric charge is the same, so overall an atom has no charge. If an atom gains or loses an electron, it is called an ion. An ion has a charge.

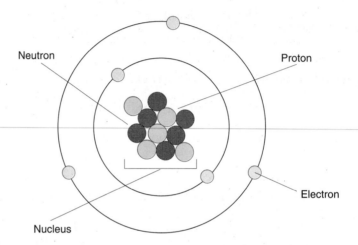

▶ **Match the name of the particle with its description. Write the letter of the particle in the blank at the left. Letters may be used more than once.**

Description	Particle
_____ **28.** has no electric charge	A. proton
_____ **29.** not found in the nucleus	B. neutron
_____ **30.** has a positive electric charge	C. electron
_____ **31.** a negatively charged ion has an extra one	

▶ **Circle the letter of the best answer.**

32. Which sentence correctly describes the atom shown in the diagram?

    A.   It has 6 electrons, 5 protons, and a negative charge.

    B.   It has 5 electrons, 5 protons, and no charge.

    C.   It has 6 neutrons, 6 protons, and no charge.

    D.   It has 5 electrons, 6 protons, and a positive charge.

States of Matter

On Earth, all matter is found in three states: **solid, liquid,** and **gas.** The table below shows the properties of these states. The state of matter of a substance depends on its temperature. Each substance changes state at different temperatures. At low temperatures, substances are solids. Sugar, salt, and plastic are solids at room temperature. If a solid is heated, it changes to a liquid. Water and alcohol are liquids at room temperature. If a liquid is heated, it changes to a gas. Air is a mixture of substances that are gases at room temperature.

State	Temperature Range	Shape	Volume
solid	lowest	definite (does not change)	definite (does not change)
liquid	middle	not definite; takes the shape of its container	definite (does not change)
gas	highest	not definite; takes the shape of its container	not definite; expands to fill the volume of its container

▶ **Circle the letter of the best answer.**

33. In which state or states of matter does the volume stay the same?

    A. solid only   C. gas only

    B. liquid only   D. solid and liquid only

34. Which of the following can you predict will happen if you cool liquid alcohol enough so that it forms a solid?

    A. Its shape will change from not definite to definite.

    B. Its shape will change from definite to not definite.

    C. Its volume will change from not definite to definite.

    D. All of its properties will remain the same.

35. Pablo has a sample of water and a sample of an unknown substance. At room temperature, both samples are clear liquids. When Pablo heats the samples, the unknown substance changes to a gas at 79°C and the water changes to a gas at 100°C. Pablo concludes that the unknown substance is water. Which of the following statements is correct?

    A. Pablo's conclusion is supported because both substances change from a liquid to a gas when heated.

    B. Pablo's conclusion is not supported because each substance changes state at a different temperature.

    C. Pablo's conclusion is supported because both substances are clear liquids at room temperature.

    D. Pablo's conclusion is not supported because only one sample has a definite volume at room temperature.

Forces

A **force** is a push or pull. In a tug of war, two teams pull on a rope. Each team exerts a force on the rope. The forces act in opposite directions. If the two forces are equal, there is no movement. The forces are said to be balanced.

Suppose an extra player joins one team. The extra player increases that team's force. Now the forces are not balanced, and there is movement. A change in movement is called acceleration. The rope accelerates, moving in the direction of the greater force. The team with the extra player wins.

If you hold a ball in your hand, the forces on the ball are balanced. **Gravity** pulls down on the ball. Your hand exerts an upward force that balances the force of gravity. If you let go of the ball, your force changes, but gravity does not. Gravity "wins," and the ball accelerates in the direction of the pull of gravity.

If you throw a ball, the forces involved get more complicated. When you throw the ball, you exert a force on it. The forward force of your hand is opposed by the force of **friction** between the ball and the air. These forces are not balanced. Because your force is greater, the ball moves in the direction you throw it. Once the ball leaves your hand, you exert no force on it. Friction continues to act on the ball. This force is not balanced, so it changes the motion of the ball. The ball slows down. At the same time, gravity pulls on the ball. This downward force is not balanced by another force. So the ball falls down as it moves forward.

▶ **Fill in the blank with the word or words that best complete each statement.**

36. A _____ is a push or a pull.

37. A change in movement is called _____.

▶ **Circle the letter of the best answer.**

38. Which of the following is an effect of an unbalanced force?

    A. acceleration

    B. gravity

    C. friction

    D. a push

39. In an experiment, Emma observes the effect of gravity acting on a block. To record her observations in a drawing, which of the following arrows should she use to show the direction that gravity acts on the block?

    A. ↑

    B. →

    C. ↓

    D. ←

Pretest Evaluation Chart

The chart below will help you determine your strengths and weaknesses in the four content areas of science.

▶ **Directions**

Check your answers on pages 246–248. Circle the number of each question that you answered correctly on the Pretest. Count the number of questions in each row that you answered correctly. Write the number in the Total Correct space in each row. (For example, in the Life Science row, write the number correct in the blank before *out of 14*). Complete this process for the remaining rows. Then add the four totals to get your total correct for the whole Pretest.

Content Area	Question	Total Correct	Practice Pages
Life Science (Pages 12–93)	1, 2, 3 4, 5, 6 7, 8, 9 10, 11, 12, 13, 14	_____ out of 14	Pages 14–19 Pages 30–35 Pages 54–59 Pages 62–67
Earth and Space Science (Pages 94–159)	19, 20, 21, 22, 23 24, 25, 26, 27	_____ out of 9	Pages 128–133 Page 137
Physical Science (Pages 160–233)	15, 16, 17, 18 28, 29, 30, 31, 32 33, 34, 35 36, 37, 38, 39	_____ out of 16	Pages 194–199 Pages 162–167 Pages 170–175 Pages 210–215

Total Correct for Pretest: _____ out of 39

If you answered fewer than 35 questions correctly, look more closely at the four content areas of science listed above. In which areas do you need more practice? Page numbers to refer to for practice are given in the right-hand column above.

Life science is the study of living things and biological processes. Living things include plants, animals, and other organisms. You use knowledge of life science when you make choices that affect your personal health and environment. Understanding life science can help you better understand yourself and your world.

List three living things you saw today. _____

_____

List two things you did today to keep yourself healthy. _____

_____

Thinking About Life Science

You may not realize how often you use life science as you go about your daily life. Think about your recent activities.

Check the box for each activity you have done recently.

☐   Did you exercise?

☐   Did you choose to eat one food over another?

☐   Did you take care of a pet?

☐   Did you water a plant?

☐   Did you go to a doctor?

☐   Did you recycle an item?

Write some other activities where you used life science.

_____

_____

_____

Previewing the Unit

In this unit, you will learn:

- what living things have in common
- how different parts of your body work
- how organisms pass traits to their offspring
- how germs cause disease
- how living things relate to one another and to their environment
- how living things can change over time

Lesson	**1**	**The Cell**
Lesson	**2**	**Blood Vessels**
Lesson	**3**	**Bones and Muscles**
Lesson	**4**	**Reproduction and Development**
Lesson	**5**	**Genetics**
Lesson	**6**	**Bacteria and Viruses**
Lesson	**7**	**Life Cycles**
Lesson	**8**	**Ecosystems**
Lesson	**9**	**Evolution**

THE CELL

Sitting in the sun feels good. It feels so good that many people find it hard to believe that the sun can be harmful. In the past, a tan was even considered a sign of good health.

Tanning is no longer considered safe. And getting a sunburn is even more dangerous. Both tanning and burning can cause skin cancer. Harmful rays in sunlight can cause skin cells to grow in abnormal ways.

Vocabulary

ultraviolet light

basal cell skin cancer

squamous cell skin cancer

melanoma

cell

cytoplasm

ribosome

mitochondria

nucleus

cell membrane

Relate to the Topic

This lesson is about skin cancer, the abnormal growth of skin cells. It explains the types of skin cancer, how sunlight can cause it, and how you can prevent it. Have you or someone you know ever had any problems from staying out in the sun?

Describe what happened.

_____

_____

What do you usually do to help yourself stay safe when you go out in the sun?

_____

_____

Reading Strategy

SCANNING BOLDFACED WORDS **Scanning** means to quickly look over something to find specific information. Scanning and skimming are two ways to preview something. Technical terms in science materials are often highlighted in **bold type**—type that is darker than the type around it. Look at the boldfaced terms on page 15. Then answer the questions.

1. What is ultraviolet light?

_____

_____

Hint: Look at the first paragraph.

2. Write the technical terms for two kinds of skin cancer.

_____

_____

Hint: Look under the heading Types of Skin Cancer.

Sunlight and Skin Cancer

Each year, millions of Americans relax at beaches, by pools, or in the mountains. Many people work outdoors in the sun. Some people go to tanning parlors to get a bronzed look. However, exposure to **ultraviolet light,** a type of light given off by the sun and by tanning lamps, can cause skin cancer. In fact, there are close to two million new cases of skin cancer in the United States each year. That makes skin cancer the most common cancer in this country. Skin cancer is also the easiest form of cancer to treat and cure.

Types of Skin Cancer

There are three types of skin cancer. They are called basal cell, squamous cell, and melanoma.

The most common and least dangerous skin cancer is **basal cell skin cancer.** It is estimated that there are more than one million new cases of this type of skin cancer each year. Basal cell skin cancer often appears on the hands or face. It may look like an open sore, reddish patch, mole, shiny bump, or scar. Basal cell skin cancer grows slowly and rarely spreads to other parts of the body. When found early and removed, basal cell skin cancer can almost always be cured.

Squamous cell skin cancer is more dangerous than basal cell skin cancer. There are about a half million new cases of this skin cancer each year. Squamous cell skin cancer looks like raised pink spots or growths that may be open in the center. This cancer grows faster than basal cell skin cancer. Squamous cell skin cancer can spread to other parts of the body. If it is not treated, this type of skin cancer may lead to death.

The most dangerous of the three types of skin cancer is **melanoma.** The most recent data shows there about 75,000 new cases each year. This type of skin cancer may grow in a mole or on clear skin. Melanomas are oddly shaped blotches that turn red, white, or blue in spots. They become crusty and bleed, and they grow fast. When melanomas reach the size of a dime, it's likely that they have spread and become deadly. About 9,500 people die of melanoma each year in the United States.

▶ Finding the Main Idea One way to make sure you understand what you read is to find the main idea of each paragraph. A paragraph is a group of sentences about one **main idea** or topic. The main idea is usually stated in one sentence which is called a **topic sentence.**

Reread the first paragraph on this page. The first sentence is the topic sentence. It makes a general statement about the topic of the paragraph. All the other sentences give details about the topic.

Which of the following is the main idea of this paragraph?

A. Melanoma is the most dangerous type of skin cancer.

B. Thousands of people die of melanoma each year.

How Sunlight Causes Skin Cancer

The human body is made of many cells. A **cell** is the smallest unit of a living thing that can carry on life processes such as growing, responding, and reproducing itself. The cells in our bodies have special jobs and work together to keep us alive. These cells are organized into different tissues, which form organs, which, in turn, make up organ systems.

A typical animal cell is shown here. This is a normal cell, not a cancer cell.

A Healthy Human Cell

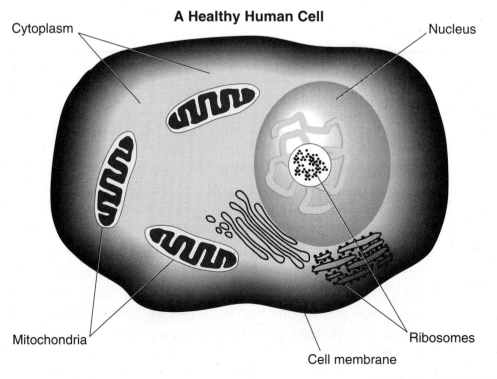

Cytoplasm

Nucleus

Mitochondria

Cell membrane

Ribosomes

A cell has many parts. A jellylike material, called **cytoplasm,** makes up most of the cell. **Ribosomes** are cell parts that make the proteins the cell needs to grow. **Mitochondria** give the cell the energy it needs to grow and reproduce.

The part of the cell that controls all cell activities is the **nucleus.** When a normal cell reproduces, it divides into two cells. Each new cell gets its own complete copy of the nucleus. The ultraviolet rays in sunlight can cause changes in the nucleus of a skin cell. When this happens, the cells divide abnormally. Cancer is cell division that is out of control.

The **cell membrane** covers the cell. Most cells stop dividing when they touch another cell. However, cancer cells keep dividing, even if they crowd the cells near them.

▶ Interpreting Diagrams   A **diagram** is a picture that explains what something looks like or how it works. A diagram usually has a title and labels. The title tells the main idea of the diagram. The labels point out different parts of the diagram. Lines usually connect each label to the part of the diagram it names.

Look at the diagram on page 16. Read the diagram's title and labels. Which of the following types of information are you likely to learn from this diagram? Circle the letter of the correct answer.

A. the growth stages of a cancer cell

B. the main parts of a healthy cell

Preventing Skin Cancer

The color of your skin has a lot to do with how likely you are to get skin cancer. In general, people with light skin are the most likely to get skin cancer. People with darker skin, including most Asians and Hispanics, are less likely to get skin cancer. African Americans are least likely to get skin cancer.

Here are some things you can do to protect yourself from skin cancer.

- Spend less time in the sun, especially between 10 A.M. and 4 P.M.

- Wear long sleeves and a hat to protect your skin.

- Always wear a sunscreen with an SPF (Sun Protection Factor) of at least 15. Apply it to all of the exposed areas of your body, including the tops of your ears and your lips. Use a sunscreen even on cloudy days. Sunscreens may not protect against melanomas, but they do give important protection against sunburn and less harmful skin cancers.

- Do not use tanning parlors.

- Check your skin for new growths or sores that do not heal. If you find any of these, see a doctor right away. Early treatment for skin cancer is very important.

Thinking About the Article

Practice Vocabulary

▶ **The terms below are in the passage in bold type. Study the way each term is used. Then match each term with its meaning. Write the letter.**

_____ **1.** cell membrane

_____ **2.** cytoplasm

_____ **3.** cell

_____ **4.** nucleus

_____ **5.** mitochondria

_____ **6.** ribosome

A. the outer covering of a cell

B. the control center of a cell

C. smallest unit of a living thing that carries on life processes

D. the jellylike material that makes up most of the cell

E. the cell part that makes proteins

F. the parts of the cell that provide energy

Understand the Article

▶ **Write or circle the answer to each question.**

7. Describe the three types of skin cancer.

_____

_____

_____

8. How can sunlight cause skin cancer?

A. The ultraviolet rays in sunlight cause bacteria and viruses to grow on skin.

B. The ultraviolet rays can cause skin cells to grow and reproduce abnormally.

9. What is the relationship between skin color and the likelihood of getting skin cancer?

A. The lighter the skin, the more likely a person is to get skin cancer.

B. The darker the skin, the more likely a person is to get skin cancer.

10. How are the cells in our bodies organized?

_____

_____

_____

Apply Your Skills

▶ **Circle the letter of the best answer for each question.**

11. What is the main idea of the first paragraph on page 15?

   A.   Millions of Americans enjoy the sun.

   B.   Sunlight can cause skin cancer.

   C.   More than one million Americans get skin cancer each year.

   D.   Skin cancer can usually be treated and cured.

12. Look at the diagram on page 16. Where in the cell are the mitochondria located?

   A.   outside the cell membrane

   B.   in the nucleus

   C.   in the cytoplasm

   D.   under the ribosomes

13. Under which heading in the article would you find information about protecting yourself from skin cancer?

   A.   Sunlight and Skin Cancer

   B.   Types of Skin Cancer

   C.   How Sunlight Causes Skin Cancer

   D.   Preventing Skin Cancer

Connect with the Article

▶ **Write your answers in the space provided.**

14. Why would it be a good idea to have any moles checked periodically by a doctor?

_____

_____

_____

15. How will you protect your skin the next time you go outdoors?

_____

_____

_____

Check your answers on pages 248–249.

SCIENCE PRACTICE FOCUS

How Long Do Cells Live?

The adult human body consists of trillions of cells. New cells replace some cells after they die. A cell reproduces by dividing, which is a process called **mitosis.** Some cells in the body are replaced every few days. Other cells may never be replaced. The table below shows the average life span of different types of cells in the human body.

Human Cell Type	Average Lifespan
Muscle	15 years
Stomach lining	2 days
Bone	25–30 years
Colon lining	4 days
Nerve	Lifetime of the person
Liver	250–500 days
Red blood	120 days

▶ **Circle the letter of the best answer.**

1. Which of the following cells has the shortest lifespan?

   A. nerve

   B. muscle

   C. stomach lining

   D. red blood

2. Which of the following cells has the longest lifespan?

   A. colon lining

   B. red blood

   C. liver

   D. bone

3. Which of the following conclusions is supported by the data in the table?

   A. The most important cells in the body have the longest lifespans.

   B. A cell's lifespan is related to its job or function in the body.

   C. At any given time, most cells in an adult human body are older than 30 years.

   D. Nerve cells are replaced more frequently than any other type of cell.

▶ **Write your answer to each question.**

4. Which sentence in the text supports the conclusion that some cells in the human body will never reproduce? Explain your choice.

_____

_____

_____

5. Why do you think the cells that line the stomach and colon have such short lifespans? Explain.

_____

_____

_____

_____

6. Why is it important to prevent damage to nerve cells? Explain.

_____

_____

_____

_____

7. Do you think that a skin cell has a short lifespan or a long lifespan? Explain.

_____

_____

_____

_____

8. Some cells in the body will self-destruct if they become damaged or infected. How do you think this process contributes to the health and well-being of the body?

_____

_____

_____

_____

Check your answers on page 249.

LESSON 2

BLOOD VESSELS

We've been hearing the message for years: Americans eat too many fatty foods, and fat is bad for the heart. Some people have listened to the message and changed their diet to include more fruits, whole grains, and vegetables and less meat and dairy products.

But it's also true that fat gives food a satisfying flavor, so many people find it hard to cut down. For those who can't resist potato chips, there are new versions of snack products to try. However, these products have pros and cons that you should consider.

Vocabulary

fat

cholesterol

saturated fat

monounsaturated fat

polyunsaturated fat

plaque

artery

Relate to the Topic

This article is about fats and cholesterol and how they affect the heart. It explains that cutting down on fats in the diet can help prevent heart disease.

List three of your favorite snack foods.

_____

_____

Do you think these foods are good for your heart? Why or why not?

_____

_____

_____

Reading Strategy

SKIMMING CIRCLE GRAPHS   A **circle graph** shows how parts of an amount are related to a whole amount. The circle represents the whole amount. The title tells you what kind of information is presented. Labels also tell you the name and amount of the parts, or wedges, that make up a circle graph. When you skim something, you read it quickly to get the main ideas. Skim the two circle graphs on page 25. Then answer the questions.

1. What is the topic of the two graphs?

_____

Hint: Look at the title.

2. What is each graph about?

_____

Hint: Look at the labels below each circle graph.

Eating Right for a Healthier Heart

Food labels can be confusing. They are full of words like *cholesterol, saturated fat, polyunsaturated fat,* and *monounsaturated fat.* Since eating too much fat and cholesterol can cause heart disease, it's important to know what's in your food.

Help with Reading the Labels

Many people confuse cholesterol and fat, although these substances are not the same. **Fats** are substances that provide energy and building materials for the body. Fats are found in oils, butter, milk, cheese, eggs, meat, and nuts. When the body takes in more food of any kind than it needs, it stores the extra food as fat. **Cholesterol** is a fatlike substance found in all animals, including humans. Some foods, such as egg yolks and shellfish, contain cholesterol. But most of the cholesterol in our bodies is made from the saturated fats in the foods we eat.

Saturated fat is a type of fat that is solid at room temperature. Most saturated fats come from animal products such as butter, cheese, meat, and egg yolks. Some vegetable oils, such as palm oil, also have saturated fat. Saturated fat increases cholesterol in the blood.

Monounsaturated fat is a type of fat found in some vegetable products, including olive oil, peanut oil, and peanut butter. Some scientists think monounsaturated fat lowers the body's cholesterol. Others believe it has no effect on cholesterol.

Polyunsaturated fat is a type of fat found in some vegetable foods and fish. Corn oil, almonds, mayonnaise, soybean oil, and fish are common sources of this fat. Polyunsaturated fat lowers the amount of cholesterol in the blood.

Meat and fried foods, such as potato chips, are usually high in fat and cholesterol.

The Effect of Fat and Cholesterol

Your body needs fat. Fat insulates the body from hot and cold. Fat stores energy. The body uses fats to build cells. Fats are needed to absorb certain vitamins. Women need fat to help regulate menstruation.

Your body also needs cholesterol. Cholesterol is an important part of all animal cells. It also helps protect nerve fibers. The body needs cholesterol to make vitamin D and other substances.

▶ Drawing Conclusions A **conclusion** is an idea that follows logically from facts or evidence. Scientists are careful not to draw a conclusion unless they have evidence to support it.

Which of the following is a conclusion that can be drawn about fats?
A. Fats are essential for the human body to function properly.
B. Cholesterol is harmful to the human body in any amount.

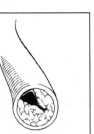

Cross sections of a healthy artery (top) and an artery clogged with plaque (bottom)

If fat and cholesterol have so many benefits, what is the problem? The problem is that too much fat and too much cholesterol can be harmful. Fat should provide less than 30 percent of the total daily calories in an average person's diet. Many people have trouble keeping their fat intake within these guidelines. Also, the body can make cholesterol.

What happens when there is too much fat and cholesterol in the diet? Extra cholesterol circulates in the blood. There it forms deposits called **plaque** on the inside walls of arteries. Too much fat can add to this problem. **Arteries** are large blood vessels that carry blood to all parts of the body. When they are clogged with plaque, arteries cannot carry as much blood. The heart must work harder to pump the same amount of blood through them. When the flow of blood to the heart muscle is blocked, a heart attack occurs. As a result, the person may die.

Studies have shown that people with a lot of cholesterol in their blood are most likely to have heart attacks. Reducing blood cholesterol can lower the risk of having a heart attack. The best way to do this is to eat less food that is high in cholesterol and saturated fats.

Food Companies Respond

Since so many people are looking for foods low in cholesterol and saturated fat, food companies have responded. One chain of fast-food restaurants changed its frying oil to one with less saturated fat and less trans fats (artificially produced solid fats). The new oil is high in polyunsaturated fats. They also added a salad bar and put more chicken and fish, which have less fat than beef, on the menu.

Some snack food companies have switched from saturated to polyunsaturated fats. Many have cut the fat content of their products. Some are using a controversial fat substitute called Olestra. Still, you have to read the labels carefully. "No cholesterol" does not mean "no saturated fat." Also, even low-fat versions of some products may still have a lot of fat.

Percent of Total Calories from Various Nutrients

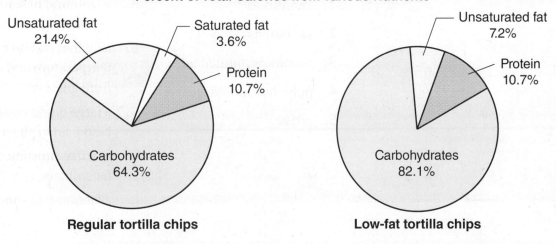

Regular tortilla chips   **Low-fat tortilla chips**

▶ Reading a Circle Graph Think of a circle graph as a pie. The circle is the whole pie. Each wedge is a piece of the pie. In the circle graphs above, the whole pie is the total percent of calories in one serving of tortilla chips (100%). Each wedge shows the percent of calories for one nutrient. Big wedges show big percents, and small wedges show small percents. For example, most of the calories in tortilla chips come from carbohydrates: 64.3 percent for the regular chips and 82.1 percent for the low-fat chips.

Look at the circle graphs to answer these questions.

1. What percent of the calories in the regular chips comes from unsaturated fat?
   A.   21.4%   B.   3.6%

2. The regular tortilla chips have about _____ times the amount of unsaturated fat as the low-fat chips.

What You Can Do

There are some simple things you can do to reduce your chances of heart disease. Start with your diet. Eat less meat, eggs, butter, ice cream, cheese, whole milk, and snack foods. Eat more whole grains, fruits, vegetables, lean meats, and low-fat dairy products. You also should get more exercise. Walking, running, swimming, and other aerobic exercises all help lower the body's cholesterol level. Stop smoking— that's also bad for your heart. Last, have your cholesterol level checked by your doctor. If it is too high, your doctor will probably suggest a diet and exercise.

Thinking About the Article

Practice Vocabulary

▶ **The terms below are in the passage in bold type. Study the way each term is used. Then match each term with its meaning. Write the letter.**

_____ **1.** cholesterol

_____ **2.** saturated fat

_____ **3.** monounsaturated fat

_____ **4.** polyunsaturated fat

_____ **5.** artery

A. a fat found in some vegetable products like olive oil

B. a fat that is solid at room temperature and usually comes from animals

C. a large blood vessel that carries blood fat to all parts of the body

D. a fatlike substance found in all fat animals

E. a fat found in some vegetables and fish

Understand the Article

▶ **Write or circle the answer to each question.**

6. What are fats?

A. substances that provide energy and building materials for the body

B. substances found only in animals, including humans

7. What happens to the extra cholesterol that the body cannot use?

_____

_____

8. Why does the heart have to work harder in a person with clogged arteries?

A. The arteries become narrower, so the heart has to work harder to pump the same amount of blood through them.

B. The heart becomes weaker because the person is not getting exercise.

9. What can you do to reduce your chance of getting heart disease? Circle the letter next to each action that will help.

A. Eat more meat, butter, and eggs.

B. Eat more whole grains, fruits, and vegetables.

C. Get more exercise.

D. Stop smoking.

Apply Your Skills

▶ **Circle the letter of the best answer for each question.**

10. This article discusses the effects of fat and cholesterol on the heart. What advice might be beneficial to someone recovering from a heart attack?

    A. Eat as many foods high in cholesterol as possible.

    B. Increase the amount of meat and eggs eaten per day.

    C. Eat foods low in saturated fat.

    D. Eat as few whole grains and vegetables as possible.

11. Look at the circle graphs on page 25. Which category contributes no calories to low-fat tortilla chips?

    A. unsaturated fat

    B. saturated fat

    C. carbohydrates

    D. protein

12. If you were on a low-salt diet, which tortilla chips would be better for you?

    A. The regular chips would be better because they have less salt.

    B. The low-fat chips would be better because they have less salt.

    C. Both types of chips would be okay.

    D. You cannot tell because the graphs do not show the salt content.

Connect with the Article

▶ **Write your answer to each question.**

13. Why should a person concerned about his or her heart health still read the labels on low-fat versions of foods?

_____

_____

_____

14. Suppose your friend finds out that his cholesterol level is high. Some of his favorite foods are cheese and bacon. If he doesn't change his eating habits, what health issues might he face in the future?

_____

_____

_____

SCIENCE PRACTICE FOCUS

Does Looking at Certain Colors Affect Blood Pressure?

Blood pressure is the force exerted on blood vessels when the heart beats. A doctor can get useful information about a person's heart and blood vessels by taking measuring his or her blood pressure. Generally, two measurements are made. The maximum blood pressure (systolic) occurs when the heart beats and pumps blood throughout the body. The minimum blood pressure (diastolic) occurs in the moments between beats when the heart is resting.

Suppose you are asked to design an investigation involving blood pressure. You are given a set of red, yellow, green, and blue cards and a blood pressure measuring device. Your assignment is to determine if looking at different colors affect a person's systolic blood pressure.

You might think that one of the colors will affect the results more than the other colors. This possible answer to a question is called a **hypothesis.** To test a hypothesis, a scientist may do a **controlled experiment.** A controlled experiment is an experiment that tests only one **variable,** or factor, at a time. The variable being changed by the scientist is called the **independent variable.** By changing just one variable, scientists can see the results of just that one change. The variable that changes as a result of the experiment is called the **dependent variable.** This variable depends on the changes made to the independent variable.

▶ **Write your answer to each question.**

1. Using the materials described above, explain how you would design an investigation to determine the effect of color on blood pressure.

   _____

   _____

   _____

   _____

   _____

2. State a hypothesis that your investigation will test.

   _____

   _____

▶ **Fill in the blank with the word or words that best complete each statement.**

3. The dependent variable in this investigation is _____ .

4. The independent variable in this investigation is _____ .

▶ **Kyle recorded the systolic blood pressures for four different subjects after looking at each of the four colors. He recorded the results of his investigation in the table below. Use the data to answer Questions 5–7.**

Subject	Maximum Blood Pressure			
	Blue	Red	Green	Yellow
1	95	105	95	104
2	94	102	95	100
3	100	108	100	107
4	102	112	102	111

5. What conclusion about color and blood pressure can you draw based on Kyle's data?

_____

_____

_____

6. Kyle did not have each subject look at the colors for the same amount of time. How might this have introduced a possible source of error in his investigation?

_____

_____

_____

▶ **Circle the letter of the best answer.**

7. Which of the following identifies a possible weakness in the design of Kyle's investigation?

  A. The subjects' names were not recorded.

  B. Too many subjects were used.

  C. Each subject's normal blood pressure was not measured and recorded.

  D. Only the systolic blood pressure for each subject was measured and recorded.

Check your answers on page 250.

BONES AND MUSCLES

Vocabulary

aerobic

osteoporosis

joint

sprain

ligament

Walking is a simple activity with excellent health benefits. It strengthens the heart, muscles, and bones. Because walking is a low-impact exercise, there is little chance of damaging your bones, muscles, or joints.

Best of all, walking doesn't require expensive gear, special clothing, or lessons. In this lesson, you will learn about the benefits of walking and other exercise to your bones and muscles.

Relate to the Topic

This lesson is about walking as a form of exercise. It explains the benefits of walking and shows its effects on muscles and joints. Suppose you wanted to convince a friend to start an exercise program.

Why might you recommend walking as a way to get started?

_____

_____

What are some of the points you would make to convince your friend of the importance of exercising regularly?

_____

_____

_____

Reading Strategy

SKIMMING DIAGRAMS   A diagram usually has a title and labels. The title tells you the topic of the diagram. You can skim a diagram to find its topic by looking at its title. Skim the diagrams on pages 32 and 33. Then answer the questions.

1. What is the topic of the diagram on page 32?

_____

Hint: Look at the title.

2. What is the topic of the diagram on page 33?

_____

Hint: Look at the title.

Walking for Fitness

Strolling through the mall or around town is a pleasant way to spend time. But did you know that by walking faster, you can improve your fitness and health? Walking at a fast pace gives the heart, lungs, muscles, and bones a good workout.

The Benefits of Walking

Walking is easy and it's convenient. You don't need expensive equipment, special clothing, or lessons to walk. All you need is a good pair of shoes and a little time. You can walk anywhere—around the block, on a track, or even indoors. Some malls open early so walkers can exercise before the shoppers arrive.

Walking is easy on the body. It doesn't jar the joints as jogging or tennis does. That makes walking safe for many people. In fact, doctors often recommend walking to patients recovering from heart attacks, operations, or some injuries.

Walking is a safe and inexpensive way to exercise.

Walking can be an aerobic exercise like jogging, swimming, or cycling. An **aerobic** exercise requires the body to take in extra oxygen. It strengthens the heart, because the heart is required to beat faster. It also increases the amount of oxygen taken in by the lungs. As you exercise, your heart delivers the oxygen-rich blood to your muscles, which helps them grow stronger.

Studies have shown that brisk walking may reduce the risk of heart disease, stroke, and high blood pressure. Other studies have shown that a brisk walk three times a week may lower cholesterol, lower stress, and even provide protection against certain types of cancer.

Walking uses up stored fat. Walking burns about the same number of calories per mile as jogging. It just takes longer to walk a mile than to jog. People who walk regularly and do not increase the amount they eat can lose weight slowly.

Improving Bones and Muscles

Walking uses major muscle groups in the legs, abdomen, and lower back. Walkers who exercise their arms as they walk can make the muscles of the upper body stronger, too.

Muscles work in pairs to move bones. The diagram below shows that when you push off the ground with your foot, you straighten your ankle. To do this, the calf muscles of the leg contract, or shorten. At the same time, the shin muscles relax, or lengthen. Then as you swing your leg forward, your foot lifts up. To bend the ankle this way, the shin muscles contract. At the same time, the calf muscles relax. This repeated movement improves the tone of the leg muscles.

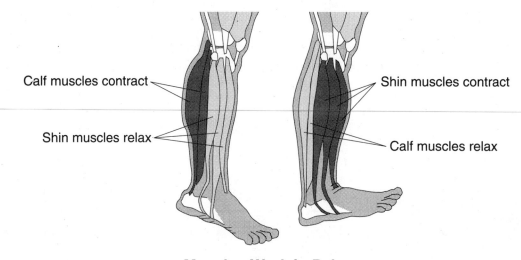

Calf muscles contract

Shin muscles relax

Shin muscles contract

Calf muscles relax

Muscles Work in Pairs

Exercise that increases muscle strength also benefits the bones. Exercise causes muscles to pull on the bones. As a result, the bones become stronger and more solid. This can help prevent **osteoporosis,** a condition of brittle bones. This problem affects many older people, especially women.

▶ Finding the Implied Main Idea Sometimes the main idea of a paragraph is not stated. Instead, it is hinted at, or **implied.** To find the implied main idea, you have to think about how the details in the paragraph are related to each other and to the topic of the article.

Reread the paragraph on this page that begins, "Exercise that increases. . . . " It discusses the effect of exercise on bones. The implied main idea is that **walking can benefit bones,** even though the word *walking* is never used.

Read the first paragraph on this page. Which of these ideas is implied?
A. Walking reduces pain in your lower back.
B. Walking strengthens muscles throughout your body.

Easy on the Joints

Walking is considered one of the safest forms of exercise because it doesn't jar the joints of the body. A **joint** is the place where two or more bones come together. There are several types of joints. Most allow some kind of movement. For example, a hinge joint works like the hinge on a door. The hinge allows the door to open and close. A hinge joint allows your knee to bend and straighten.

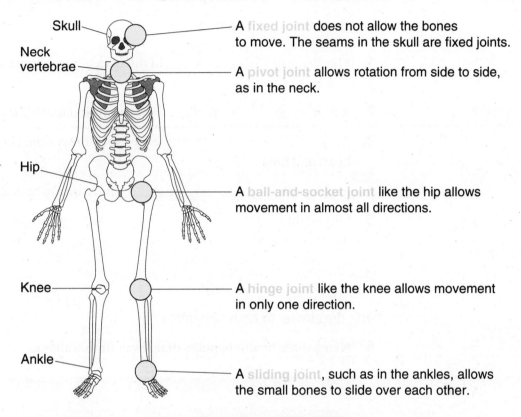

Skull

Neck vertebrae

Hip

Knee

Ankle

A fixed joint does not allow the bones to move. The seams in the skull are fixed joints.

A pivot joint allows rotation from side to side, as in the neck.

A ball-and-socket joint like the hip allows movement in almost all directions.

A hinge joint like the knee allows movement in only one direction.

A sliding joint, such as in the ankles, allows the small bones to slide over each other.

The Joints of the Body

Some physical activities, such as jogging, can put a lot of stress on joints. In some cases, runners sprain a leg or ankle. A **sprain** is a joint injury in which the ligaments are stretched too far or torn. **Ligaments** are strong bands of tissue that connect bones at joints. A ligament stretches much like a rubber band. Unlike joggers, walkers rarely hurt their ligaments.

▶ Comparing and Contrasting with Diagrams   When you tell how things are alike, you are **comparing**. When you tell how things are different from one another, you are **contrasting**.

Look at the diagram above. How do neck joints and knee joints differ? Circle the letter of the correct answer.

A.   Neck joints are fixed, while knee joints have a ball and socket.

B.   Neck joints are pivot joints, while knee joints are hinge joints.

Thinking About the Article

Practice Vocabulary

▶ **The words below are in the passage in bold type. Study the way each word is used. Then complete each sentence by writing the correct word.**

aerobic	osteoporosis	joint
sprain	ligament	

1. The _____ in the neck allows rotation from side to side.

2. A torn _____ is a common injury for runners.

3. A(n) _____ exercise improves the condition of your heart and lungs.

4. People with _____ have brittle bones.

5. You might _____ an ankle if you run on a hard, uneven surface.

Understand the Article

▶ **Write the answer to each question.**

6. Name three health benefits that result from walking.

   _____

   _____

   _____

7. Why is it necessary for muscles to work in pairs?

   _____

   _____

   _____

8. You decide to go for a fast walk to get some exercise. How can you tell whether you are walking fast enough for your exercise to be aerobic?

   _____

   _____

Apply Your Skills

▶ **Circle the letter of the best answer for each question.**

9. How can walking and jogging burn about the same number of calories per mile?

    A. Both walking and jogging reduce the risk of heart disease.

    B. It takes longer to walk a mile than to jog one.

    C. Both kinds of exercise can help you lose weight.

    D. Both kinds of exercise help to increase muscle strength.

10. Reread the paragraph below the diagram on page 33. Which of the following main ideas is implied?

    A. Sprains heal slowly.

    B. Ligaments stretch or tear easily.

    C. Walking does not put a lot of stress on joints.

    D. Jogging is an unsafe form of exercise.

11. Look at the diagram on page 32. How is the leg on the left different from the leg on the right?

    A. The calf muscles are relaxed.

    B. The calf muscles are contracted.

    C. The shin muscles are contracted.

    D. Both the shin and the calf muscles are relaxed.

Connect with the Article

▶ **Write your answer to each question.**

12. Choose one of the types of joints from the diagram on page 33. Explain how the joint works by comparing it to a common object.

    _____

    _____

    _____

13. Suppose you want to start an exercise program to lose weight and improve your overall health. Would you choose walking or jogging? Why?

    _____

    _____

    _____

 Check your answers on page 251.

SCIENCE PRACTICE FOCUS

Levels of Organization

There are five levels of cellular organization in multicellular organisms. The simplest level is the cell, the basic building block of all living things. **Tissue** is made up of similar cells that perform the same function. An **organ** is made up of a group of tissues that work together to perform a specific function. An **organ system** is a group of two or more organs. An organism is often composed of two or more organ systems.

The skeletal system is composed of many different kinds of bones. Bones are made up of two main types of bone tissue: compact and spongy. Osteocytes are mature bone cells found in compact bone tissue.

▶ **Complete the diagram using the terms below to show the levels of organization from least complex to most complex.**

bone   osteocyte

skeletal system   compact tissue

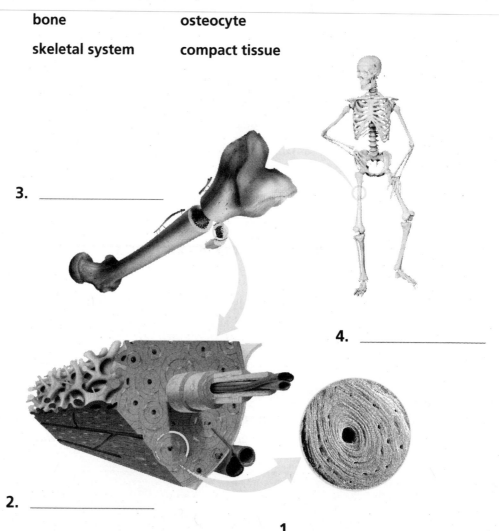

3. _____

4. _____

2. _____

1. _____

Body Systems

Body systems often work together to perform specific functions. The model below demonstrates how the biceps and triceps muscles work with bones to move the forearm.

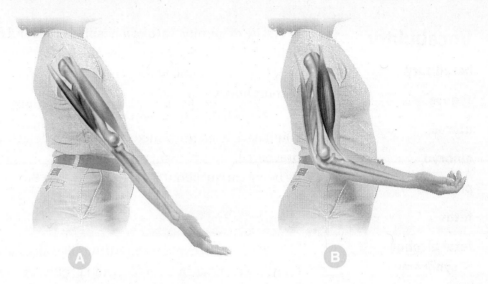

▶ **Circle the letter of the best answer.**

5. Which of the following statements is true for A?

   A. The biceps muscle is contracted.

   B. The triceps muscle is contracted.

   C. Both muscles are contracted.

   D. Neither muscle is contracted.

6. Which of the following statements is true for B?

   A. The biceps muscle is contracted.

   B. The triceps muscle is contracted.

   C. Both muscles are contracted.

   D. Neither muscle is contracted.

▶ **Write your answer to each question.**

7. Use the model to explain how muscles and bones work together to raise and lower the forearm.

_____

_____

_____

_____

REPRODUCTION AND DEVELOPMENT

Vocabulary

hereditary

zygote

uterus

embryo

placenta

fetus

fetal alcohol syndrome

The maternity ward of a hospital is a joyful place. Beaming relatives hold healthy babies. In contrast, the neonatal intensive care unit is stressful. Tiny babies are hooked up to tubes and monitors. Nurses and worried parents hover over them.

Some babies in a neonatal intensive care unit have conditions that could have been prevented. Not all birth defects and problems can be prevented, but pregnant women can help their babies during development by being careful about what they take into their bodies.

Relate to the Topic

This lesson explains how drugs like alcohol can pass from mother to baby. It describes birth defects and problems caused by certain drugs.

List three substances that might affect the development of an unborn baby.

_____

How would you persuade a friend not to drink alcohol during pregnancy?

_____

_____

Reading Strategy

ASKING QUESTIONS   Ask yourself questions as you read. This will help you understand what you read by making you more aware of important details and ideas. Read the first paragraph on page 39. Then answer the questions.

1. What is one question you could ask after reading the first paragraph?

_____

Hint: Follow your own interests.

2. What is one question that is likely to be answered later in the article?

_____

Hint: Look at the last sentence in the first paragraph.

Check your answers on pages 251–252.

Having a Healthy Baby

Scientists once thought that almost all birth defects were **hereditary.** This means that a problem is passed from parent to child through the father's sperm or the mother's egg. People did not realize that what a mother did during pregnancy could affect the health of her unborn child.

Then in the 1950s and 1960s, many pregnant women in Europe took a drug called *Thalidomide.* Thousands of these women had babies born with misshapen arms and legs. Over a 30-year period in the United States, millions of women took a drug called *DES.* This drug prevented miscarriages. But by 1970, daughters of many of these women had cancer. Studying the effects of these two drugs helped scientists focus their research. Since then, scientists have learned that unborn babies are affected by what their mothers eat, drink, and smoke.

A mother and her healthy baby

The Development of an Unborn Baby

In nine months, a new human being develops from one cell into an organism with billions of cells. A developing baby goes through three stages before it is born. First it is a zygote, then an embryo, and finally a fetus.

Zygote. A sperm from the father joins with the egg produced by the mother. This fertilized egg is called a **zygote.** The zygote divides and forms a hollow ball of cells, which makes its way toward the **uterus,** or womb. It floats freely in the uterus for a few days. Around the tenth day, the zygote attaches to the woman's uterus.

Embryo. From the third to the eighth week, the developing baby is called an **embryo.** The embryo is attached to the uterus by the placenta. The **placenta** is a structure that allows substances to pass between the embryo and the mother.

The placenta is like a filter. The mother's blood passes along one side of the placenta. The embryo's blood passes along the other side. The two bloodstreams are separated by thin blood vessels, through which nutrients and oxygen pass from the mother's blood to the embryo's blood. Waste and carbon dioxide pass from the embryo's blood to the mother's blood. Other substances in the mother's blood, such as drugs or chemicals, can pass through, too.

During this stage, the baby's main body organs and systems form. Birth defects are most likely to occur at this time. A harmful substance in the mother's blood can cause serious damage to the embryo.

Fetus. From the ninth week until the end of the ninth month, the developing baby is called a **fetus.** During these months, the fetus grows. Harmful substances are less likely to cause birth defects during this stage because the main systems and body have been formed. If damage occurred in the embryo stage, the damaged organ or system in the fetus may not work properly.

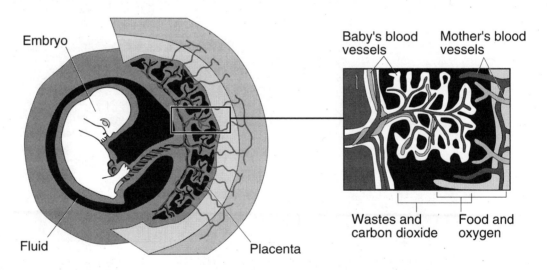

The Exchange of Substances Between Mother and Embryo

▶ Finding the Main Idea of a Diagram A diagram is a picture that helps you see how something looks or works. Like a paragraph or an article, a diagram has a main idea. You can figure out the main idea by looking at the diagram or by studying its title. Look back at the diagram on page 16. The title tells you the main idea: *This is what a healthy human cell looks like.*

Which of the following tells the main idea of the diagram above?
A.   Substances pass between mother and embryo.
B.   The embryo is attached to the mother by the placenta.

The Effects of Drugs

What happens when a pregnant woman smokes a cigarette, drinks a beer, or takes an aspirin? It's hard to prove what is harmful and what is not. But over the years, scientists have started to link some substances with certain problems.

Cocaine. The mother's use of cocaine can cause a miscarriage, early labor, or stillbirth (death of the fetus). Cocaine babies are often underweight. They may have damage to the brain, lungs, urinary system, or sex organs.

Cigarettes. The nicotine in cigarettes makes the blood vessels in the placenta shrink. Less oxygen and fewer nutrients reach the developing baby. Smoking has been linked to miscarriages and stillbirths. Babies born to smokers are often underweight at birth.

▶ Finding Details Details are specific facts that describe or explain the main idea of a paragraph, article, or diagram. For example, the main idea of the previous paragraph is that smoking cigarettes during pregnancy can affect a developing baby. A detail that supports this main idea is that the babies of smokers often are underweight at birth.

Place a check mark beside any details that you can find in the paragraph about smoking cigarettes during pregnancy.

_____ A. Nicotine shrinks placenta blood vessels.

_____ B. Nicotine can damage the baby's brain.

_____ C. Smoking is linked to stillbirths.

_____ D. Fewer nutrients reach the baby's blood.

Alcohol. A condition called **fetal alcohol syndrome (FAS)** can occur when the mother drinks alcohol while pregnant. Children with FAS may have abnormal heads, faces, arms, or legs. They often have low birth weights. Some have intellectual disabilities.

Common Medications. Few medications are known to cause serious harm to a developing baby. This doesn't mean, however, that most medications are safe. A pregnant woman should not take any medication without consulting her doctor. Even over-the-counter medications should be avoided. For example, some headache medications can cause problems when taken during the last three months of pregnancy.

Preventing Birth Defects

There is no way to guarantee a healthy baby. However, women can help lower the risks to their babies. A pregnant woman should eat a well-balanced diet. She should get regular medical care. A woman who is pregnant should not smoke or drink alcohol. She should not take cocaine or other illegal drugs. Also, she should check with her doctor before taking any medicines.

Check your answers on page 252.

Thinking About the Article

Practice Vocabulary

▶ The words below are in the passage in bold type. Study the way each word is used. Then complete each sentence by writing the correct word.

zygote　　　　**uterus**　　　　**embryo**

placenta　　　**fetus**

1. The fertilized egg, called a(n) _____ , attaches to the

   wall of the _____ , or womb, by the tenth day.

2. Main body organs and systems form while a developing baby is called a(n)

   _____ .

3. The _____ is a structure through which substances
   pass between mother and baby.

4. Harmful substances are less likely to cause birth defects after

   the developing baby becomes a(n) _____ .

Understand the Article

▶ Write or circle the answers to each question.

5. What two drugs helped focus research on what happens when a woman
   takes drugs during pregnancy?

   _____

6. How do nutrients and wastes pass between mother and baby in the
   placenta?

   _____

7. During which stage of development is the most serious damage to the
   unborn baby likely to occur?

   _____

8. List three drugs that have been linked with problems for babies.

   _____

9. What can a pregnant woman do to help ensure she has a healthy baby?
   Circle the letter next to each correct answer.

   A. eat a well-balanced diet　　　C. drink alcohol in moderation

   B. not smoke at all　　　　　　D. check with her doctor before
   　　　　　　　　　　　　　　　　　taking medicine

Apply Your Skills

▶ **Circle the letter of the best answer for each question.**

10. The diagram on page 40 has two parts. What is the main idea of the part on the left?

    A. The placenta is part of the mother, not the baby.

    B. The embryo is connected to the placenta, which is connected to the mother.

    C. The baby and mother exchange substances via the placenta.

    D. Food and oxygen pass from the mother to the baby.

11. Why are harmful substances least likely to cause birth defects in the last few months of pregnancy?
    By the last few months of pregnancy,

    A. all of the body organs have formed

    B. the placenta blocks harmful substances

    C. the fetus has stopped growing

    D. the fetus is not connected to the placenta

12. What should a pregnant woman who wants to have a healthy baby do?

    A. eat a well-balanced diet

    B. stop smoking if she smokes

    C. stop drinking alcohol if she drinks

    D. do all of the above

Connect with the Article

▶ **Write your answer to each question.**

13. Suppose a pregnant woman occasionally has a glass of wine with dinner. What problems might her baby have after she gives birth?

    _____

    _____

    _____

14. If you saw a friend who was pregnant smoking a cigarette, how would you explain to her that it was harming the baby?

    _____

    _____

SCIENCE PRACTICE FOCUS

Human Reproduction

For the human reproductive process to occur, sex cells need to be produced. Males produce sperm cells and females produce egg cells. Sperm and egg cells are formed through a process called **meiosis.** Meiosis involves two different cell divisions. It results in four new cells, each containing only one copy of each chromosome—a total of 23 chromosomes. When a sperm and egg cell come together during fertilization, the fertilized egg has a full set of 46 chromosomes.

Hormones are chemicals that are made in small organs called **glands.** Hormones can control the functions of different organs. The three hormones necessary for human reproduction are estrogen, testosterone and progesterone. Estrogen is the hormone that causes the growth and development of sexual characteristics in females. Testosterone is the hormone that causes the growth and development of sexual characteristics in males. Progesterone is produced in the female reproductive system and plays an important role in the menstrual cycle and pregnancy.

▶ **Write the answer to each question.**

1. What is meiosis?

_____

_____

2. Why does a human sex cell have only 23 chromosomes?

_____

_____

3. How do you think a gland can control the function of an organ?

_____

_____

_____

4. What role does estrogen play in the human body?

_____

_____

_____

Hormones and Menstrual Cycle

The menstrual cycle is controlled by the hormones estrogen and progesterone. The cycle is about 28 days long, and in the middle of the cycle, ovulation occurs. During ovulation, an unfertilized egg is released from the ovary and travels to the uterus. If the egg is fertilized by a sperm cell, then it will implant on the wall of the uterus and develop into an embryo. If the egg is not fertilized, then it will leave the body during the last half of the menstrual cycle.

The data table below shows the levels of estrogen and progesterone in the bloodstream during the menstrual cycle.

Hormone Levels During the Menstrual Cycle		
Day	Estrogen (pg/ml)	Progesterone (ng/ml)
1	50	0
4	50	0
7	90	0
10	100	0
13	400	2.5
16	100	3
19	175	8
22	290	11
25	150	4
28	50	0

▶ **Use the data table to answer the following questions.**

5. During which part of the menstrual cycle does estrogen rise to its highest level?

_____

_____

6. During which part of the menstrual cycle does progesterone fall to its lowest level?

_____

_____

7. What is the relationship between the estrogen and progesterone levels during the second half of the menstrual cycle?

_____

_____

8. Predict the progesterone level on Day 21 of the menstrual cycle. Explain your answer.

_____

_____

GENETICS

Do you and your mother have the same eye color or the same hair color? Do you have a nose shaped like your father's? Parents pass on features like these to their children. In fact, parents pass on more than appearance to their children.

For example, parents can pass on certain disorders or diseases to their children. Tests can detect if people are likely to get a disorder passed on by their parents. These tests cannot tell for sure whether a person will get a disorder—only if they are likely to get it.

Vocabulary

inherit

traits

heredity

genetics

dominant trait

recessive trait

Punnett square

genetic screening

amniocentesis

Down syndrome

chromosome

Relate to the Topic

This lesson is about genetics. It explains how some features, including disorders, are passed from parents to children. Think about your family.

List a disorder that runs in your family. _____

If you could take a test to determine whether you are likely to develop the disorder, would you? Why or why not?

_____

_____

Reading Strategy

RELATING TO PERSONAL EXPERIENCE   Link your personal experiences to the topic you are reading about. Look at the photograph on page 47. Then answer the questions.

1. In what ways do you look like your parents?

    _____

    _____

    Hint: Has anyone told you that you look like your parents?

2. What features do you share with your other relatives?

    _____

    _____

    Hint: Think about ways that you resemble different relatives.

Genetic Screening

When Kristi Betts was 15, her mother came down with Huntington's disease. This disorder, which starts in middle age, slowly attacks the brain. People with Huntington's lose control over their physical and mental functions. This takes place over a period of about 20 years. There is no cure.

At first, Kristi was concerned only for her mother. Then she realized that she and her sisters and brothers were at risk for Huntington's disease, too. You cannot catch Huntington's disease like a cold or the flu. You **inherit** the disease. This means that you receive genetic material from one or both of your parents that causes you to develop the disease. Huntington's disease is passed on in the same way as brown eyes or curly hair. Each child of a parent with Huntington's disease has a chance of inheriting it.

How Traits Are Passed from Parent to Child

All organisms inherit features, or **traits,** from their parents. Some traits, such as hair color, are easily seen. Others, such as blood type, cannot be seen. **Heredity** is the passing of traits from parents to their young, or offspring. Traits are passed on when organisms reproduce. The study of how traits are inherited is called **genetics.**

Each parent gives its offspring genetic material for a form of the trait. In some cases, one form of a trait shows and the other does not. The form of a trait that shows whenever it is present is called a **dominant trait.** The form of a trait that doesn't always show is called a **recessive trait.** In humans, for example, dark hair and dark eyes are dominant traits. Light hair and light eyes are recessive traits. A person must inherit a recessive trait from both parents in order for it to show.

A four-generation birthday party

Scientists show how traits combine by using a diagram called a **Punnett square,** which shows all the possible combinations of traits among the offspring of two parents. Look at the Punnett square on the left. It shows the combinations that may result when one parent has the trait for Huntington's disease and the other parent does not. The trait for Huntington's disease is a dominant trait. It is labeled with a capital *H*. The healthy form of the trait is recessive. It is labeled with a lowercase *h*.

Mother

	H	h
h	Hh	hh
h	Hh	hh

Father

In this Punnett square, the mother with the trait for Huntington's disease is shown on top. She has a dominant and a recessive form of the trait. The healthy father is shown on the left. He has two recessive forms of the trait. When these two people have a child, each gives one form of the trait to the child. Their traits can combine as shown in the four boxes. A child who inherits a dominant and a recessive form (Hh) or two dominant forms (HH) will develop Huntington's disease as an adult. A child who inherits two recessive forms (hh) will not develop the disease.

▶ Using Details   Details are very important in science. When you come to a passage with a lot of details, slow down. The previous paragraph explains how to read the Punnett square. Reread the paragraph one sentence at a time. If you read slowly and carefully, you will understand the details. For example, you will find out that the father is healthy because he has two recessive forms of the trait for Huntington's. The mother has Huntington's because she has one dominant and one recessive form of the trait.

Look back at the paragraph to find the details to help you answer these questions.

1. Will a child who inherits hh develop Huntington's disease? _____

2. Will a child who inherits Hh develop Huntington's disease? _____

Testing for Inherited Disorders

You can see from the Punnett square above that Kristi Betts had a two out of four chance of inheriting Huntington's disease. At one time, people had to live with this uncertainty. Since Huntington's disease doesn't appear until middle age, young people with an ill parent didn't know their own fate. But now people at risk can be tested. **Genetic screening** is the name for tests that can tell people if they have inherited certain disorders.

It is hard to decide whether to be tested for Huntington's disease. Is it better to know or not know if you are going to get the disease? Kristi decided it was better to know. She was lucky. She found out that she had not inherited Huntington's disease.

Unlike Huntington's, many genetic diseases are recessive. In such cases, when two recessive forms combine, the child inherits the disorder even though both parents may be healthy. There are tests to see if adults carry the recessive traits for certain disorders, such as sickle-cell anemia.

Genetic Screening of the Unborn

Genetic screening of fetuses is becoming more common, even among people with no history of genetic disorder in their families. For example, **amniocentesis** is a test that can be performed after the sixteenth week of pregnancy. This test can detect several disorders caused by genetic abnormalities, including Down syndrome. **Down syndrome** is a disorder caused by the presence of an extra **chromosome.** Children who have Down syndrome are mildly to severely mentally retarded. They may also have other health problems.

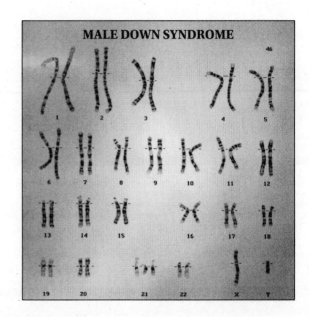

MALE DOWN SYNDROME

The developing baby receives genetic material from each parent in the form of chromosomes. Each baby should have 23 pairs of chromosomes, with one in each pair coming from the mother, and the other coming from the father. In amniocentesis, the baby's chromosomes are photographed and examined. The extra chromosome 21 in this photograph indicates that this baby has Down syndrome.

When genetic screening shows a disorder, prospective parents must make a decision. Genetic counselors help them explore their choices. People may decide not to have children. They may also accept the risk and the possible outcome of having a disabled child. Some people believe that genetic screening is wrong. Others feel that the knowledge, even if it is bad news, is worth having.

▶ Distinguishing Fact from Opinion **Facts** are things that can be proved true. **Opinions,** on the other hand, are beliefs. They may or may not be true. When reading a science text, it's important to distinguish fact from opinion. One way to do this is to look for words that signal an opinion: *believe, feel, think,* and *opinion.* For example, in the previous paragraph the phrase "Some people believe" signals that an opinion is about to be expressed.

Write the word *fact* or *opinion* next to each statement. If the statement includes an opinion, circle the word that signals an opinion.

1. Genetic counselors help parents explore their choices. _____

2. Some people feel that even bad news is knowledge worth having. _____

Check your answers on page 253.

Thinking About the Article

Practice Vocabulary

▶ **The terms below are in the passage in bold type. Study the way each term is used. Then complete each sentence by writing the correct term.**

traits	**heredity**	**genetics**
dominant trait	**recessive trait**	

1. In humans, dark hair is a _____ that always shows when it is present.

2. _____ , or characteristics, are features inherited from parents.

3. _____ is the study of how traits are inherited.

4. The passing on of traits from parents to their children is called

   _____ .

5. Light hair is a _____ .

Understand the Article

▶ **Write or circle the answer to each question.**

6. Unlike a cold or pneumonia, Huntington's disease is not spread by contact with other people's germs. How is Huntington's disease transmitted?

   A. You inherit it from a parent.

   B. You get it from contact with poisonous chemicals.

7. Name a human trait that is dominant.

   _____

8. Name a disorder or disease that results when a child inherits two recessive forms of the trait.

   _____

9. Name a disorder that can be identified by performing amniocentesis.

   _____

10. Why is it impossible for a person to develop Down syndrome later in life?

   _____

   _____

▶ **Circle the letter of the best answer for each question.**

11. Which of the following is a genetic screening test for a fetus?

   A. traits

   B. amniocentesis

   C. Punnett square

   D. heredity

12. According to the Punnett square on page 48, what is the chance that a child of a parent with Huntington's disease will inherit the disease?

   A. zero out of four

   B. one out of four

   C. two out of four

   D. three out of four

13. Which of the following statements includes an opinion rather than a fact?

   A. To test whether a person has inherited a disease, he or she undergoes genetic screening.

   B. A person with one parent who has Huntington's has a chance of inheriting the disease.

   C. Some young people think it is better to be tested and know whether they will develop Huntington's in middle age.

   D. Some parents undergo amniocentesis to find out whether their unborn babies have Down syndrome or other disorders.

Connect with the Article

▶ **Write your answer to each question.**

14. If both of your parents had Hh traits for Huntington's, what would be your chances of inheriting this disease?

15. Suppose a Punnett square shows a cross between two parents that results in four offspring with Huntington's disease. One parent has Hh traits for the disease. What is the other parent's traits for the disease?

SCIENCE PRACTICE FOCUS

Using a Pedigree Chart

A **pedigree chart** is a diagram that shows family relationships and the occurrence of particular genetic traits in the family. The chart uses symbols to represent individuals and their relationships. Males are represented by squares and females are represented by circles. A horizontal line between a square and a circle indicates a parental cross. Lines coming from the parental cross indicate the offspring of the cross. Each row in the chart indicates another generation in the family. Each generation is indicated by a Roman numeral and each individual by an Arabic number.

For a particular genetic trait, individual phenotypes within the family are represented by colors. When a square or circle is filled in with a color, it indicates the individual has both genes for the trait and expresses the trait. When a square or circle is half filled, it indicates that the individual carries the trait on only one gene and does not express it. An empty square or circle indicates that the trait is not present on either gene.

This pedigree chart shows the occurrence of a hereditary heart defect in a family. The trait is recessive and requires that both genes in the individual carry the defect. Study the chart and then answer the questions that follow.

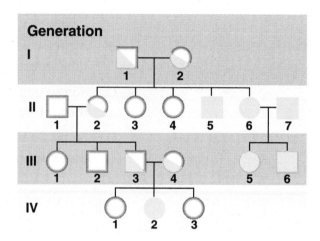

▶ **Write the answers to the questions.**

1. How many offspring are in the second generation?

   _____

2. How many of the offspring in Generation II have the heart defect?

   _____

3. Do any of the healthy offspring in Generation II carry the trait? If so, how many?

   _____

▶ **Circle the letter of the best answer.**

4. Which of the following individuals in Generation III does not carry the trait?

A.   Individual 2

B.   Individual 3

C.   Individual 4

D.   Individual 5

5. How many individuals on the pedigree chart have the heart defect?

A.   0

B.   2

C.   4

D.   6

6. Which of the following pairs of individuals in Generation III are not related by blood?

A.   Individuals 1 and 2

B.   Individuals 2 and 3

C.   Individuals 2 and 4

D.   Individuals 5 and 6

▶ **Write the answers to the questions.**

7. Pedigree charts often are used by dog and other animal breeders. How might a pedigree chart be a useful tool for a dog breeder?

_____

_____

_____

_____

8. Suppose Individual 2 in Generation IV marries someone who does not carry the trait. What are the chances that an offspring will have the defect? Explain.

_____

_____

_____

_____

Check your answers on page 254.

BACTERIA AND VIRUSES

Vocabulary

rhinovirus

virus

influenza (flu)

vaccination

antibody

pneumonia

bacteria

antibiotic

Colds can make you feel miserable. That's why many people try to avoid them. You may have heard of different ways to avoid getting a cold or to treat a cold so it doesn't get worse.

If you've ever had a cold, then you probably know that colds can be passed from person to person. Colds and certain other diseases are caused by germs. Sharing germs is one way to get sick. Scientists are trying to find out exactly how cold germs are passed from person to person and how to treat diseases effectively.

Relate to the Topic

This lesson is about the viruses and bacteria that cause some common diseases. Think back to a time when you had a cold or the flu.

How do you think you caught it? _____

_____

What were your symptoms? _____

_____

What did you do to make yourself feel better? _____

_____

_____

Reading Strategy

RELATING TO WHAT YOU KNOW   The topic of this lesson is bacteria and viruses. As you read, think about what you already know about the topic. Answer the questions to help get you thinking.

1. What are bacteria and viruses?

_____

Hint: Think about what you have heard about them.

2. What kinds of illnesses can bacteria and viruses cause?

_____

_____

Hint: Think about some illnesses you have had.

Colds, Flu, and Pneumonia

First you feel a small ache or a tickle in your throat. Soon your nose is running, your head is congested, and your eyes are watering. Your throat is now sore, too. Yes, it's another cold.

Catching a Cold

In spite of what your mother may have told you, simply getting wet and chilled won't give you a cold. Instead, you catch a cold from another person who is sick.

For many years, scientists have researched ways that colds are passed from person to person. Jack Gwaltney, a scientist at the University of Virginia, thinks that colds are passed by touch. Gwaltney says that people with colds have many cold-causing viruses on their hands. When these people touch something, such as a telephone, they leave viruses on the surface. You come along and touch the telephone. Then you touch your nose or eyes, and the virus settles in.

Another scientist, Elliot Dick, focused on a different theory. While at the University of Wisconsin, he performed an experiment in which he gathered 60 card players for a 12-hour poker game. 20 players had colds. Of the 40 healthy players, half wore braces or collars that kept them from touching their faces. The other half were free to touch their faces. Players in both healthy groups caught colds. Since players who could not touch their faces also got sick, Dick concluded that cold viruses spread through the air. Someone who is sick sneezes or coughs, and you breathe in the virus. Soon you are sick, too.

Treating a Cold

Protein covering

Genetic material

A Rhinovirus

Stroll through any drugstore and you'll see hundreds of sprays, pills, capsules, and syrups to make the cold sufferer feel better. Many of these products do help. But none can cure a cold. For years, scientists have been trying to find a cure for the common cold. The problem is that colds are caused by about 200 different viruses. About half of all colds are caused by a group of viruses called **rhinoviruses.**

Just what is a virus? A **virus** is a tiny particle made up of genetic material with a protein covering. The genetic material holds directions for making more viruses. The protein covering protects the virus.

▶ **Finding Details in a Diagram** Besides providing a general picture of something, a diagram has many specific things, or details, in it. You have to look carefully to find the details. Often there's help: The most important details are labeled. The words with lines pointing to parts of the diagram are called *labels*. Labels direct your attention to important details. In the diagram of a rhinovirus above, labels point out two details: the protein covering and the genetic material.

Now look at the diagram of a bacterial cell on the next page. List the details you can find in this diagram.

....

....

Viruses are not cells, and they are not made of cells. They don't grow. To make more viruses, they must be inside a living cell. For example, a rhinovirus latches onto a cell in the nose. The virus injects its genetic material into the cell and uses the cell's materials to make more viruses. Then the cell bursts open and dies. The new viruses are released to infect other cells.

Infections caused by viruses are hard to cure. The best way to fight viruses is to stop them before they invade. Researchers are looking for ways to block the rhinoviruses from attaching to cells in the nose.

The Flu

Another illness caused by a virus is **influenza,** usually called the **flu.** The difference between a cold and the flu is sometimes hard to know. A cold usually starts slowly, with a scratchy throat. Other symptoms follow in a day or two. Usually there is little or no fever. In contrast, the flu starts quickly. Within twelve hours you may have a fever over 101 degrees. Besides having a sore throat, stuffy nose, and a cough, you ache and feel very tired. Recovering from the flu can take up to three weeks. Although there are some drugs to help people feel better, there is no cure.

One defense against the flu is to get a flu vaccination each year. A **vaccination** is an injected dose of a dead or weakened disease-causing agent. This causes the body to form antibodies. An **antibody** is a substance the body makes to fight a disease. Once antibodies form, you are protected against that specific agent. This protection lowers your chance of getting the disease.

Pneumonia

People weakened by a bad cold or the flu are more likely to develop pneumonia. Symptoms include a high fever, chest pain, breathing problems, and a bad cough. **Pneumonia** is an infection of the lungs caused by a virus or bacterium. **Bacteria** are one-celled organisms and are many times larger than viruses. A bacterial cell is shown in the following diagram.

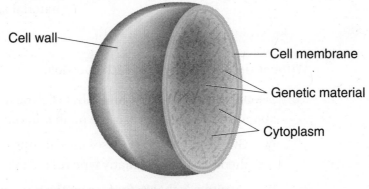

Cell wall

Cell membrane

Genetic material

Cytoplasm

A Bacterial Cell

About 90 percent of flu-related pneumonia is caused by bacteria. As the infection takes hold, the lungs produce fluid and mucus to fight the bacteria. The fluid blocks the air passages in the lungs. The person has trouble breathing and may have to go to a hospital. He or she is given **antibiotics,** or drugs that fight bacteria. The antibiotics kill the disease-causing bacteria, and the person gets better.

▶ Making Inferences When you read, you can sometimes figure out things that the author hints at but doesn't actually tell you. A fact or idea that is not stated in the text but that you figure out is an **inference.** Reread the first paragraph about pneumonia. The author says that people who have the flu sometimes develop an infection called pneumonia. One thing you can infer is that a good way to avoid getting pneumonia is to avoid getting the flu.

Which of the following ideas can be inferred from the information in the paragraph that begins "About 90 percent"? Circle the letter of the correct inference.

    A. About 10 percent of flu-related pneumonia is caused by a virus.

    B. Antibiotics can help cure pneumonia caused by a virus.

Thinking About the Article

Practice Vocabulary

▶ **The words below are in the passage in bold type. Study the way each word is used. Then match each word with its meaning. Write the letter.**

_____ **1.** virus

_____ **2.** influenza

_____ **3.** pneumonia

_____ **4.** bacteria

_____ **5.** antibiotic

A. one-celled organisms

B. an infection of the lungs caused by bacteria or a virus

C. an illness caused by a virus; also called the flu

D. a drug that fights bacteria

E. a tiny particle made of genetic material and a covering

Understand the Article

▶ **Write or circle the answer to each question.**

6. Scientists Jack Gwaltney and Elliot Dick have focused on different theories about cold viruses. What is the main difference between their theories?

   A.   Gwaltney's theory focuses on only one type of cold virus, while Dick's theory focuses on many types of cold viruses.

   B.   Gwaltney's theory focuses on the transmission of cold viruses through touch, while Dick's theory focuses on the transmission of cold viruses through the air.

7. What can cause each of the following diseases? Write _bacteria_ and/or _virus_ in the space provided.

   A.   a cold _____

   B.   the flu _____

   C.   pneumonia _____

8. How does a virus make more copies of itself?

   A.   It splits in half, as in cell division.

   B.   It takes over a cell and uses the cell to copy itself.

9. What is a vaccination?

_____

_____

10. What is an antibody?

_____

Apply Your Skills

▶ **Circle the letter of the best answer for each question.**

11. Which of the following is found in both a bacterial cell and in a virus?

    A.   cell membrane

    B.   antibody

    C.   genetic material

    D.   cytoplasm

12. Based on the information in this article, what can you infer is the best way to prevent getting a cold?

    A.   Avoid touching anything that people with colds touch.

    B.   Avoid breathing air in spaces where people with colds are.

    C.   Avoid people with colds.

    D.   Get a vaccination against colds.

13. Antibiotics are not used to treat colds and the flu. What can you infer from this?

    A.   Antibiotics do not fight viruses.

    B.   Antibiotics do not fight bacteria.

    C.   People with colds or the flu do not go to the hospital.

    D.   Antibiotics cost too much to use them on colds and the flu.

Connect with the Article

▶ **Write your answer to each question.**

14. Winter is the season when most cases of colds, flu, and pneumonia occur. Why do you think that is so?

15. What can you do to keep yourself and your family healthy next winter?

SCIENCE PRACTICE FOCUS

Bacterial Population Growth

Bacteria are single-celled organisms and most of them reproduce by dividing into two cells. The two daughter cells are about the same size and contain the same genetic material. Some kinds of bacteria can reproduce every hour. That means that the number of bacteria doubles each hour. As a result, a population of bacteria can increase very quickly!

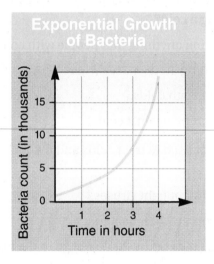

Exponential Growth of Bacteria

Data Table	
Time	Bacteria count
0	1,000
1	2,000
2	4,000
3	8,000
4	16,000

▶ **Write the answers to the following questions. Refer to the graph and table.**

1. How large is the bacteria count after 3 hours?

_____

2. Based on the data, predict the bacteria count after 5 hours.

_____

3. Cooking guidelines recommend heating meat until all of the bacteria are killed. Explain why it is dangerous to leave even a few live bacteria in cooked meat.

_____

_____

_____

_____

Preventing Viral Infection

A virologist is a scientist who studies viruses. Many virologists look for ways to stop viruses from making people sick. One strategy to combat viruses is to prevent them from reproducing. If a virus cannot multiply, then it cannot make a person sick.

The diagram shows the steps that viruses use to multiply themselves. Use the diagram to answer the questions below.

How a Virus Multiplies

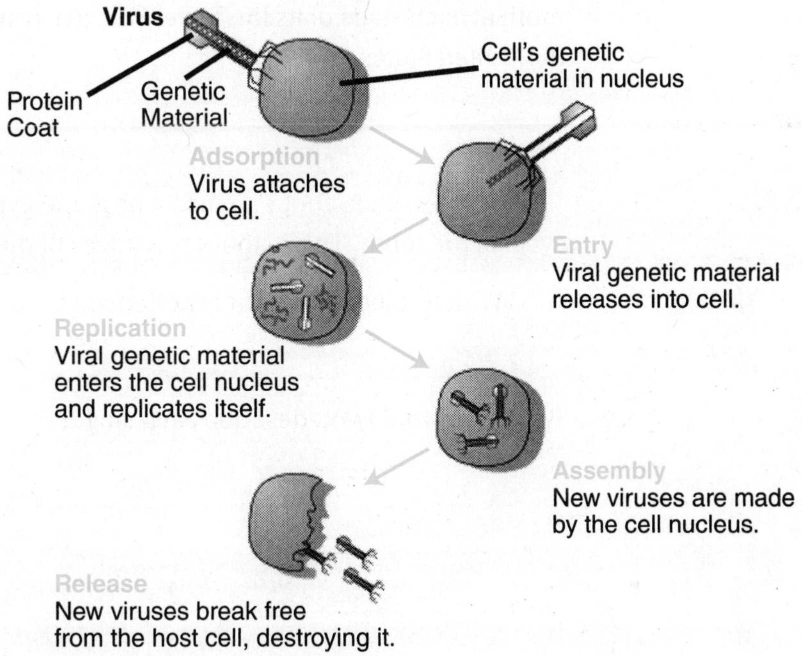

Virus

Protein Coat

Genetic Material

Cell's genetic material in nucleus

Adsorption
Virus attaches to cell.

Entry
Viral genetic material releases into cell.

Replication
Viral genetic material enters the cell nucleus and replicates itself.

Assembly
New viruses are made by the cell nucleus.

Release
New viruses break free from the host cell, destroying it.

▶ **Circle the letter of the best answer.**

4. Which of these drugs might keep a virus from making people sick?

A. A drug that prevents the Entry step.

B. A drug that prevents the Replication step.

C. A drug that prevents the Release step.

D. All of the above

▶ **Write your answer to the question.**

5. Explain the reasoning you used to answer Question 4. Cite evidence from the text to support your answer.

_____

_____

_____

LIFE CYCLES

Roaches, silverfish, carpenter ants, termites, aphids—the list of insect pests is long. One destructive pest is the gypsy moth. Gypsy moths are leaf-eating insects that have damaged millions of acres of trees. They can strip all the leaves off a tree in just a few weeks.

One way to fight insect pests is to try to attack them at different stages of their life cycles. People have tried many methods of wiping out the gypsy moth at each stage of its life cycle. Still, gypsy moths continue to spread in the United States.

Vocabulary

life cycle

egg

egg mass

caterpillar

pupa

adult

parasite

Relate to the Topic

This lesson is about an insect pest, the gypsy moth. It describes the life cycle of the moth. Think about the stages of the human life cycle.

Which stages have you experienced so far?

_____

How would you describe each stage?

_____

_____

_____

Reading Strategy

SCANNING DIAGRAMS   Science materials often use diagrams to display important concepts. A diagram usually has a title and labels. The title tells you what the diagram is about. The labels name the different parts of the diagram. Scan the diagram on page 64. Then answer the questions.

1. What is the diagram about?

_____

Hint: Look at the title.

2. What are the four forms of the gypsy moth?

_____

Hint: Look at the labels.

Fighting the Gypsy Moth

You may take the trees in your neighborhood for granted. Yet in the Northeast, gypsy moth caterpillars have stripped the leaves off millions of oak, birch, aspen, gum, and other trees. People in the northeastern United States have been fighting the gypsy moth for a hundred years.

The Spread of the Gypsy Moth

A Frenchman brought gypsy moth eggs from Europe to Massachusetts in the 1860s. He hoped to breed the moths with American silk-producing moths. Unfortunately, several moths escaped from his house. Within 50 years, the gypsy moth had spread throughout the Northeast. Today many scientists, government agencies, and private citizens are fighting the gypsy moth as far south as North Carolina and as far west as Wisconsin. The moths have been seen even in California and Oregon.

Gypsy moth caterpillars do a great deal of damage. They will eat every leaf on trees they like, such as oak trees. However, they skip other types of trees, such as spruce. Healthy trees can survive a gypsy moth attack. The leaves usually grow back the next year. But trees weakened by disease or inadequate rainfall may die after a year or two.

In addition to damaging trees, gypsy moth caterpillars make a mess. They leave half-eaten leaves everywhere. Their droppings ruin the finish on cars. The caterpillars make their way onto porches, screens, and windows. When they die, the smell of decay is terrible.

A gypsy moth caterpillar

The Life Cycle of the Gypsy Moth

To find ways to get rid of gypsy moths, scientists study the insect's life cycle. A **life cycle** is the series of changes an animal goes through in its life. There are four stages in the life cycle of a gypsy moth.

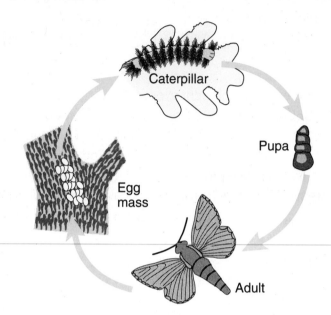

The Gypsy Moth's Life Cycle

1. **Egg.** Gypsy moth eggs are laid during the summer. Each female lays from 75 to 1,000 eggs in a clump called an **egg mass.** Egg masses are tan and slightly fuzzy.

2. **Caterpillar.** Gypsy moth eggs hatch into caterpillars. The caterpillars climb up trees to find leaves to eat. They grow to more than two inches long.

3. **Pupa.** During the pupa stage, the caterpillar encloses itself in a case for about two weeks. Its body changes into an adult moth.

4. **Adult.** When the pupa case breaks open, the adult moth comes out. Adult gypsy moths do not eat, so they do not live long. The female gives off a smell that attracts males. After mating, the male dies. The female lives long enough to lay eggs, and then she dies.

▶ **Understanding Sequence in a Diagram** A **sequence** is the order in which things happen. Often, arrows are used to indicate a sequence, as they are in the diagram of the gypsy moth life cycle above.

1. In the life cycle of the gypsy moth, what stage comes after the caterpillar?

   _____

2. What three stages come before the adult stage?

   _____

Check your answers on page 255.   UNIT 1 LIFE SCIENCE

A life cycle is often shown in the circular style used on page 64. However, it can also be shown in a timeline, such as the one below.

Life Cycle of a Gypsy Moth

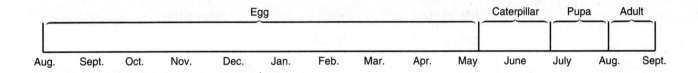

Aug. Sept. Oct. Nov. Dec. Jan. Feb. Mar. Apr. May June July Aug. Sept.

▶ Reading a Timeline A **timeline** is a way to show a sequence. In addition to showing the sequence of events, a timeline shows when an event happens. When you see a timeline, look at its title first. It will tell you what the timeline is about. This one is about the life cycle of the gypsy moth. Next, look at the labels. The labels along the bottom of this timeline are months. The labels at the top show the stages of a gypsy moth's life. For example, you can see that most adult gypsy moths emerge in August and die in September. This stage only lasts a month.

1. How long does the caterpillar stage of the life cycle last? _____

2. When do caterpillars go into the pupa stage?

_____

Controlling the Gypsy Moth

The gypsy moth damages trees during the caterpillar stage. The caterpillars can be killed by spraying the trees. Some sprays are chemicals that can harm other animals and the environment. Other sprays contain bacteria that kill only the moths. Caterpillars can be caught by wrapping sticky tape around trees. When the caterpillars climb, they get stuck on the tape and die. Gypsy moths can also be killed by destroying their eggs. Egg masses can be found on trees, buildings, fences, and outdoor furniture. They can be scraped into a bucket of kerosene, bleach, or ammonia. These chemicals kill the eggs.

Pupa cases can be removed from trees and crushed. Adult males can be caught in scented traps, which contain a bait that smells like a female moth. The male flies into the trap and dies there.

Some birds prey on gypsy moths. Birds that eat the moths can be attracted into an infested area. People can put out food, water, and nesting materials to encourage the birds to stay. Another natural control method uses parasites. A **parasite** is an organism that lives on or in another organism and harms it. Many parasites have been released in areas with gypsy moths.

Diseases can lower the number of moths. One year there was a very rainy spring, and many moths died of a fungus disease. Perhaps one day scientists will be able to use the fungus to kill gypsy moths.

Check your answers on page 255.

Thinking About the Article

Practice Vocabulary

▶ **The terms below are in the passage in bold type. Study the way each term is used. Then complete each sentence by writing the correct term.**

life cycle	**egg**	**caterpillar**
pupa	**adult**	

1. The _____ is the first stage of the gypsy moth's life.

2. The caterpillar is enclosed in a case during the

   _____ stage.

3. During the _____ stage, the gypsy moth crawls around and damages trees.

4. A mature gypsy moth, capable of laying eggs, is in the

   _____ stage.

5. An animal goes through stages during the course of its life, which are

   called its _____ .

Understand the Article

▶ **Write the answer to each question.**

6. How were gypsy moths introduced into the United States?

   _____

   _____

   _____

7. What damage does the gypsy moth caterpillar do?

   _____

   _____

▶ **Match the stage of the gypsy moth's life cycle with the control method used during that stage.**

_____ **8.** egg	A.	spraying insecticide
_____ **9.** caterpillar	B.	soaking in ammonia, kerosene, or bleach
_____ **10.** pupa	C.	putting out scent traps
_____ **11.** adult	D.	crushing

66

▶ **Circle the letter of the best answer for each question.**

12. Look at the diagram on page 64. Which of the following is the correct sequence of stages in the gypsy moth life cycle?

    A. egg, pupa, caterpillar, adult

    B. egg, adult, pupa, caterpillar

    C. egg, caterpillar, adult, pupa

    D. egg, caterpillar, pupa, adult

13. According to the timeline on page 65, which is the longest stage of the gypsy moth's life cycle?

    A. egg

    B. caterpillar

    C. pupa

    D. adult

14. During the month of March, which control method can people use to destroy gypsy moths?

    A. Crush the pupa cases.

    B. Spray the caterpillars with insecticide.

    C. Put out scented bait traps for adult male moths.

    D. Soak the egg masses in kerosene, bleach, or ammonia.

▶ **Write your answer to each question.**

15. What other animals do you know about that look different at different stages of their life cycles? Pick one of these animals and describe how it looks and acts during different parts of its life cycle.

_____

_____

_____

16. Describe an experience you or someone you know has had with gypsy moths or other insect pests. What did you do to control them?

_____

_____

_____

SCIENCE PRACTICE FOCUS

The Life Cycle of a Frog

The life cycle of a frog is very different from the human life cycle. Study the diagram. Then use the information to answer the questions below.

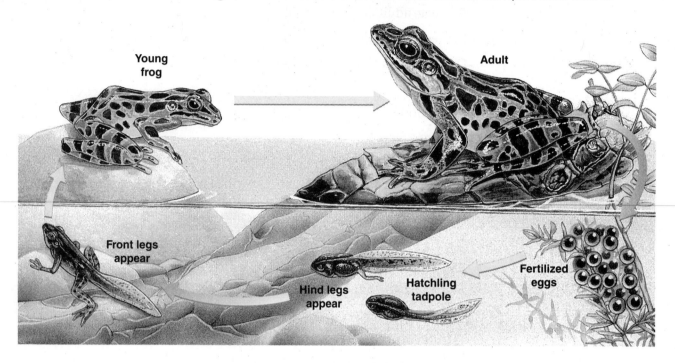

Young frog

Adult

Front legs appear

Hind legs appear

Hatchling tadpole

Fertilized eggs

▶ **Fill in the blank with the word or words that best complete each statement.**

1. Frogs swim in the water but have no legs in the _____ stage.

2. Frogs lay eggs in the _____ stage.

▶ **Write the answers to the following questions.**

3. Look back at the diagram of the gypsy moth life cycle on page 64. Identify two ways in which the frog and the gypsy moth life cycles are similar.

   _____

   _____

4. Identify two ways in which the frog and gypsy moth life cycles are different.

   _____

   _____

5. Suppose that people built a housing development and filled in all of the local ponds with dirt. Predict what would happen to the frog populations nearby. Explain your reasoning in a sentence or two.

_____

_____

_____

6. Create your own diagram showing the life cycle of an animal. Draw each stage of the life cycle, label each stage, and draw arrows connecting each stage to the one that follows it.

▷ **Circle the letter of the best answer.**

7. The life cycle of every kind of animal includes

   A. a stage that lays eggs

   B. adults

   C. a stage that lives in the water

   D. tadpoles

Check your answers on page 256.

ECOSYSTEMS

Vocabulary

tropical rain forest

ecosystem

equator

photosynthesis

respiration

**carbon dioxide–
    oxygen cycle**

greenhouse effect

climate change

What do Brazil nuts, mahogany, and natural rubber have in common? They are all products of tropical rain forests. Tropical rain forests are warm, wet regions near the equator.

Although tropical rain forests cover only a small part of Earth, they contain a large proportion of the world's plants and animals. Tropical rain forests benefit the whole world, but they are disappearing because of farming, logging, and ranching.

Relate to the Topic

This lesson is about tropical rain forests. Think about what you already know about tropical rain forests.

Describe something you know or have heard about tropical rain forests.

_____

_____

Imagine that you are in a tropical rain forest. What do you see, hear, and feel?

_____

_____

Reading Strategy

SCANNING MAPS   Maps are a simple way to present a lot of information. You can preview a map to find out what kind of information it includes. Scan the title, labels, and key for the map. The key tells what the colors or symbols on the map represent. Scan the map on page 73. Then answer the questions.

1. What is the topic of the map?

_____

Hint: Look at the title.

2. What do the colors on the map represent?

_____

Hint: Look at the map key.

Tropical Rain Forests

Do you like rice cereal with bananas? Coffee with sugar? Did you know that the foods in this breakfast first came from a **tropical rain forest?** Tropical rain forests are the source of many foods that are now grown commercially.

Take a look around you. Offices, libraries, and department stores may have furniture made of mahogany or teak. These woods grow in tropical rain forests. Check out your medicine cabinet. About 40 percent of all drugs have ingredients that first came from tropical rain forest plants.

What Is a Tropical Rain Forest?

A tropical rain forest is a large ecosystem. An **ecosystem** is an area in which living and nonliving things interact. Tropical rain forests are found near the **equator** (the imaginary line that goes around the middle of Earth, halfway between the poles). In these areas, there is a great deal of rainfall, and it is warm throughout the year. The temperature may vary more from day to night than from season to season.

The conditions in tropical rain forests—such as space, food, and water—support a wealth of plant and animal life. More than half of all types of plants and animals live in tropical rain forests. The variety of life is tremendous. Just one square mile of rain forest in Peru has over 1,000 types of butterflies. Together, the United States and Canada have fewer than 750!

A tropical rain forest

The Global Effects of the Rain Forests

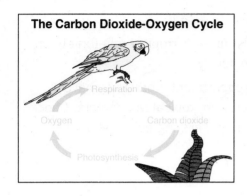

The Carbon Dioxide-Oxygen Cycle

The plants of the rain forests absorb carbon dioxide from the atmosphere. Through the process of **photosynthesis,** plants use energy from sunlight to combine carbon dioxide and water to make food. This process gives off oxygen. Oxygen is used by animals for respiration. **Cellular respiration** is the process by which living things use oxygen to get energy from food. This process gives off carbon dioxide. Carbon dioxide is also given off when fuels are burned and when organic material, such as plants and animals, decompose. The carbon dioxide is then used by plants, completing the **carbon dioxide–oxygen cycle.**

▶ Recognizing Cause and Effect There are many situations in which one thing (a cause) makes another thing (an effect) happen. For example, plants make their own food during photosynthesis (cause). The process of photosynthesis results in plants' giving off oxygen (effect). Science is full of cause-and-effect relationships. Watch for words such as *cause, effect, because, result, leads to, due to, therefore, thus,* and *so.* These words often signal cause-and-effect relationships.

In the first paragraph of the article, you learned about the carbon dioxide–oxygen cycle. According to the text, what effect does burning fuels have on the atmosphere?
  A. Burning fuels releases oxygen into the atmosphere.
  B. Burning fuels releases carbon dioxide into the atmosphere.

The amount of carbon dioxide in the air affects Earth's temperature. Carbon dioxide absorbs heat and helps keep Earth warm. The role of carbon dioxide and other gases in warming Earth is known as the **greenhouse effect.** By taking carbon dioxide from the air, the plants of the rain forests help control Earth's temperature.

Destruction of the Rain Forests

Over 50,000 square miles of tropical rain forests are destroyed each year by farmers, ranchers, and loggers. Many tropical countries don't have enough farmland, so farmers clear forests and burn the trees. When the soil is no longer able to nourish crops, they move on and clear new places. Ranchers cut down trees to make room for their cattle. Loggers also destroy the forests by cutting down trees for the wood.

This destruction affects the carbon dioxide–oxygen cycle in two ways. First, many trees are burned to clear the land. This burning adds tons of carbon dioxide to the air. Second, destroying trees means there are fewer plants to take carbon dioxide from the air. Scientists think that more carbon dioxide in the air is causing **climate change,** an increase in the average surface temperature of our planet.

Tropical rain forests cover about one-twentieth of Earth's land area. They are found along the equator, as shown in the map below. Large areas of the rain forests have already been destroyed.

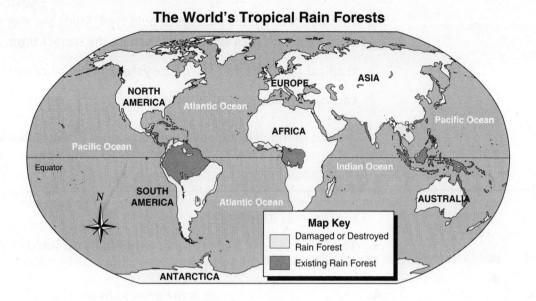

The World's Tropical Rain Forests

▶ Reading a Map To study a map, first look at the title. It tells you what the map shows. This map shows the world's tropical rain forests. Then look for the map key. The map key tells you how information is shown on the map. In this map, existing rain forests are in dark gray, and damaged or destroyed forests are in dark blue. Look at the compass rose in the lower left. It shows the directions north, south, east, and west.

Study the map above. Which of the following continents has the smallest area of tropical rain forest? Circle the letter of the correct answer.

A. North America C. Africa
B. South America D. Asia

Stopping the Destruction

People in tropical countries do not destroy the forests with bad intentions. In these countries, the forests are a source of land, fuel, food, and income for the expanding population. It's not possible to keep farmers, ranchers, and loggers out of the rain forests. Many countries are now trying to save some areas in the forests by making them off-limits. Some areas are set aside for tourism. In addition, new methods of farming and logging can help people use the forests without destroying them.

Other countries can help, too. They can buy products, such as Brazil nuts, that are grown without damaging the forests. They can refuse to buy products that damage the forests. This includes tropical woods, such as teak. It also includes beef ranched on lands that were once tropical rain forests.

Check your answers on page 256.

Thinking About the Article

Practice Vocabulary

▶ **The terms below are in the passage in bold type. Study the way each term is used. Then complete each sentence by writing the correct term.**

> tropical rain forests   ecosystem   photosynthesis
>
> carbon dioxide–oxygen cycle   cellular respiration

1. An area in which living and nonliving things interact is called a(n)

   _____ .

2. _____ is the process by which living things use oxygen to get energy from food.

3. The _____ describes how carbon dioxide and oxygen circulate through the world.

4. _____ is the process by which plants use carbon dioxide, water, and energy from sunlight to make food.

5. Scientists think that the destruction of the _____ is contributing to climate change.

Understand the Article

▶ **Write or circle the answer to each question.**

6. What are three basic things in a rain forest that can affect the number of animals that can live there?

   _____

   _____

7. What role do animals play in the carbon dioxide–oxygen cycle?

   A. Animals take in oxygen and give off carbon dioxide during the process of cellular respiration.

   B. Animals take in carbon dioxide and give off oxygen during the process of photosynthesis.

8. Which three industries are most destructive to the tropical rain forest? Explain why.

   _____

   _____

   _____

Apply Your Skills

▶ **Circle the letter of the best answer for each question.**

9. People burn more fuel now than ever before. What effect does this have on the amount of carbon dioxide in the air?
Carbon dioxide has

   A. increased

   B. decreased

   C. first increased, then decreased

   D. remained the same

10. Which of the following is the cause of climate change?

    A. a decrease in the amount of oxygen in the atmosphere

    B. an increase in the amount of oxygen in the atmosphere

    C. a decrease in the amount of carbon dioxide in the atmosphere

    D. an increase in the amount of carbon dioxide in the atmosphere

11. Some monkeys that live in rain forests rely on trees for food and shelter. How might the destruction of a rain forest affect a population of monkeys that live there?

    A. The monkey population would increase.

    B. The monkey population would remain the same.

    C. The monkey population would first increase and then remain the same.

    D. The monkey population would decrease.

Connect with the Article

▶ **Write your answer to each question.**

12. List three ways that tropical rain forests are important to human health and to the health of Earth's ecosystems.

    _____

    _____

    _____

13. What can you do to help prevent the destruction of tropical rain forests?

    _____

    _____

    _____

    _____

Check your answers on pages 256–257.

SCIENCE PRACTICE FOCUS

Investigating Ecosystems

Chelsea is designing an investigation about ecosystems. She is studying how the amount of rainfall in an ecosystem affects the number of species in the ecosystem. She plans to compare the number of plant and animal species in a wet ecosystem to the number in a dry ecosystem. Before she begins the investigation, Chelsea hypothesizes that more rainfall will allow more kinds of animals and plants to live in the ecosystem. She expects to find more species in the wet ecosystem.

Chelsea spends a week surveying the wet temperate forest near her home. She keeps careful records of every species she sees. She finds 42 species of plants and 49 species of animals.

The second ecosystem is a dry grassland in a state park. Unfortunately, Chelsea is unable to visit the park. Instead, she finds a list of all of the species in the grassland on the state park's website. According to the website, naturalists have spotted 216 species of plants and 444 species of animals in the dry grassland.

▶ **Write your answers to the following questions:**

1. What question is Chelsea's science project designed to answer?

_____

_____

_____

2. What is Chelsea's hypothesis?

_____

_____

_____

3. Do Chelsea's results support or contradict her hypothesis? Explain your reasoning.

_____

_____

_____

_____

_____

4. Do you think that Chelsea's results are accurate? Explain your reasoning.

5. Suggest one way that Chelsea could improve her investigation.

6. When Chelsea's teacher sees her report, he is not satisfied. He tells her that she needs to count species at the grassland herself. He gives her an extra week to complete the project. Chelsea identifies 21 species of plants and 39 species of animals in the grassland. Do Chelsea's new results support her original hypothesis? Explain your answer.

7. Why do you think that Chelsea didn't identify all of the species listed on the state park website?

Check your answers on page 257.

EVOLUTION

In one scene of the movie *Jurassic Park,* dinosaurs hunt children who are hiding in a kitchen. The dinosaurs turn the knob to open the kitchen door. These dinosaurs can open doors because they have flexible wrists that allow them to swivel their hands.

Flexible wrists are also characteristic of birds. A flexible wrist allows powered flight. This—and other shared characteristics—have led many scientists to hypothesize that birds and dinosaurs are related.

Relate to the Topic

This lesson is about the theory of evolution. It explains how birds probably evolved from small, feathered dinosaurs. Think about birds you have seen.

What do birds look like?

_____

_____

What are some characteristics of birds that help you recognize them as birds?

_____

_____

Reading Strategy

SKIMMING PICTURES   Science articles often use photographs and illustrations to help the reader understand the text. Skimming a picture and its caption can also help you preview an article. Skim the illustration on page 79 and the photograph on page 81. Then answer the questions.

1. What does the picture on page 79 show?

_____

Hint: Read the caption.

2. What does the picture on page 81 show?

_____

Hint: Read the caption.

Vocabulary

fossil

paleontologist

adaptation

mutation

natural selection

theory

evolution

convergence

Dinosaurs with Feathers

Mammals have fur or hair, fish have scales, and dinosaurs have—feathers? New fossils indicate that some dinosaurs did indeed have feathers. A **fossil** is a trace or the remains of an organism that lived in the distant past. By comparing fossils over time, scientists can trace the development of species over time. Some scientists think that these feathered fossils settle the longstanding debate over the dinosaur-bird link. According to this view, feathered dinosaurs provide evidence that modern birds evolved from dinosaurs.

Dinosaur-Bird Links

The first scientist to suggest that birds and dinosaurs are related was Thomas Henry Huxley. His theory was based on the 1861 discovery of a primitive bird fossil, *Archaeopteryx* (ar-kee-AHP-tuhr-iks). This creature had many similarities to dinosaurs, including clawed fingers and a long bony tail. It also had feathers. While many scientists accepted Huxley's theory, there was little evidence to support it. However, **paleontologists**—scientists who study prehistoric life—predicted that fossils of birdlike dinosaurs would eventually be discovered. In recent decades, this prediction was proved correct. During the 1990s, a number of fossils of birdlike dinosaurs were found. All of the different species of birdlike dinosaurs had feathers.

A drawing of the feathered dinosaur *Caudipteryx*

One kind of birdlike dinosaur is *Protoarchaeopteryx* (proh-toh-ar-kee-AHP-tuhr-iks). It is similar in many ways to the fast, meat-eating dinosaur *Velociraptor* (vuh-LAH-suh-rap-tuhr), made famous by the movie *Jurassic Park.* *Protoarcheopteryx* had a cluster of long feathers at the end of its tail.

Another kind, *Caudipteryx* (caw-DIP-tuhr-iks), may have been even more feathery. Feathers covered the arms, much of the body, and the tail. Some feathers were tiny and soft like down, and others were large and stiff like quills.

A third kind of birdlike dinosaur, *Confuciusornis* (con-few-shus-OR-nis), may have actually been able to fly. *Confuciusornis* may provide evidence for how a dinosaur's grasping limb evolved into a flying limb. *Confuciusornis* had unique wing feathers that were longer than its body, and the male had very long, narrow tail feathers.

The Usefulness of Feathers

Despite their feathers, neither *Protoarchaeopteryx* nor *Caudipteryx* could fly. Instead, scientists think that the short feathers may have provided insulation. The long feathers may have been used by males to attract females. Many modern birds have down to keep warm and colorful feathers to display during courtship.

Once feathers developed, they may have given some birdlike dinosaurs a competitive edge. They may have enabled these dinosaurs to run faster or balance better than their nonfeathered relatives. In other species, feathers may have aided gliding or flying. A trait, such as feathers, that makes an organism better able to live in its environment is called an **adaptation.** Another example of an adaptation is an arctic fox's white fur. The color helps the arctic fox blend into the background of snow. Its enemies have trouble seeing it, so the fox has a better chance of surviving.

Many adaptations occur through mutation. A **mutation** is a change in genetic material. Mutations happen by chance and most have no noticeable effect. Some are harmful. But, sometimes, a mutation produces a trait, such as feathers on a dinosaur or white fur on a fox, that helps an organism survive.

▶ Making Inferences An inference is a fact or idea that follows logically from what has been said. Readers make inferences all the time from the information in what they read. Review the previous paragraph about mutations. The author states in the paragraph that some mutations cause traits which can help an organism to survive. From what the author says, you can infer that harmful mutations can cause an individual to die.

Which of the following can you infer from the paragraph about adaptations? Circle the letter of the correct inference.

    A. White fur is a useful adaptation any place that foxes live.

    B. White fur is a useful adaptation only in places with lots of snow.

Evolution through Natural Selection

There are always variations in any population due to mutation. When feathers first appeared, a few dinosaurs may have had them. A dinosaur with this adaptation was more likely to survive, reproduce, and pass the trait to offspring.

Charles Darwin, a nineteenth-century English scientist, called this process natural selection. **Natural selection** means that the organisms best suited to their environments are most likely to survive and reproduce. In this case, feathers may have helped some dinosaurs in the competition for resources. However, survival of an individual organism is not enough. It must reproduce to pass on the adaptations to its offspring.

Fossils of Archaeopteryx revealed evidence of feathers.

Darwin's idea's are commonly referred to as the theory of evolution. A **theory** is a well-supported explanation for observations made in the natural world. A theory can be revised over time as more data are gathered and analyzed.

Darwin concluded that the make-up of a population of organisms changes slowly over time. Those with useful adaptations have offspring with a better chance of surviving and reproducing than others. Over time, the adaptation may be found in most of the population. This gradual change of a species over time is called **evolution.**

Convergence

Some scientists are not convinced that the feathered dinosaurs show that birds evolved from dinosaurs. They argue that birds and dinosaurs could have developed traits such as feathers independently, a process called **convergence.** Convergence results in similarities among groups of animals that are not closely related through evolution. For example, crows, bats, and butterflies all have wings, but they are not closely related. Crows are birds, bats are mammals, and butterflies are insects. Their wings evolved independently as an adaptation to life in the air.

However, most scientists accept the general theory that birds and dinosaurs are related. They point to more than a hundred shared traits, including feathers, air-filled skull bones, and wishbones. Says one scientist, "Dinosaurs are not extinct after all. They're alive and well and represented by more than 10,000 species of living birds."

▶ **Applying Knowledge to Other Contexts** Using the knowledge you gain in one situation and applying it to another can give you new insights about the world around you. For example, you just learned that birds, bats, and butterflies all have wings but are not closely related. Their traits converge because they each have adapted to their environment by taking up flight, and controlled flight requires wings.

Which of the following is another example of convergence?

A. Sharks and dolphins have similarly shaped bodies and fins, but sharks are fish and dolphins are mammals.

B. Humans and chimpanzees have thumbs that allow them to grasp objects, and both are mammals.

Check your answers on page 258.

Thinking About the Article

Practice Vocabulary

▶ The terms below are in the passage in bold type. Study the way each term is used. Then complete each sentence by writing the correct term.

| adaptation | mutation | natural selection |

| evolution | convergence |

1. A(n) _____ is a change in a gene.

2. A trait that makes a plant or animal better able to live in its environment is called a(n) _____.

3. _____ is the independent evolution of similar characteristics among unrelated organisms.

4. _____ means that organisms best suited to their environments are most likely to survive and reproduce.

5. The gradual change in a species over time is called

_____.

Understand the Article

▶ Write or circle the answer to each question.

6. What do all species of birdlike dinosaurs discovered so far have in common?

_____

_____

7. What do scientists think flightless dinosaurs might have used feathers for?

_____

_____

_____

8. How do species evolve?

A. Individuals with useful adaptations survive, reproduce, and pass the adaptations to their offspring.

B. Individuals may develop traits during their lifetime and teach them to their offspring.

▶ **Circle the letter of the best answer for each question.**

9. You can infer that birds, bats, and butterflies are not closely related because they

A. are very different types of animals

B. have wings instead of arms

C. can fly

D. have feathers

10. Antibiotics are drugs that fight disease-causing bacteria. Over time, bacteria can develop resistance to an antibiotic, and the drug no longer works. The resistance of bacteria to antibiotics is an example of a(n)

A. fossil

B. convergence

C. adaptation

D. paleontologist

11. Which would most likely happen over time if people had to do more standing, walking, and running to survive?

A. Humans would develop bird-like wings.

B. Humans would develop stronger legs.

C. Humans would gradually die out.

D. Humans would develop flexible ankles.

Connect with the Article

▶ **Write your answer to each question.**

12. Which do think is more likely: that birds evolved from dinosaurs, or that the similarities between birds and dinosaurs are the result of convergence? Cite evidence from the article to support your answer.

_____

_____

13. How did reading this article change the way you think about dinosaurs or birds?

_____

_____

_____

Check your answers on page 258.

SCIENCE PRACTICE FOCUS

Evolution in a Population of Deer

Study the diagram below and then answer the questions that follow.

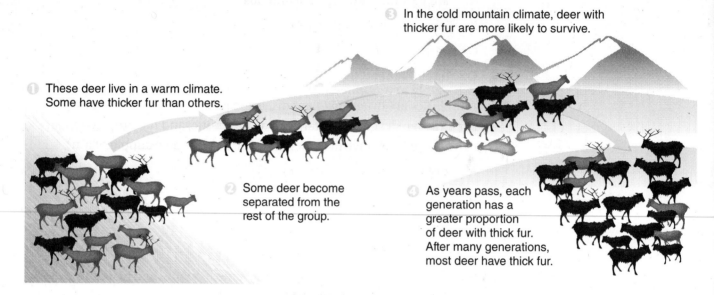

③ In the cold mountain climate, deer with thicker fur are more likely to survive.

① These deer live in a warm climate. Some have thicker fur than others.

② Some deer become separated from the rest of the group.

④ As years pass, each generation has a greater proportion of deer with thick fur. After many generations, most deer have thick fur.

▶ **Circle the letter of the best answer.**

1. If the deer move back to a warmer climate, which of the following is most likely to happen?

A. The population will gradually include more thin-furred individuals again.

B. The population will gradually include an even greater proportion of thick-furred individuals.

C. The proportion of thin-furred individuals will stay the same.

D. The population will all die out.

2. More thick-furred individuals survive in the colder climate because of

A. convergence

B. mutation

C. natural selection

D. extinction

3. Thick-furred in a cold climate is an example of a(n)

A. species

B. fossil

C. population

D. adaptation

Symbiosis

Symbiosis is the interaction between two different species that have evolved a close relationship. One example of symbiosis is the bacteria that live in a cow's stomach and help the cow digest its food. Without the cow, the bacteria would have nowhere to live. Without the bacteria, the cow would not be able to get nutrients from grass. Both species survive together better than they survive apart. Through natural selection, cows and bacteria have evolved a very close relationship.

A symbiotic relationship in which both species benefit (like the cow and bacteria) is called **mutualism**. Other kinds of symbiotic relationship are not so equal. A symbiotic relationship in which one partner is helped and the other is hurt is called **parasitism**. In **commensalism**, one species benefits in the relationship but does not help or hurt the other species.

▶ **Fill in the blank with the word or words that best complete each statement.**

4. The relationship between humans and bedbugs is an example of

   _____.

5. Hermit crabs live in the shells of dead snails. The relationship between hermit crab and snail is an example of _____.

▶ **Write your answer to each question:**

6. Humans and housecats live in a symbiotic relationship. Which type of relationship do you think this is? Explain your answer.

   _____

   _____

7. Honeyguides are birds that lead humans to bee colonies. Once people have broken open the beehive, the honeyguides eat the young bees and beeswax. Describe how natural selection could result in honeyguides living in symbiosis with humans.

   _____

   _____

   _____

   _____

Check your answers on pages 258–259.

SCIENCE AT WORK

HEALTH:
FITNESS INSTRUCTOR

Health and fitness has become a huge industry in our country. People enjoy exercising because it helps them mentally and physically. Fitness instructors teach people to exercise safely and effectively. They design workout routines, demonstrate exercises and gym equipment, teach classes, and monitor clients' progress. Fitness instructors must be able to answer clients' questions clearly and correctly. Because they work closely with people most of the day, they should have excellent communication skills.

Fitness instructors need a good understanding of life science, especially the human body. They need to understand how the body and its systems work. They must know about human anatomy, or the parts of the body, and physiology—how the body parts work and how they interact. Fitness instructors must pay great attention to their clients' bones and muscles and cardiovascular and respiratory systems. They are responsible for helping their clients achieve their workout goals without injury.

Look at the chart showing some of the careers in health and fitness.

- Do any of the careers interest you? If so, which ones?

- What information would you need to find out more about those careers? On a separate piece of paper, write some questions that you would like answered. You can find more information about those careers in the *Occupational Outlook Handbook* at your local library or online.

Aerobics Instructor conducts fitness classes for groups of people

Assistant Aerobics Coordinator helps choose and schedule classes; selects instructors and conducts training sessions

Water Fitness Instructor conducts fitness classes in swimming pools for groups of people

Personal Trainer works individually with clients on fitness needs

> **Use the following memo to answer the questions below.**

FROM: Fitness Instructor Diane

TO: Client Tom

Tom, I have designed an exercise program for you. To get your body in good shape, it is important that you complete all three parts. Only use this workout program 3–4 times a week. Give yourself a day of rest between each day of exercise to avoid injury or stress to your body. Be sure to start each workout session by stretching.

Part 1 – Cardiovascular Workout – to get your heart working more efficiently. Choose one of the following machines: step machine; treadmill; rowing machine; or stationary bicycle. These machines will strengthen lower body muscles. Do a 5-minute warm up, 10 minutes at peak working heart rate, and a 5-minute cool down.

Part 2 – Strength Training – to build muscle and bone density. Use either the weight machines, or leg and hand weights. While using the weights, rotate between body parts to give each part time to rest. For example, first work on an arm muscle, then on a leg muscle. Start with light weights. Lift each weight 15 times. Do this twice. Work on at least 3 muscles in the leg and arm areas.

Part 3 – Stretching – to help your body cool down, relax, and resume its normal state. Stretch the same muscles you worked on in Part 2. Stretch and hold the position for 5–8 seconds. Do each muscle one time.

1. Which of the following will help Tom build muscle and bone density?

   A. stretching

   B. step machine

   C. hand weights

   D. stationary bicycle

2. Why is it important for Tom to rest between the days he works out?

   A. He will get too tired at the gym.

   B. He might get hurt from too much exercising.

   C. Diane won't be there to help him.

   D. Stretching is too difficult.

3. Match the recommended exercise with its benefit.

   _____ treadmill   A. build muscle and bone density

   _____ weight machines   B. cool down

   _____ stretching   C. improve efficiency of the heart

How Cells Reproduce

The **nucleus** of a cell is the control center. The nucleus contains the chromosomes, which in turn contain the genetic material, or **DNA.** This material has all the instructions the cell needs to live. When the cell reproduces, this information is passed on to the new cells.

A cell reproduces by dividing. This five-step process is called mitosis. In **mitosis,** one cell becomes two cells. Before a cell divides, it makes a copy of its DNA. Each new cell receives one copy of the DNA. These two new cells can then grow and divide.

Nucleus   Chromosomes

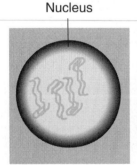   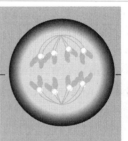 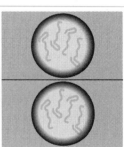

| DNA doubles in parent cell | Chromosomes shorten | Chromosomes line up | Chromosomes split | Two new cells form |

▷ **Fill in the blank with the word or words that best complete each statement.**

1. The genetic material is called _____.

2. Cells reproduce in a process known as _____.

▷ **Circle the letter of the best answer.**

3. Which of the following can you infer from the diagram?

A.   Chromosomes in new cells are fatter than those in the parent cell.

B.   New cells have twice as many chromosomes as parent cells do.

C.   Parent cells pass only half their chromosomes to new cells.

D.   An X-shaped chromosome consists of two copies of a parent chromosome.

The Heart

Your heart is a large, muscular pump. As you read this, your heart is pumping blood to your lungs, where the blood absorbs oxygen. Your heart is also pumping blood throughout your body. The blood carries oxygen to the body. The parts of the heart are shown below.

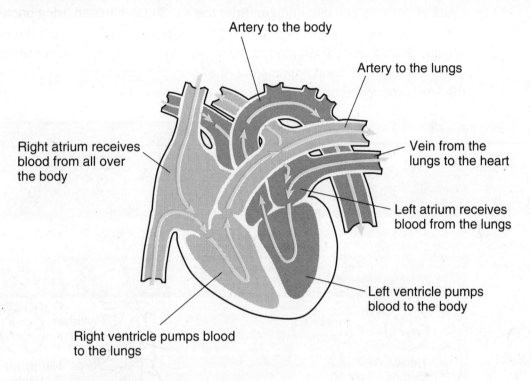

Artery to the body

Artery to the lungs

Right atrium receives blood from all over the body

Vein from the lungs to the heart

Left atrium receives blood from the lungs

Left ventricle pumps blood to the body

Right ventricle pumps blood to the lungs

▶ **Fill in the blank with the word or words that best complete each statement.**

4. If blood is flowing away from the heart, it is in a(n)

   _____.

5. Blood coming from the lungs flows through a vein to the

   _____ of the heart.

▶ **Circle the letter of the best answer.**

6. Which is the correct sequence of blood flow in the heart?

   A. right atrium, right ventricle, lungs, left atrium, left ventricle

   B. left atrium, left ventricle, lungs, right atrium, right ventricle

   C. right atrium, lungs, left ventricle, right atrium, left ventricle

   D. right ventricle, left ventricle, lungs, right atrium, left atrium

The Nitrogen Cycle

All living things need nitrogen in some form. Nitrogen is an important part of proteins. Proteins make up much of the structures of living things. For example, muscles are made mostly of protein.

The air around you is 78 percent nitrogen, which your body cannot use. Only a few kinds of bacteria can use nitrogen from the air. These nitrogen-fixing bacteria live in the soil. They change nitrogen into a form called **nitrates.** Plants take in the nitrates from the soil. Plants use the nitrates to make proteins, which animals get when they eat the plants. When plants and animals die, they decay. Some bacteria return the nitrogen to the soil. Other bacteria release nitrogen into the air.

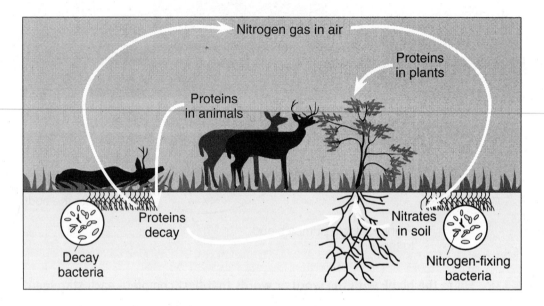

▷ **Match each organism with its source of nitrogen.**

Organism	Nitrogen source
_____ **7.** animals	A. air
_____ **8.** plants	B. protein
_____ **9.** nitrogen-fixing bacteria	C. nitrates

▷ **Write your answer to the question.**

10. Some animals do not eat any plants. How do you think these animals get the nitrogen that their bodies need to survive?

_____

_____

UNIT 1 LIFE SCIENCE

The Ant and the Acacia

You have probably seen ants swarming all over a piece of candy dropped on the sidewalk. Cleaning up such bits of food and eating other dead animals is the role that most species of ants fill in nature. These ants are called scavengers.

Not all ant species are scavengers. Some species of ants live in a partnership with acacia plants. Many partnerships in nature involve a give and take. A relationship in which two species help each other is called **mutualism.** Each partner gives the other something it needs. The need may be food, shelter, water, or protection from an enemy. In the case of the ant and the acacia plant, the trade is food and shelter for defense.

The acacia makes a sugary sweet nectar, which the ants eat. The ants also live in the thorns of the acacia plant. The ants protect the plant from insects and other animals that might eat it. If a deer starts nibbling on an acacia leaf, the ants swarm and sting it all over. The deer will probably avoid eating that plant in the future. If any other plants start to grow near the acacia, the ants chew them down.

▶ **Fill in the blank with the word that best completes each statement.**

11. In its relationship with the ant, the acacia plant gets

_____.

12. Animals that eat other dead animals are called

_____.

▶ **Circle the letter of the best answer.**

13. Which of the following is an example of mutualism?

    A.   A bird eats ticks that are on the back of an ox.

    B.   Ants carry bits of leaves back to the anthill.

    C.   A wild dog eats what is left of an antelope after lions have finished eating.

    D.   Two chimpanzees remove fleas from each other's fur.

▶ **Write the answer to the question.**

14. Suppose a population of ants lives among acacia plants. During a severe storm, most of the acacia are damaged or destroyed. What do you think will happen to the ant population? Explain.

_____

_____

Check your answers on page 259.

MINI-TEST

This is a 15-minute practice test. After 15 minutes, mark the last number you finished. Then complete the test and check your answers. If most of your answers were correct but you did not finish, try to work faster next time.

▶ **Directions: Choose the <u>one best answer</u> to each question.**

Questions 1 and 2 refer to the following diagram.

How West Nile Virus Is Spread

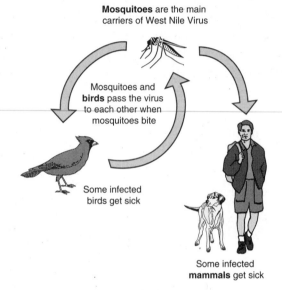

Mosquitoes are the main carriers of West Nile Virus

Mosquitoes and **birds** pass the virus to each other when mosquitoes bite

Some infected birds get sick

Some infected **mammals** get sick

1. A mosquito infected with West Nile virus bites a bird. According to the diagram, what will happen next?

   A. The mosquito will get infected with the virus.

   B. The bird will get infected with the virus.

   C. A mammal will pass the virus to a bird.

   D. A mammal will pass the virus to a mosquito.

2. Less than 1% of people infected with West Nile virus get very sick. What are the chances of getting seriously ill if you are bitten by a mosquito infected with West Nile virus?

   A. certain   C. unlikely

   B. very likely   D. impossible

Questions 3 and 4 refer to the following information.

Germs are all around us, but they rarely make healthy people ill. Thanks to our immune system, any germs that enter the body are seen as foreign substances. A foreign protein is called an **antigen.** When an antigen enters a healthy body, white blood cells begin to make antibodies. An antibody is a protein that the body makes to defend itself. Antibodies attack and kill germs. When your white blood cells produce sufficient antibodies against invading germs, you remain healthy.

3. Based on this information, what can you infer about infections?
   When a person has an infection, his or her white blood cells are

   A. not producing enough antibodies

   B. producing too many antibodies

   C. not producing enough antigens

   D. producing too many antigens

4. Why do healthy people rarely become ill?

   A. Our environment is generally germ-free.

   B. Most germs do not attack humans.

   C. White blood cells protect the body.

   D. Antigens attack invading germs.

5. Your physical traits are determined by genetic material that you inherit from your parents. For every trait you inherit, each of your parents has contributed genetic material for that trait. Some traits are dominant or recessive. For example, the ability to roll the tongue is a dominant trait; the inability to roll the tongue is a recessive trait. If you have a recessive trait, you inherited recessive genetic material for that trait from both of your parents. If you have a dominant trait, you inherited dominant genetic material for that trait from one or both parents. Dominant genetic material for a trait can mask the recessive genetic material.

Right-handedness is a dominant trait. Can two right-handed parents produce a left-handed child?

A. No, since one parent has recessive genetic material for the handedness trait.

B. Yes, if both parents have recessive genetic material for the handedness trait.

C. No, since one parent has dominant genetic material for the handedness trait.

D. Yes, since handedness is a trait that does not show dominance.

Questions 6 and 7 refer to the following information.

A biologist wanted to answer the question "How much time do plant cells spend in each phase of cell division?" She used a chemical to stop cell division in an onion root tip. Then she examined a sample of the cells and counted the number of cells in each phase of division. The biologist knew that the percentage of cells in

each phase was equal to the amount of time the cells spent in that phase. She then summarized her observations in the circle graph below.

Time Cells Spend in Cell Division

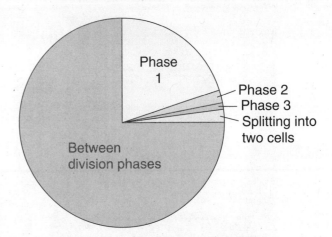

6. Which of the following statements is supported by the biologist's observations? Most of the cells she observed were

A. not actively dividing

B. in Phase 1

C. in Phase 2

D. in Phase 3

7. Which of the following is a valid comparison based on the biologist's data? The plant cells spent

A. more time in Phase 2 than in Phase 1

B. more time in Phase 1 than in Phase 2

C. more time in Phase 3 than in Phase 1

D. more time in Phase 3 than in Phase 2

Earth and space science is the study of our world—from deep inside our planet, to Earth's surface where we live, to beyond the atmosphere and into outer space. Earth and space science covers topics as large as the universe and as small as a pebble.

Understanding Earth and space science can help you to better understand our planet and its place in the universe. It can also help you to take better care of yourself and the world you live in. Here are examples of very basic ways that Earth and space science is a part of everyday life.

Describe today's weather. _____

Describe one way to use water wisely. _____

List natural objects you've recently seen in the sky. _____

_____

Thinking About Earth and Space Science

You may not realize how often you use Earth and space science as you go about your daily life. Think about your recent activities.

Check the box for each activity you have done recently.

☐ Did you check a weather forecast?

☐ Did you use water?

☐ Did you turn over soil for a garden plot or dig a hole?

☐ Did you ride in an airplane?

☐ Did you go hiking, camping, or to the beach?

☐ Did you watch the sun rise or set?

☐ Did you look at the moon or the stars?

Write some other activities in which you used Earth and space science.

_____

_____

_____

Previewing the Unit

In this unit, you will learn:

- how scientists measure and study the history of Earth

- how the Earth is a continually changing planet

- how scientists predict and explain the weather

- how Earth is warmed

- how people can affect Earth

- how the planets, including Earth, are arranged in the solar system

- how scientists are learning about outer space

Lesson 10	**Geologic Time**
Lesson 11	**Earth's Interior**
Lesson 12	**Weather**
Lesson 13	**The Atmosphere**
Lesson 14	**Resources**
Lesson 15	**The Solar System**
Lesson 16	**The Universe**

GEOLOGIC TIME

Suppose you wanted to write the story of your personal history. How would you use time to tell your story? Most likely, you would describe periods of time in terms of decades, years, months, weeks, days, or hours.

To tell the story of Earth's history, scientists also use periods of time. But since Earth is significantly older than you are, scientists use significantly longer periods of time to tell the story. They divide Earth's history into eons, eras, periods, and epochs. To do this, they use evidence provided by Earth's rocks.

Vocabulary

geologist

geology

absolute age

relative age

radiometric dating

radioactive decay

geologic time scale

Relate to the Topic

This article describes Earth's history. Think about your own history.

What are some of the major events in your life?

_____

_____

How would you use different periods of time to describe events in your history? Give two examples.

_____

_____

Reading Strategy

SKIMMING CHARTS   Information is often summarized in **charts.** A chart usually has a title and labels. The title tells you what kind of information the chart contains. The labels help you locate specific information in the chart. Skim the chart on page 99. Then answer the questions.

1. What is the topic of the chart?

_____

Hint: Look at the title.

2. What unit of time do the numbers in the chart represent?

_____

_____

Hint: Look at the labels above each column.

Earth's History

Your history may not be very long or complicated, but Earth's history is both. Understanding this long and complicated history is the task of **geologists,** or scientists who study Earth and its history. The study of Earth and its history is called **geology.** By studying the various kinds of rocks, the rock layers, and the evolution of life, geologists reconstruct the sequence of events that make up Earth's history.

Just as your history begins the day you were born, Earth's history begins when the planet formed. Scientist estimate that Earth formed approximately 4.6 billion years ago. But how do scientists know the age of Earth?

Dating Rocks

An important part of finding Earth's age and reconstructing Earth's history is dating rocks, or determining their age. When dating rocks, geologists use two concepts: absolute age and relative age. **Absolute age** refers to how many years ago a rock formed. **Relative age** refers to how old one rock is compared to another rock.

For example, some of the oldest rocks discovered so far on Earth are found in the Acasta Gneiss (pronounced *nice*), a large outcropping of rock in the Northwest Territories of Canada. These rocks have an absolute age of 4.03 billion years.

To measure absolute age of rocks, scientists use a method called **radiometric dating.** This process uses the decay of radioactive elements found in rocks. Elements are the building blocks of all things on Earth. Radioactive elements are unstable substances that emit particles. Giving off these particles changes the unstable element, called the parent. It changes into a more stable element, called the daughter. This process of decay is called **radioactive decay.** Radioactive decay occurs at a constant rate specific to each unstable element. So scientists can measure the amount of parent and daughter elements in a rock and use the decay rate to calculate the age of the rock.

Rocks on Earth change constantly, so the oldest rocks probably do not exist any longer. However, moon rocks and meteorites have been dated at 4.4 to 4.6 billion years using radiometric dating. Evidence indicates that these objects formed about the same time that Earth formed. Therefore, scientists infer Earth's age to be approximately 4.6 billion years.

Radiometric dating indicates that this rock from the Acasta Gneiss is one of the oldest on Earth.

Some types of rocks cannot be dated using radiometric dating. Instead, their relative age must be determined. One of the main ways to determine relative age is using the principle of superposition. This principle states that, as layers accumulate over time, older layers get buried beneath younger layers. In general, that means older rocks lie below younger ones.

Recall that, by comparing fossils over time, scientists can trace the development of species over time. Scientists also use the fossils preserved in sequences of rock layers to find the relative age of rocks using the principle of faunal succession. This principle says that fossil species succeed each other in a recognizable order. The same sequence of changes in fossil species occurs in different places on Earth. As a result, fossils can be used to identify rocks of the same or different ages.

▶ Drawing Conclusions A conclusion is an idea that follows logically from facts or evidence. For example, suppose a geologist observes three undisturbed rock layers: a shale located beneath a sandstone, and a limestone located above the sandstone. Using the principle of superposition, the geologist can conclude that the shale is older than the sandstone.

Which of the following is another conclusion that can be drawn from the evidence provided about the three rock layers? Circle the letter of the correct answer.

A. The limestone is younger than the sandstone.
B. The sandstone formed after the limestone.

The Geologic Time Scale

The history of the Earth is a long and complicated story of constant change. The landscape changed as oceans formed and dried up, and mountain ranges were lifted higher and worn down. Organisms evolved as the environments they inhabited changed. But dating methods enable scientists to organize Earth's rocks, fossils, and the events they represent in chronological order on chart called a time scale. The **geologic time scale** is a record of the major events in Earth's history, with the oldest events at the bottom and the youngest at the top.

On the geologic time scale, Earth's history is divided into time periods of eons, eras, periods, and epochs. An eon is the largest division of geologic time. Eons are divided into eras, and eras are divided into periods. Periods are divided into epochs.

Divisions on the geologic time scale are based on major events in Earth's history. For example, life first appeared on Earth during the Archean Eon. The Paleozoic Era began with an explosion in diversity of multi-celled animals and ended with the wiping out of approximately 90% of all marine animal species. Dinosaurs evolved in the Triassic Period and became extinct at the end of the Cretaceous Period.

Geologic Time Scale

Era	Period	Epoch	Millions of years ago
Cenozoic	Quaternary	Holocene	0.01
		Pleistocene	1.8
	Tertiary	Pliocene	5.3
		Miocene	23.8
		Oligocene	33.7
		Eocene	54.8
		Paleocene	65
Mesozoic	Cretaceous		144
	Jurassic		206
	Triassic		248
Paleozoic	Permian		290
	Pennsylvanian		323
	Mississippian		354
	Devonian		417
	Silurian		443
	Ordovician		490
	Cambrian		543

PHANEROZOIC EON

PROTEROZOIC EON

Proterozoic Eon
The first cells appeared during this eon.

2,500

ARCHEAN EON

Archean Eon
Life first appeared on Earth during this eon.

3,800

HADEAN EON

Hadean Eon
The oldest known rocks on Earth date from near the end of this eon.

4,600

The geologic time scale is a record of Earth's history.

▶ **Interpreting Charts** Charts can provide a large amount of information in a small space. To find the information you are looking for in a chart, you must read the labels at the top of each column. These labels tell you what types of information are listed in each column. Once you find the information you are looking for in one column, trace your finger across the row to find related information. The geologic time scale is a special kind of chart.

Refer to the chart above. When did the Mesozoic Era begin? Circle the letter of the best answer.

    A. with the Cretaceous Period 65 million years ago

    B. with the Triassic Period 248 million years ago

Thinking About the Article

Practice Vocabulary

▶ The terms below are in the passage in bold type. Study the way each term is used. Then complete each sentence by writing the correct term.

geology   absolute age   relative age

radiometric dating   radioactive decay

1. How old a rock is compared to another rock is the rock's

   _____ .

2. _____ is process of the decay of radioactive elements.

3. The science of _____ is the study of Earth and its history.

4. _____ involves using the decay of radioactive elements to find the absolute age of rocks.

5. How many years ago a rock formed is the rock's

   _____ .

Understand the Article

▶ Write or circle the answer to each question.

6. Name one method of determining a rock's absolute age and two ways of determining a rock's relative age.

   _____

   _____

   _____

7. What is the approximate age of Earth?
   A. 4.6 million years
   B. 4.6 billion years

   _____

   _____

8. What is the geologic time scale?

   _____

   _____

Apply Your Skills

▷ **Circle the letter of the best answer.**

9. Which of the following would a geologist most likely study?

    A.   how sunlight affects plants

    B.   when a distant star formed

    C.   what makes up skin cells

    D.   when rock layers formed

10. A scientist observes and compares the fossils in two rocks discovered in different locations. Based on her observations, she concludes that the two rocks are the same age. Which statement most likely describes her conclusion?

    A.   She used radiometric dating to determine relative age.

    B.   She used the principle of faunal succession to determine absolute age.

    C.   She used the principle of superposition to determine relative age.

    D.   She used the principle of faunal succession to determine relative age.

11. According to the geologic time scale on page 99, during which time period did the Acasta Gneiss form?

    A.   Phanerozoic Eon

    B.   Hadean Eon

    C.   Proterozoic Eon

    D.   Mesozoic Era

Connect with the Article

▷ **Write your answer to each question.**

12. According to the geologic time scale on page 99, what eon, era, period, and epoch do you live in?

_____

_____

13. Use absolute age and relative age to describe yourself or someone you know.

_____

_____

_____

SCIENCE PRACTICE FOCUS

The Geologic Time Scale

The chart below shows the major biologic (life) events and geologic (earth) events that happened during the Mesozoic and Cenozoic eras of Earth's history. Study the chart and then answer the questions that follow.

Era	Period	Epoch	Major Biologic Events	Major Geologic Events
Cenozoic	Quaternary	Holocene	Modern humans; agricultural development	Ice Age ends; uplift of continents
		Pleistocene	Early human development	Ice Age begins
	Tertiary	Pliocene	Large carnivores and mammoths	Cold climate; N. and S. America connected
		Miocene	Pigs, cattle, deer, camels, giraffes, grasslands	Warm climate; Andes Mountains form
		Oligocene	Birds of prey, elephants, primates	Cold climate; marine life moves to Equator
		Eocene	Many modern species of small mammals	Warm climate; separation of large continents
		Paleocene	Early horses, rodents, rabbits, ferns	Cold climate; most continents still connected
Mesozoic	Cretaceous		Extinction of dinosaurs; development of flowering plants	Supercontinent Pangaea splits; asteroid hits Earth in Yucatan Peninsula, Mexico
	Jurassic		First birds and mammals; development of many dinosaur species	Beginning of Rocky Mountain formation
	Triassic		First dinosaurs	Supercontinent Pangaea begins to split

▶ **Circle the letter of the best answer.**

1. The development of birds of prey, elephants, and primates occurred during which of the following epochs?

   A. Pleistocene   C. Miocene

   B. Pliocene   D. Oligocene

▶ **Fill in the blank with the word or words that best complete each statement.**

2. The Ice Age ended during the _____ Epoch.

3. The Rocky Mountain began to form during the _____ Period.

4. The Eocene Epoch is part of the _____ Era.

▶ **Write your answer to each question.**

5. Early dinosaur fossils have been found on each of Earth's modern continents. Since most of these dinosaurs could not swim, how were they able to travel from Antarctica to North America?

6. How might an asteroid hitting Earth at the end of the Cretaceous Period be connected to the extinction of the dinosaurs?

7. The complete geologic time scale with the length of time each time period lasted is shown on page 99. Suppose you are given a 5-meter long strip of butcher paper, a meter stick, and a set of colored pencils. You are asked to construct an accurate model of the geologic time scale. Describe how the model might be created.

8. Why would it be difficult to indicate the history of the United States on the your model?

9. Use the information on page 99 to predict which eon would be longest on your model. Explain your answer.

 Check your answers on page 261. 103

EARTH'S INTERIOR

Some people may think that mountains and oceans last forever, but features on Earth's surface are shifting, rising, and falling every day. That's because Earth's surface is constantly changing.

The changes on Earth's surface are related to changes that occur deep inside the planet. These changes can make the ground shake and crack open, and they can make rock melt and explode onto the surface. Earth is a dynamic place inside and out.

Relate to the Topic

This article describes Earth's interior and how changes under the ground affect features on the surface. Think about changes to Earth's surfaces that you have seen.

What is the most dramatic change to Earth's surface that you have witnessed, either in person or in the news?

_____

_____

In what ways do you think the dramatic change impacted people who lived there?

_____

_____

Reading Strategy

PICTURING AN EVENT   When you read about an event or experience, it can help if you try to imagine what is happening by forming a picture of something in your mind. Look at the first paragraphs on page 105. Then answer the questions.

1. What does the first paragraph on page 105 ask you to imagine?

_____

Hint: Look for a sentence with the word imagine *in it.*

2. How do you think imagining this event might help you understand the topic of this lesson?

_____

Hint: Look for words such as also *or* like *to find out how what you imagine relates to the lesson topic.*

Vocabulary

crust

mantle

core

lithosphere

plates

asthenosphere

plate tectonics

plate boundaries

landform

trench

volcano

earthquake

fault

Earth's Structure

Imagine that you have a hard-boiled egg, and you use a knife to slice right through the shell to cut the egg in half. What would you see inside the egg? You would see three main layers: the shell on the outside, the white in the middle, and the yoke in the center. Earth is also made up of three main layers: the crust, the mantle, and the core.

The **crust** is Earth's outermost and thinnest layer, ranging from about 5 to 70 km thick. It is thinnest under the oceans and thickest under the continents, particularly under mountains. It is made up of solid but brittle rock that can break. The layer beneath the crust is the **mantle**, which is a dense, hot layer of rock about 2,900 kilometers thick.

The innermost layer is the **core**. It is mostly made up of the metals iron and nickel. The core has a liquid outer region of about 2,200 kilometers thick and a solid inner region of about 1,250 kilometers thick. This inner part of the core is under such intense pressure from the surrounding layers that the melting points of the metals are affected. The pressure allows this inner core to remain solid, even at temperatures as hot as the sun's surface.

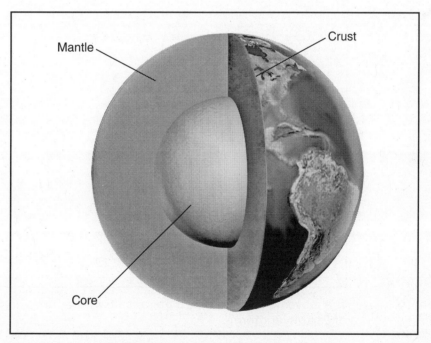

Earth's three main layers are the crust, mantle, and core.

▶ Reading a Diagram A diagram is a picture that shows how something is put together or explains how something works. Some diagrams have labels and leader lines that show you the parts of something. In the diagram above, the leader lines point to the different layers of Earth and the labels tell you the names of those layers.

According to the diagram, which of the following layers is located at Earth's center?
A. mantle   B. core

Plate Tectonics

The crust and uppermost mantle form a rigid layer of rock called the **lithosphere**. It is broken up into the moving pieces that contain the oceans and continents. These pieces of the lithosphere are called **plates**, and they fit together like pieces of a jigsaw puzzle. The rigid lithosphere floats or moves around on the soft, less-rigid region of the mantle below it. This region of the mantle is called the asthenosphere. It slowly flows as a result of currents caused by heat in the mantle. As a result, the plates float along the **asthenosphere**. The idea that Earth's lithosphere consists of plates that slowly move as a result of currents in the mantle is known as the theory of **plate tectonics**.

Tectonic plates move away from, toward, or past each other. The edges of plates where two plates meet are known as **plate boundaries**. Both earthquakes and volcanic activity are common along plate boundaries. Let's find out why.

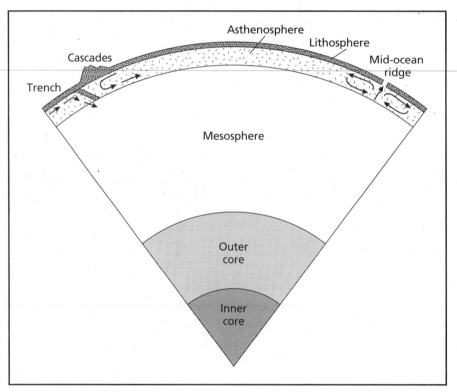

The movement of tectonic plates results in the formation of many of Earth's landforms.

▶ **Recognizing Cause and Effect** When one event causes another event to happen, the events are related by cause and effect. To find cause-and-effect relationships, look for words and phrases such as *caused by, as a result of,* and *because of.* The temperature increases with depth below Earth's surface, making the mantle a very hot layer. Heat in the mantle causes currents to flow in the solid but soft rock. Which of the following is an effect of theses currents flowing in the mantle?

A. Tectonic plates move around Earth's surface.

B. Earth's inner core remains solid instead of melting.

Earth's Landforms

Movements of Earth's tectonic plates cause many of the changes that have formed Earth's landforms. A **landform** is a feature of Earth's surface, such as a mountain, canyon, or ridge.

Where two plates move toward each other and collide, one or both plates may buckle and get pushed upward, and a mountain range can form. Earth's tallest mountains, the Himalaya Mountains, formed as a result of the collision of two plates. When plates move together, one plate may sink below the other and partially melt. A deep canyon called a **trench** forms along the plate boundary. Where the melted rock rises and erupts on the surface, a chain of volcanoes often forms parallel to the boundary. A **volcano** is an opening in the crust from which melted rock erupts. The volcanic mountains known as the Cascades in the northwestern United States formed in this way. One of those mountains, Mount St. Helens in Washington, erupted in 1980.

When one plate sinks below another plate, volcanoes can form. Melted rock from the asthenosphere can rise through the lithosphere and erupt onto Earth's surface through the volcano.

Where plates move past each other, volcanoes don't usually form. But the rocks do get ground up and broken, often creating gaps in the surface called fault valleys or undersea canyons. Grinding of rock along the plate boundaries results in the shaking of the ground know as an **earthquake**. In fact, earthquakes often occur along all types of plate boundaries where tremendous stresses build up and get released.

Along the west coast of North America, the Pacific Plate and North American Plate grind past each other, causing many earthquakes and the famous San Andreas Fault. A **fault** is a fracture in the crust along which rocks slide past each other. Faults commonly occur along plate boundaries, and they provide another example of how changes on Earth's surface result from changes inside Earth.

Thinking About the Article

Practice Vocabulary

▶ **The words below are in the passage in bold type. Study the way the words are used. Then complete each sentence by writing the correct words.**

landform	plates	earthquake	volcano

1. A(n) _____ is an opening in the crust from which melted rock erupts.

2. A(n) _____ is a shaking of the ground that often occurs along plate boundaries.

3. The lithosphere is broken up into moving pieces called

    _____ .

4. A _____ is a feature of Earth's surface.

Understand the Article

▶ **Match each layer of Earth with its description. Write the letter of the layer in the space provided.**

Description

_____ 5. innermost layer made mostly of iron and nickel

_____ 6. region of the mantle on which plates float

_____ 7. outermost and thinnest layer

_____ 8. rigid layer of crust and upper mantle rock

_____ 9. dense, hot layer beneath the crust

Layer

A. lithosphere

B. core

C. mantle

D. asthenosphere

E. crust

▶ **Write the answer to each question.**

10. Which layer of Earth has a liquid outer region and a solid inner region?

    _____

11. What is the theory of plate tectonics?

    _____

    _____

Apply Your Skills

▶ **Circle the letter of the best answer.**

12. According to the diagram on page 105, which of the following lists Earth's main layers from innermost to outermost?

    A.   core, crust, mantle

    B.   mantle, core, crust

    C.   crust, mantle, core

    D.   core, mantle, crust

13. Which of the following is most likely to occur where the one tectonic plate moves past another plate?

    A.   earthquakes

    B.   volcanic eruptions

    C.   new crust forming

    D.   ocean basin being destroyed

14. The Juan de Fuca Trench is located off the west coast of North America along the boundary of the Juan de Fuca Plate and the North American Plate. Which of the following most likely caused this landform to form?

    A.   the Juan de Fuca Plate moving away from the North American Plate

    B.   the Juan de Fuca Plate moving past the North American Plate

    C.   the Juan de Fuca Plate sinking under the North American Plate

    D.   the Juan de Fuca Plate colliding with and buckling the North American Plate

Connect with the Article

▶ **Write your answer to each question.**

15. The word *tectonics* comes from a Greek word meaning "to build." Why do you think the theory was named plate tectonics?

16. Why do you think it is generally considered to be riskier to live near plate boundaries than in the middle of plates?

SCIENCE PRACTICE FOCUS

The Theory of Continental Drift

Geologists around the world accept that the continents move. Few scientists would argue that the land masses have stayed in one place for billions of years. That acceptance, however, is a surprisingly recent development.

Alfred Wegener (VEH geh nuhr) first proposed the theory of continental drift in 1912. Wegener was a German weather scientist, or meteorologist. He noticed that the edges of the continental shelves fit together like a puzzle. Wegener studied rock formations and compared fossils at the edges of different continents. The evidence led him to conclude that all of the continents once fit together into a single giant land mass.

Wegener presented his theory at scientific meetings and in writing. A majority of geologists at the time dismissed his ideas. They did not take Wegener seriously because he was not a geologist and he did not speak English well enough to defend his ideas at meetings. In addition, Wegener could not explain *how* the continents moved.

Wegener died in 1930 on an Arctic expedition to Greenland. In the 1950s, other scientists began to collect data about Earth's interior that supported Wegener's theory of continental drift. With new tools, geologists could measure the spreading of the ocean floor and the movement of landmasses. Decades after his death, Wegener was finally recognized as the father of plate tectonics, one of the most important scientific theories of the 20th century.

▶ **Fill in the blank with the word or words that best complete each statement.**

1. Before Wegener, most geologists thought that the

_____ remained fixed in their places.

2. The modern-day theory that grew out of Wegener's work is

_____ .

▶ **Write the answer to each question.**

3. What kinds of evidence helped Wegener to develop his theory of continental drift?

_____

_____

4. How was Wegener's theory first received by geologists when he proposed it?

_____

_____

5. List three reasons that Wegener struggled to get other scientists to accept his theory of continental drift.

_____

_____

_____

6. Why did geologists eventually change their minds about Wegener's theory?

_____

_____

_____

7. How did Wegener react when his theory finally was accepted by other scientists?

_____

_____

8. How did reading this article change the way you think about scientific progress?

_____

_____

_____

_____

▶ **Circle the letter of the best answer.**

9. Which of the following is consistent with Wegener's theory of continental drift?

   A.   The continent of Africa has stayed in the same position for billions of years.

   B.   The continent of North America once covered the entire planet.

   C.   The fossils and rocks found on one continent are completely different from the fossils and rocks found on every other continent.

   D.   A world map of early Earth would look very different from a modern world map.

Check your answers on pages 262–263.

WEATHER

Vocabulary

air mass

continental polar
   air mass

continental tropical
   air mass

maritime polar air
   mass

maritime tropical
   air mass

front

stationary front

weather map

precipitation

meteorologist

forecast

Imagine what it would be like to have a hurricane or blizzard hit your area without warning. In the past—just decades ago—severe weather often took people by surprise. Today, thanks to weather satellites, global weather stations, and meteorologists, we can predict and prepare for all types of weather.

Weather maps also play a role in forecasting coming weather. Weather moves from one place to another. One day's snow in Buffalo may be the next day's snow in Boston. Weather maps show the weather over large areas and how it moves.

Relate to the Topic

This lesson is about weather and weather maps. Think about a time when you experienced really bad weather.

Did you know in advance that bad weather was coming? If so, how did

you know? _____

_____

Describe what happened. _____

_____

_____

Reading Strategy

PREVIEWING A MAP   A map is a picture that gives information about a place. Maps usually have a title, labels, and a key. The title tells the main idea of the map. The key tells what the colors or the symbols on the map represent. Refer to the map on page 114. Then answer the questions.

1. What is the topic of the map?

_____

Hint: Look at the title.

2. What does a line of triangles represent?

_____

Hint: Look at the map key.

Weather Systems

You've probably noticed that weather can change dramatically overnight. One day is hot, humid, and drizzling, and the next day is clear and dry. It feels as if the air has changed. In fact, the air *has* changed. One large body of air has replaced another.

Air Masses

Large areas of air near Earth's surface take on the same temperature and moisture as the surface. For example, the air over a tropical ocean becomes warm and humid. A large body of air with a specific temperature and moisture is called an **air mass.** The term used to describe an air mass tells you where it came from. The word *continental* refers to a continent. The word *maritime* refers to the sea. There are four main types of air masses that influence the continental United States:

- **Continental polar air masses** are cold and dry. They form over Canada and the northern United States.

- **Continental tropical air masses** are warm and dry. They form over the southwestern United States.

- **Maritime polar air masses** form over the northern Atlantic Ocean and the northern Pacific Ocean. These air masses are cold and moist.

- **Maritime tropical air masses** form over the Caribbean Sea, the middle of the Atlantic Ocean, and the middle of the Pacific Ocean. These air masses are warm and moist.

Air masses do not stay where they form. They may move thousands of miles. Think of a moving air mass as a large, flattened bubble of air. In the United States, air masses are usually pushed from west to east by winds. As the air mass moves, it may keep nearly the same temperature and moisture.

Fronts

The weather changes when one air mass moves out of an area and another moves in. The leading edge of a moving air mass is called a **front.** A cold front is at the front of a cold air mass. A warm front is at the front of a warm air mass. The weather can change quickly when a front passes through. A front often brings rain or snow to an area as it passes. When air masses stop moving for a while, the zone between them is called a **stationary front.**

Stormy weather often accompanies the passing of a front.

What Does a Weather Map Show?

Most newspapers print a **weather map** each day. A weather map shows where cold, warm, and stationary fronts are. It shows temperature and **precipitation,** such as rain, snow, and sleet.

Weather maps also show areas of high and low pressure. These areas of pressure are important because certain types of weather go with each. Most of the time, a high-pressure area means fair weather and no clouds. A low-pressure area is often cloudy with rain or snow.

High Temperatures and Precipitation for June 28

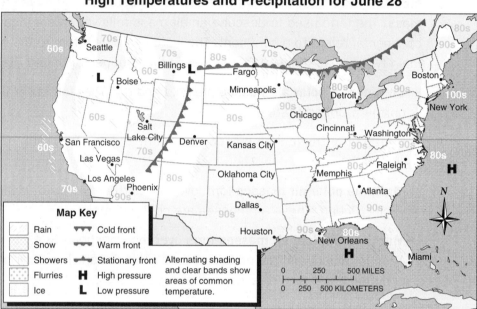

▶ Reading a Map When you read a map, look at the title first. That gives you the main idea of the map. This map shows the weather for June 28, with high temperatures in degrees Fahrenheit, the temperature scale we usually use in the United States. It also shows precipitation. Next, look at the map key to see how information is shown. On this weather map, for example, cold fronts are shown by a line of triangles. The triangles point in the direction in which the front is moving. Finally, look at the map itself. Find details that will help you understand it. For example, look at Dallas. Dallas is in the shaded area that shows places with a high temperature in the 90s. There is no precipitation shading over Dallas. On this day Dallas is very hot and dry.

1. The symbol for a warm front looks like
   A. a row of semicircles   B.   a row of triangles

2. The city closest to a warm front is
   A. Fargo   B.   Chicago

3. A cold air mass is behind a cold front. The high temperature in the cold air mass over the western United States is in the
   A. 80s and 90s   B.   60s and 70s

Weather Forecasts

Meteorologists are scientists who study the weather. Meteorologists study present weather conditions. Then they decide where the air masses and fronts will probably be the next day. From this data they **forecast,** or predict, the next day's weather. Suppose a meteorologist in Dallas studied the June 28 map. Her forecast for the next day might have said the high temperature would again be in the 90s and there would be no rain. Look at the map for June 29 below. Was the forecast correct?

High Temperatures and Precipitation for June 29

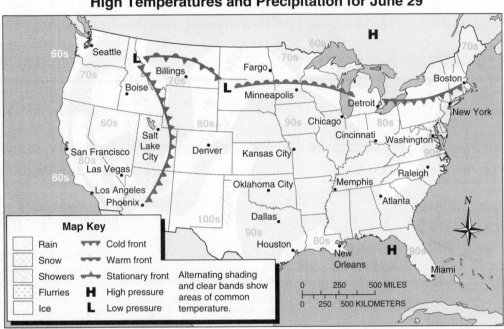

Map Key

Rain	⋁⋁⋁ Cold front
Snow	⌒⌒⌒ Warm front
Showers	⋁⌒⋁⌒ Stationary front
Flurries	**H** High pressure
Ice	**L** Low pressure

Alternating shading and clear bands show areas of common temperature.

▶ **Making Predictions** Like a meteorologist, you can use what you know to predict what will happen to the weather. Look at the map for June 28. In the upper right, there is a cold front moving south toward the northeastern United States. Now look at the map for June 29. The cold front has reached Boston. You can predict that soon the high temperature in the Boston area will drop from the 80s to the 70s. Use the map to answer these questions.

1. What is the weather like in New York City on June 29?
   A. high temperature in the 70s, rain
   B. high temperature in the 90s, dry

2. What kind of weather would you predict for New York City on June 30?
   A. high temperature in the 70s, dry
   B. high temperature in the 90s, rain

People often make jokes about the accuracy of weather forecasts. Yet meteorologists are pretty good at predicting tomorrow's weather. However, their long-range forecasts are not so accurate. Many factors can affect the weather. So forecasting more than a few days in advance involves guessing as well as predicting.

Thinking About the Article

Practice Vocabulary

▶ The terms below are in the passage in bold type. Study the way each term is used. Then complete each sentence by writing the correct term.

air mass	stationary front	front	weather map
precipitation	meteorologists	forecast	

1. A large body of air with similar temperature and moisture is called a(n)

   _____ .

2. The edge of a moving air mass is called a(n) _____ .

3. A(n) _____ is a prediction about the weather.

4. Scientists who study weather are called _____ .

5. A(n) _____ can be used to help predict the coming weather.

6. The zone between air masses that have stopped moving is called

   a(n) _____ .

7. Rain and snow are the most common forms of

   _____ .

Understand the Article

▶ Match the air mass with its characteristics. You may have more than one answer for each air mass.

Air Mass		Characteristic
_____	8. continental polar	A. cold
_____	9. continental tropical	B. warm
_____	10. maritime polar	C. dry
_____	11. maritime tropical	D. moist

▶ Write the answer to each question.

12. In what direction does weather in the United States generally move?

    _____

13. Why are long-range weather forecasts often inaccurate?

    _____

▶ **Circle the letter of the best answer for each question.**

14. On a weather map, there is a line of alternating triangles and half circles pointing in opposite directions. Look at the map key on page 114. What does this symbol indicate?

    A. cold front

    B. warm front

    C. stationary front

    D. high-pressure area

15. Refer to the map for June 29 on page 115. What do you predict the temperature will be in Fargo on June 30?

    A. 40s

    B. 60s

    C. 70s

    D. 90s

16. Refer to the map for June 29 on page 115. What do you predict the next day's weather forecast for Salt Lake City is likely to be?

    A. occasional showers, high temperature in the 60s

    B. occasional showers, high temperature in the 90s

    C. clear, high temperature in the 90s

    D. clear, high temperature in the 50s

▶ **Write your answer to each question.**

17. Refer to the map for June 28 on page 114. Which of the four types of air masses do you think is covering the western states? Give reasons for your answer.

_____

_____

_____

18. Describe today's weather in your area. What kind of air mass is in your area now?

_____

_____

Check your answers on page 263.

SCIENCE PRACTICE FOCUS

How Hurricanes Form

Hurricanes are among some of the most violent weather events on Earth. These storms form over the warm ocean waters near the equator and rely on warm, moist air for fuel. As the sun heats up ocean water, the water evaporates into the atmosphere. As the warm, moist air rises, it cools and clouds begin to form. More cool air rushes in to replace the rising warm, moist air. As a result, the whole system continues to spin and grow. Heavy rains and high winds begin to increase. As the storm system spins faster and faster, an eye usually forms in the center. The eye has very low air pressure and is calm and clear. The diagram below shows the process of hurricane formation. Study the diagram and then answer the questions that follow.

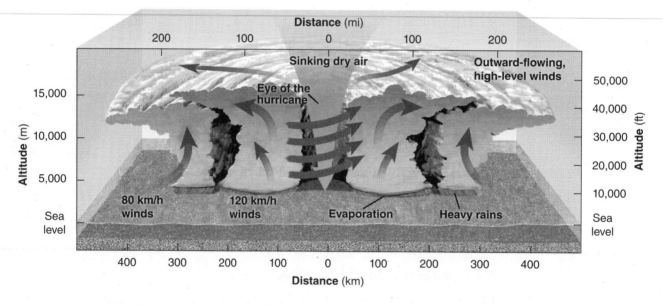

▶ **Circle the letter of the best answer.**

1. The distance across the eye of the storm system is about

   A. 50 kilometers   C. 200 kilometers

   B. 100 kilometers   D. 400 kilometers

2. How high into the atmosphere does the hurricane in the diagram reach?

   A. about 15,000 m   C. about 7,500 m

   B. about 11,000 m   D. sea level

Classifying Hurricane Strength

The tropical systems that begin around the equator do not start out as hurricanes. When the winds in the large, rotating storm reach 39 miles per hour, the storm is considered a tropical storm. When the wind speeds reach 74 miles per hour, the storm reaches hurricane status. When hurricanes make landfall, they can cause flooding due to heavy rain and severe wind damage. Hurricanes also can result in storm surges. A storm surge is a rapid rise in the level of water that moves onto land as the eye of the storm makes landfall.

The chart below shows the system used to categorize for hurricane intensity.

Category	Wind Speed (mph)	Storm Surge (ft)	Damage at Landfall
1	74–95	4–5	Minimal
2	96–110	6–8	Moderate
3	111–130	9–12	Extensive
4	131–155	13–18	Extreme
5	greater than 155	greater than 18	Catastrophic

▶ **Write the answer to each question.**

3. What are the expected wind speeds, storm surge, and land damage of a Category 3 hurricane?

4. A hurricane has a wind speed of 102 mph and a storm surge of 7 ft. What category storm is this hurricane?

5. What is the relationship between the wind speed and the storm surge of a hurricane?

6. A friend says that a recent hurricane completely destroyed some structures and caused major damage to other structures. He concludes it was a Category 2 storm. Is he correct? Explain your answer.

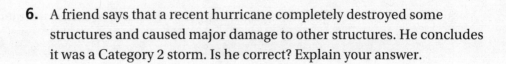

Check your answers on pages 263–264. **119**

THE ATMOSPHERE

The air that surrounds Earth helps keep our planet within a range of temperatures that support life at its surface. Like a blanket, the atmosphere holds in heat from the sun. Without the atmosphere, Earth would be very cold.

Human activities have changed the composition of the atmosphere. Many scientists think that these changes have caused Earth's temperature to increase. They are concerned that Earth will become even warmer—maybe too warm.

Vocabulary

atmosphere

radiant energy

infrared radiation

fossil fuels

Relate to the Topic

This lesson explains how the atmosphere keeps Earth warm. It also describes climate change, a trend that scientists have linked to burning fossil fuels like oil and gas.

How do you and your family use oil and gas?

_____

_____

What can you do to use less oil and gas?

_____

Reading Strategy

USING WHAT YOU KNOW   Use what you already know about a topic to help you understand an article. Think about what you already know about increasing global temperatures. Then answer the questions.

1. What have you read about climate change?

    _____

    _____

    Hint: Think about things you've seen or heard in the news.

2. What might happen if the Earth becomes warmer?

    _____

    _____

    Hint: Think about how warm temperatures affect snow and ice.

The Greenhouse Effect

The last few decades have been unusually warm. Since the mid 1970s, the average global temperature has risen by about one degree Fahrenheit (abbreviated 1 °F). This is about 0.5 degrees Celsius (0.5 °C) as measured on the scale used by scientists. Scientists attribute this warming to human activities, focusing people's attention on global, or worldwide, climate change.

How Earth is Warmed

The air around us, called the **atmosphere,** plays an important role in the warming of Earth. When the gases in the atmosphere absorb energy, they become warmer. But from where does the energy come? It comes from two places, the sun and Earth.

Energy from the sun is called **radiant energy.** When you are outside on a bright day, the radiant energy of sunlight is what warms you. The atmosphere absorbs about 20 percent of the sun's radiant energy and reflects about 30 percent back into space. The remaining 50 percent of the sun's radiant energy is absorbed by Earth.

Earth radiates energy back into the atmosphere as **infrared radiation.** We feel infrared radiation as heat. You can feel heat rising from the pavement or from sand on a beach. These are examples of infrared radiation.

Not all the infrared radiation reflected from Earth's surface escapes into space. Instead, water vapor, carbon dioxide, and other gases in the atmosphere absorb the heat. So, both the sun and the atmosphere warm the surface of Earth. This is called the greenhouse effect.

Earth's atmosphere helps keep temperatures on Earth stable.

Are People's Activities Increasing the Greenhouse Effect?

The greenhouse effect is a natural process. Without it, Earth would be much colder. But, after much research and debate, scientists who study the climate have confirmed that the greenhouse gases in the atmosphere have been increasing because of human activity. The scientific community is in consensus, or general agreement, that the average temperature on Earth is rising as a result.

In the last hundred years, people have burned more and more **fossil fuels.** Fossil fuels include coal, oil, gasoline, and wood. When these fuels burn, they increase the amount of carbon dioxide, a greenhouse gas, in the air. Also, people have destroyed many forests throughout the world. Plants absorb carbon dioxide during photosynthesis. Fewer plants means that more carbon dioxide remains in the atmosphere. More carbon dioxide in the atmosphere means that more heat is absorbed close to Earth.

Carbon dioxide is the main greenhouse gas, but there are several others. Ozone, chlorofluorocarbons (CFCs), methane, and nitrogen oxide all absorb infrared radiation, warming the atmosphere and Earth's surface. These greenhouse gases have increased as a result of pollution from cars, factories, and farms.

If greenhouse gas emissions continue at their present level or increase, scientists think that Earth's average temperature will increase 2.2 ° to 10 °F (1.4 ° to 5.8 °C) by 2100. We are already witnessing some of the effects of climate change on our planet. The ice caps at the North and South poles are already shrinking, and sea levels are rising globally.

▶ **Understanding the Relationships among Ideas** When you read, you are thinking all the time. Your mind is busy linking facts and ideas to one another and to things you already know. Reread the section of the article under the heading *Are People's Activities Increasing the Greenhouse Effect?* The main ideas are: (1) People are burning more fossil fuels. (2) People are destroying forests. (3) People are producing more air pollution. (4) Carbon dioxide and other greenhouse gases are increasing. (5) Global temperature is increasing. The first three main ideas are related. They are all things people do that affect the atmosphere.

1. How are Ideas 4 (increased greenhouse gases) and 5 (increased global temperature) related to one another?
   A. Idea 5 may be the result of Idea 4.
   B. Idea 4 may be the result of Idea 5.

2. What is the relationship of Ideas 1, 2, and 3 to Ideas 4 and 5?
   A. Ideas 1, 2, and 3 are the causes of Ideas 4 and 5.
   B. Ideas 4 and 5 are parts of Ideas 1, 2, and 3.

Check your answers on page 264.

What Can Be Done About Global Warming?

The Intergovernmental Panel on Climate Change (IPCC) was formed in 1998 and is considered an authority on climate change. It assesses the scientific data on climate change and makes policy recommendations for governments. Industrial nations have committed themselves to reducing their production of greenhouse gases. Individuals also can do many things that will help. Almost anything a person does that saves energy means that less fossil fuels are burned. If less fossil fuels are burned, there is less air pollution and less greenhouse gases are put into the air.

Reducing air pollution might help slow global warming.

People can save energy at home by adding insulation and turning down the thermostat in the winter and turning it up in the summer. Conserving electricity, which is usually produced by burning fossil fuels, will also help. Driving a car that gets many miles per gallon of gasoline saves energy. Or don't drive at all. Walking, bicycling, and taking public transportation help save energy and reduce carbon emissions.

Recycling also saves energy. When recycled materials are used in manufacturing, less energy is used. Also, recycling can help reduce the amount of garbage in landfills and incinerators. Landfills produce methane gas when garbage breaks down. Garbage burned in incinerators produces carbon dioxide.

In addition, people can contact their local, state, and federal representatives to make sure environmental regulations are passed and reinforced to reduce greenhouse gases and protect the future of our planet.

▶ **Understanding Compound Words** Science books are full of long words. Most of these words are compound words: long words that are made of smaller parts. Some familiar compound words are *baseball, sunshine,* and *supermarket.* Often you can figure out what a compound word means if you know what each part means. There are several compound words in the article you just read. *Sunlight* is light energy from the sun. A *landfill* is a place to bury trash (fill) in the ground (land).

1. What does *worldwide* mean (page 121, first paragraph)?

   _____

2. What does *greenhouse* mean (page 121, last paragraph)?

   _____

Check your answers on page 264.   123

Thinking About the Article

Practice Vocabulary

▶ **The terms below are in the passage in bold type. Study the way each term is used. Then complete each sentence by writing the correct term.**

fossil fuels	atmosphere	greenhouse effect
infrared radiation	climate change	

1. The air that surrounds Earth is called the _____ .

2. The trend toward higher average temperatures worldwide is called

   _____ .

3. The heat you feel rising from hot pavement is called

   _____ .

4. Gases in the atmosphere absorb heat energy radiated from Earth.

   This is known as the _____ .

5. There is scientific consensus that burning _____ contributes to the warming trend.

Understand the Article

▶ **Write the answer to each question.**

6. What kind of energy warms you when you sit out in the sun?

7. How is the greenhouse effect like a blanket?

8. List the major greenhouse gases.

9. What did many nations agree to do to help deal with climate change?

Apply Your Skills

▶ **Circle the letter of the best answer.**

10. Which of the following events might occur if greenhouse gas emissions continue to rise?

    A.   The polar ice caps will melt.

    B.   The average global temperature will increase.

    C.   Sea levels will rise.

    D.   All of the above

11. Carbon dioxide is a greenhouse gas. Planting trees may help reduce levels of greenhouse gases. Which statement links these two ideas?

    A.   Trees take in carbon dioxide during the process of photosynthesis.

    B.   The emissions of greenhouse gases are on the rise.

    C.   Burning fossil fuels releases carbon dioxide.

    D.   Cutting down trees may decrease the amount of carbon dioxide in the atmosphere.

12. Why does the sea level rise when the temperature on Earth becomes warmer?

    A.   Less ocean water would evaporates.

    B.   Some land is no longer suitable for farming.

    C.   The ice caps at the North and South poles melt.

    D.   There are more waves.

Connect with the Article

▶ **Write your answer to each question.**

13. Why do industrialized nations produce more greenhouse gases than nonindustrialized nations?

_____

_____

14. Why do you think it is important for there to be scientific consensus on an issue like climate change?

_____

_____

_____

SCIENCE PRACTICE FOCUS

The Layers of the Atmosphere

Earth's atmosphere is divided into four layers: troposphere, stratosphere, mesosphere and thermosphere. The **troposphere** is the layer closest to Earth's surface. Almost all of the weather occurs in the troposphere. The **stratosphere** is the layer above the troposphere. This layer is very dry and contains Earth's protective ozone layer. Above the stratosphere is the **mesosphere.** Most meteors that enter Earth's atmosphere burn up in the mesosphere. The uppermost layer is the **thermosphere.** Satellites and the International Space Station orbit Earth in the thermosphere and this is where auroras occur. Study the diagram below showing temperature and air pressure in the layers of Earth's atmosphere. Then answer the questions that follow.

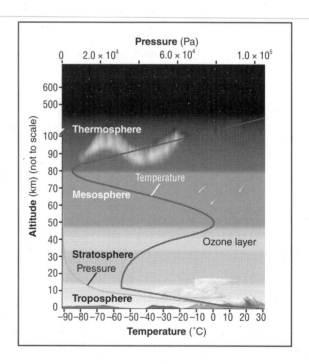

▶ **Circle the letter of the best answer.**

   1. The temperature at the top of the troposphere is about

   A. 25 degrees Celsius   C. −55 degrees Celsius

   B. 0 degrees Celsius   D. −75 degrees Celsius

▶ **Fill in the blank with the word or words that best complete each statement.**

   2. The temperature at the top of the stratosphere is about

   _____ .

▶ **Write the answer to each question.**

3. What is the relationship between air pressure and altitude in Earth's atmosphere?

....

....

4. Describe the relationship between altitude and temperature in the troposphere, stratosphere, mesosphere, and thermosphere.

....

▶ **The gas carbon dioxide (CO_2) makes up about 0.03% of Earth's atmosphere. The chart below shows the concentration of carbon dioxide in the air at the Mauna Loa Observatory in Hawaii between the years 1960–2010. Use the chart to answer Questions 5–7.**

Atmospheric CO_2 at Mauna Loa Observatory	
Year	Concentration (parts per million)
1960	315
1970	325
1980	338
1990	354
2000	370
2010	390

5. What was the change in carbon dioxide concentration in the air between 1990 and 2000?

....

....

6. What happened to the level of carbon dioxide gas in the atmosphere from 1960 to 2010?

....

....

7. Use the data in the chart to predict the level of carbon dioxide in the air at the Mauna Loa Observatory in the year 2020.

....

....

RESOURCES

Vocabulary

glacier

resource

groundwater

water cycle

renewable resource

reservoir

aqueduct

Most of us just turn on the faucet to get fresh water. We often take an endless supply of water for granted. But if you lived in a place where you had to haul water every day from a distant well, you would soon come to value water more. Fresh water is one of Earth's most precious resources.

Some communities can get all the fresh water they need from nearby lakes and rivers. But many other communities exist in areas that are far from any lake or river. These communities must go to a lot of extra effort to get fresh water.

Relate to the Topic

This article is about the supply of fresh water. It describes what a water-poor area like California does to ensure fresh water for its farms, businesses, and homes. Think about the tap water in your own home.

Where does your tap water come from? _____

_____

What would you do if you had no tap water? _____

_____

Reading Strategy

SCANNING BOLDFACED WORDS   Science materials often highlight technical terms in bold type—type which is darker than the type around it. Look at the boldfaced terms on pages 129 and 130. Then answer the questions.

1. What are glaciers?

_____

Hint: Look at the last paragraph on page 129.

2. What is the technical term for a lake created by a dam?

_____

Hint: Look under the heading Water Supplies.

Supplying Fresh Water

California is well known for its extreme variations in weather and natural disasters. Storms, earthquakes, and mud slides in California often make the national news. But these are single events lasting a few days at most. In contrast, one of California's major everyday problems—its water supply—gets much less attention.

California, like many areas of the West, is mostly desert. But you would never guess this when touring the state. In the Central Valley, a low-lying area that runs more than half the length of the state, green orchards and crops are planted in neat rows, mile after mile. In the Los Angeles area, sprinklers water lush lawns and gardens, and swimming pools dot the backyards. Yet normal rainfall in Los Angeles is just 15 inches per year—about the same as Tripoli, Libya, another desert city.

Most of the precipitation that falls in California falls in the northern mountains. Yet most of the people and agriculture are in the southern part of the state. A complex system of trapping and moving water from the north and from other states allows California to supply water to its farm industry and more than 38 million people.

Some California farms depend on water that has been moved over great distances.

Water as a Resource

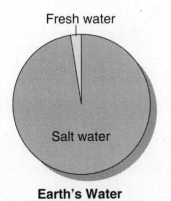

Fresh water

Salt water

Earth's Water Resources

Astronauts often call Earth the blue planet because it is covered by water. Earth has plenty of water, but most of it is in the oceans. Ocean water is salty, and you cannot drink it. Less than three percent of Earth's water is fresh water. Most of this fresh water is frozen in ice at the poles and in **glaciers,** which are large masses of ice that form where more snow falls than melts. Only about one percent of all Earth's water is available as a resource. A **resource** is a substance that is needed for human life and activities. Usable fresh water is a resource that is found in rivers, lakes, and the atmosphere. Water is also found underground in **groundwater.**

The supply of fresh water is constantly being renewed in an endless **water cycle.** Water that evaporates from lakes, rivers, and the salty oceans falls as saltless precipitation. In this way, water can be considered a **renewable resource.** However, the amount of fresh water used worldwide continues to grow. As the population expands, more people need more water for drinking, cooking, sanitation, crops, livestock, factories, and power plants. At the same time, more human activity means more water pollution. Due to natural conditions, such as geography, water is often scarce or not present where it is most needed. Like California, some regions are water-poor, while others are water-rich.

▶ Drawing Conclusions A conclusion is an idea that follows logically from the information you have. Conclusions must be supported by facts. For example, from the facts in the paragraph above you can conclude that the supply of fresh water may eventually be too small to meet the world's needs.

You can conclude that water pollution cuts the supply of fresh water because
A. less of the available water is fit for drinking and cooking
B. rivers with polluted water eventually dry up

Water Supplies

The United States as a whole has more than enough water for everyone. Moving the water where it is needed is the problem. For example, most precipitation in the West falls in the mountains, such as the Rockies and the Sierra Nevada. It flows as surface water in rivers, such as the Sacramento and Colorado. **Reservoirs,** lakes created by dams, store water. Large pipes called **aqueducts** carry the water to Southern California, Arizona, and other dry areas of the West.

California's Water Supply System

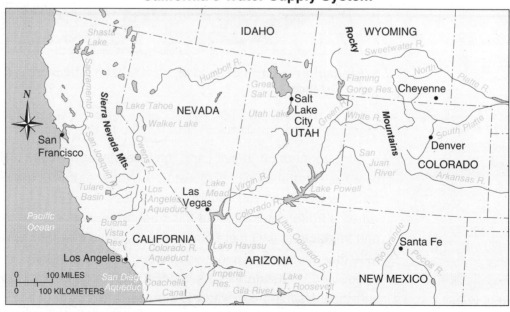

Another problem is that supplies of surface water depend on precipitation. If less than the normal amount of rain or snow falls over a long period of time, a drought occurs in that area. Groundwater, rivers, lakes, and reservoirs become low. During a drought, water use may have to be restricted.

Groundwater supplies are threatened by overuse and pollution. When a lot of water is taken from wells, the groundwater levels may go down. In West Texas, water for irrigating crops has been pumped for over 100 years. In that time the level of the groundwater has dropped about 100 feet. In other areas polluted wells have been shut down.

Finally, as the population of an area grows, competition for water increases. Southern California's population has been growing since the early 1900s. More and more people are moving to California's cities. Some people in California feel that the state has enough water. But they think that farms are getting more than their fair share. The farmers and their supporters argue that California supplies most of the country with food products. These people feel that irrigated open land adds to the quality of life for everyone in the country. While California tries to solve its long-term water problems, all Californians must conserve water.

▶ Reading a Map A map is a picture that gives information about a place. To read a map, first look at the title. It tells you the main idea of the map. Then look at the labels. They point out different parts of the map. On the map on page 130, the blue labels are the names of rivers, aqueducts, lakes, and reservoirs. The black labels are the names of states, cities, and mountain ranges.

The map on page 130 shows that water is supplied to Southern California by the
A. Sacramento River
B. Colorado River Aqueduct

Conserving Water

Many areas, not just California, have problems with their water supply. That is why it's important to get into the habit of conserving water. Here are some things you can do.

- Take shorter showers and install a water-saving shower head.
- Fix leaks. A dripping faucet can waste 300 to 600 gallons of water per month.
- Put a brick in the toilet's tank to cut the amount of water used for each flush. Or install a new low-flow toilet: they use 1.6 gallons per flush, while older toilets use 3.5 to 7 gallons per flush.
- Run the washing machine and dishwasher only with full loads.
- If you're doing dishes in the sink, don't run the water. Use one basin to wash and another to rinse.
- Turn off the water when you're brushing your teeth or shaving. A bathroom faucet uses up to 5 gallons of water per minute.

Thinking About the Article

Practice Vocabulary

▶ **The terms below are in the passage in bold type. Study the way each term is used. Then complete each sentence by writing the correct term.**

glaciers	resource	groundwater
water cycle	renewable resource	

1. A _____ is one for which there is a replaceable supply.

2. Water that is found underground is called _____ .

3. Water is a _____ that many of us take for granted.

4. _____ are large masses of ice that form where more snow falls than melts.

5. The endless movement of water from oceans to atmosphere to land is called the _____ .

Understand the Article

▶ **Write the answer to each question.**

6. Where does most of the water used in California come from?

_____

7. Where is the world's supply of usable fresh water found?

_____

_____

8. What causes a drought?

_____

_____

9. List two ways to conserve water.

_____

_____

_____

Apply Your Skills

▶ **Circle the letter of the best answer.**

10. Suppose there is a drought in California. Which of the following conclusions are you most likely to draw?

    A.   There is too little precipitation in the northern part of the state.

    B.   The reservoir levels are high all over the state.

    C.   The system of aqueducts is not transporting enough water.

    D.   Farm crops will not be affected by the lack of water.

11. Why are there water shortages in parts of the United States?

    A.   Not enough rain falls in the United States each year.

    B.   Most of the water in the United States is polluted.

    C.   Much of the water in the United States is groundwater.

    D.   Some areas get too much precipitation, while others do not get enough.

12. Refer to the map on page 130. Which of the following statements about the Los Angeles Aqueduct is correct?

    A.   It carries water from Los Angeles to Las Vegas.

    B.   It carries water from the Owens River to Los Angeles.

    C.   It carries water from northern California to Los Angeles.

    D.   It delivers water to the Sacramento River.

Connect with the Article

▶ **Write your answer to each question.**

13. If the world's supply of drinkable fresh water were running low, what alternative source of water can you think of to use?

_____

_____

14. Describe ways in which you or someone you know has conserved water.

_____

_____

_____

SCIENCE PRACTICE FOCUS

Energy Resources

Energy resources allow us to produce electricity and heat for our homes and businesses. Renewable energy resources can be replaced by nature, so there is always a good supply. Solar, wind, wood, and moving water are all example of renewable energy resources. Nonrenewable energy resources are only available in a limited supply. Once we use these resources, they are gone. Oil, natural gas, and coal, are nonrenewable energy resources.

Earth's population continues to grow and use more and more energy. Nonrenewable energy sources will gradually get harder to find and use. Logically, we need to shift to use more renewable energy resources. Renewable energy also moves human populations toward sustainability. The goal of sustainability is to continue for a long time without hurting people, the environment, or the economy.

Oil Rig

Windmills

▶ **Fill in the blank with the word or words that best complete each statement.**

1. Two example of nonrenewable energy resources are

_____ .

2. Using renewable energy helps us toward the goal of

_____ .

▶ **Write your answer to each question.**

3. Explain why wind power is considered a renewable energy resource.

_____

_____

_____

UNIT 2 EARTH AND SPACE SCIENCE

4. Some power plants generate electricity by burning garbage. Is garbage a renewable resource? Explain your answer.

_____

_____

_____

5. Predict what will happen if people continue to rely on nonrenewable resources for most of our energy needs.

_____

_____

_____

_____

6. The town of Summerville is facing a decision. Part of the town wants to invest in sustainable energy. This group wants the town to put solar panels on top of each of the town's school buildings. The solar panels would generate low-cost energy for many years. Other people opposed to spending the money. These people want to continue to purchase all of the town's electricity from a coal-fired electric plant in a nearby city. Are Summerville's energy options renewable or nonrenewable?

_____

_____

_____

7. Would a vote to install the solar panels in Summerville be a vote in favor of or against sustainable energy use?

_____

8. Think about the renewable energy resources in the area where you live. Do you have a lot of sun, or wind, running water, or trees available near your home? Describe how your community uses renewable energy now or how it could use renewable energy resources in the future.

_____

_____

_____

_____

THE SOLAR SYSTEM

Vocabulary

solar system

inner planets

silicon

erode

conglomerate

outer planets

space probe

People have been studying the solar system for centuries. Until fairly recently, observations of the solar system were made only from Earth.

Over the last 40 years, several unmanned space probes have explored the far reaches of the solar system. By sending photos and data back to Earth, these space probes have given us a closer look at Jupiter, Saturn, Uranus, and Neptune.

Relate to the Topic

This article describes some of the unmanned space missions that have been sent to the outer planets. Think about what it might be like to travel to another planet.

If you had the chance to visit another planet, would you go? Why or why not?

_____

_____

What would you hope to learn if you went to another planet?

_____

_____

Reading Strategy

USING HEADINGS TO ASK QUESTIONS   A heading usually summarizes the information that follows it. Think of questions you might have about the heading topic. Look for answers as you continue reading. Read the headings on pages 137 through 139. Then answer the questions.

1. What is one question that is likely to be answered on page 137?

_____

Hint: Read the heading.

2. Where would you expect to find information about Neptune?

_____

Hint: Look for a heading that contains the word Neptune.

The Planets

The first spacecraft to visit planets were launched in the 1960s. Since then, scientists have been learning new things about the solar system. The **solar system** is made up of the sun and the objects that revolve around the sun. These objects include the planets and their moons. Mercury, Venus, Earth, and Mars are called the **inner planets** because they are fairly close to the sun. They are all rocky planets. We know from the explorations of *Sojourner,* a robotic rover, that two of these rocky planets, Earth and Mars, have similar kinds of rocks. For example when *Sojourner* explored the surface of Mars in 1997, it found **silicon,** a common element found in Earth rocks. Also, the rounded shape of some Mars rocks suggests that they were **eroded,** or worn away. Some Mars rock is similar to **conglomerate,** rock formed when water rounds pebbles and larger stones that eventually become cemented together. Both processes have shaped rocks on Earth as well.

Jupiter, Saturn, Uranus, and Neptune are called the **outer planets.** Each of the outer planets is a gas giant, or a huge ball of various gases. They are much farther from the sun than the inner planets. The outer planets are so far away that only unmanned spacecraft, often called **space probes,** can be sent to explore them. It takes these spacecraft years to reach the outer planets.

Missions to the Outer Planets

Pioneer 10 was the first space probe to visit an outer planet. It was launched in 1972 and provided the first close-up pictures of Jupiter and its moons. The following year *Pioneer 11* sent back photos of Saturn and its rings.

Like *Pioneer 10* and *11,* most space probes are designed to visit only one planet. But scientists got a bonus with *Voyager 1* and *Voyager 2.* When these probes were launched in 1977, four of the outer planets were on the same side of the sun. These planets would not be in this position again for 175 years. So after reaching Jupiter, the *Voyager* space probes were able to fly on to Saturn, Uranus, and Neptune. They used the gravity of one planet to speed on to the next. Despite problems with radio reception, cameras, and computers, scientists on Earth guided *Voyager 1* and *Voyager 2* through an almost perfect grand tour of the outer reaches of our solar system.

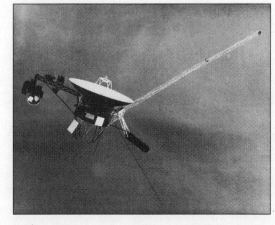

Each *Voyager* space probe had three computers, scientific instruments, and cameras mounted on a movable platform.

The *Pioneer* and *Voyager* probes flew by the outer planets and then continued out of the solar system. But the *Galileo* spacecraft was designed to orbit only its target planet, Jupiter. Launched in 1989, *Galileo* took pictures of the 1994 collision of comet Shoemaker-Levy with Jupiter. *Galileo* reached Jupiter in 1995 and began orbiting the planet. It lowered a separate probe into the atmosphere. Then it continued to circle Jupiter, sending back data about the planet and its moons.

All the space probes sent back spectacular photos. They also sent back data about Jupiter, Saturn, Uranus, Neptune, and their moons. Some basic data about these four planets and Earth are shown in the following table.

Earth and the Outer Planets					
	Earth	**Jupiter**	**Saturn**	**Uranus**	**Neptune**
Diameter (miles)	8,000	89,000	75,000	32,000	30,000
Mass (compared to the mass of Earth)	1	318	95	15	17
Distance from the sun (millions of miles)	93.5	486.4	892	1,790	2,810
Time of one revolution around sun (years)	1	12	29	84	165
Time of one rotation (length of day in hours)	24	10	11	17	16
Number of known moons	1	50	53	27	13

▶ Reading a Table   One way to present a set of facts is to organize them in a **table,** or chart. When you read a table, start with the title to get the main idea. From the title of this table, you know you will find information about Earth and the four outer planets. The column headings ("Earth," "Jupiter," and so on) tell you which planet's information is in that column. The entries in each row of the left-hand column tell you what information appears in that row. For example, the first row of the table gives you information about diameter in miles. To find Saturn's diameter, you look along that row until you reach the Saturn column. Its diameter is 75,000 miles.

1. How many known moons does Jupiter have? ....

2. How long does it take Uranus to revolve around the sun? ....

Jupiter and Saturn

Photos sent back by the spacecraft showed that Jupiter has rings. Jupiter also has a swirling, stormy atmosphere into which *Galileo*'s probe parachuted. The atmosphere is made mostly of hydrogen and helium gases. The Great Red Spot of Jupiter is a storm several times larger than Earth.

Saturn's rings photographed by *Voyager 2* when it was 27 million miles away

Jupiter's four largest moons were first seen by the astronomer Galileo with a telescope in 1610. Ganymede, the largest moon in the solar system, looks similar to our moon. Io has active volcanoes, and its surface looks like pizza. Europa has a smooth surface of ice with a network of grooves. Callisto also has ice, but its surface has many deep craters.

Like Jupiter, Saturn is made mostly of hydrogen and helium. Saturn rotates quickly, causing bands of clouds to form in its atmosphere. Wind speeds of 500 miles per hour have been measured.

Galileo's biggest surprise for scientists was Saturn's rings. Scientists discovered that the planet has thousands of narrow rings, instead of a few very wide rings. Saturn's rings are made of particles ranging from specks of dust to large rocks. Some rings have "spokes" that appear and disappear. This new information has raised many questions about Saturn's rings.

Uranus and Neptune

It took almost five years for *Voyager 2* to travel the distance between Saturn and Uranus. Uranus is made mostly of hydrogen and helium. The temperature in the atmosphere is about −330 °F. At Uranus, *Voyager 2* found ten new moons.

The last planet *Voyager 2* flew by was Neptune. Neptune, made mostly of hydrogen, also has a stormy atmosphere. One feature seen by *Voyager 2* is the Great Dark Spot. This spot is a storm almost as big as Earth. Data sent back to Earth suggests that Neptune's winds, moving over 1,200 miles per hour, might be the fastest in the solar system. *Voyager 2* also discovered six new moons orbiting Neptune.

▶ **Drawing Conclusions** Conclusions are ideas that are based on facts. They follow logically from the facts. This article describes four of the outer planets and some of their moons. From the fact that the author refers to the number of "known" moons of Uranus and Neptune, you can reach the conclusion that further exploration may lead to the discovery of more moons.

Refer to the table on page 138. What can you conclude about a planet's distance from the sun and the time it takes to revolve around the sun?

A. The farther away it is from the sun, the longer a planet takes to revolve around the sun.

B. The closer it is to the sun, the longer a planet takes to revolve around the sun.

The Missions Continue

A new space probe called *Cassini* was launched in 1997, which reached Saturn and its largest moon, Titan, in 2004. Scientists continue to analyze *Galileo*'s data, and *Voyager 1* and *Voyager 2* are still speeding out of the solar system. Some *Voyager* instruments will continue to send data until about 2015. If aliens ever come across one of the *Voyager* space probes, they will find a recording aboard. It has greetings from Earth in sixty languages.

Check your answers on page 267.

Thinking About the Article

Practice Vocabulary

▶ The words below are in the passage in bold type. Study the way the words are used. Then complete each sentence by writing the correct words.

solar system   inner planets   outer planets   space probes

1. All of the _____ are gas giants.

2. _____ like *Pioneer, Voyager,* and *Galileo* send data about the planets and moons back to Earth.

3. The _____ consists of the sun and all the objects revolving around it.

4. Earth is one of the _____ , which are small and rocky.

Understand the Article

▶ Match each planet with its description. Write the letter of the planet in the space provided.

Description		Planet
_____	5. Largest planet in the solar system	A. Earth
_____	6. Planet with the most rings	B. Saturn
_____	7. Has longest time of revolution	C. Jupiter
_____	8. Rotates in 24 hours	D. Uranus
_____	9. Has 27 known moons	E. Neptune

▶ Write the answer to each question.

10. Name all of the planets in the solar system.

_____

_____

11. Why must we use space probes to explore the outer planets?

_____

_____

12. What is the most distinctive characteristic of Saturn?

_____

Apply Your Skills

▶ **Circle the letter of the best answer.**

13. According to the table on page 138, which planet is about twice as far from the sun as Saturn?

    A. Earth

    B. Jupiter

    C. Uranus

    D. Neptune

14. According to the table on page 138, which planet has the most known moons?

    A. Jupiter

    B. Saturn

    C. Uranus

    D. Neptune

15. Saturn's composition is most similar to which other planet?

    A. Titan

    B. Earth

    C. Jupiter

    D. Mars

Connect with the Article

▶ **Write your answer to each question.**

16. What conclusion can you draw from the discovery of conglomerate on the surface of Mars? Explain you answer.

    _____

    _____

17. How would our knowledge of the solar system be affected if we did not use space probes? Cite a specific example to support your answer.

    _____

    _____

    _____

SCIENCE PRACTICE FOCUS

10 Facts About Earth's Moon

1. If the sun were as tall as a typical front door, Earth would be the size of a nickel and the moon would the size of a green pea.

2. The moon is Earth's satellite and orbits the Earth at a distance of about 384,000 km (239,000 miles) or 0.00257 AU.

3. The moon makes a complete orbit around Earth in 27 Earth days and rotates or spins at that same rate, or in that same amount of time. This causes the moon to keep the same side or face towards Earth during the course of its orbit.

4. The moon is a rocky, solid-surface body, with much of its surface cratered and pitted from impacts.

5. The moon has a very thin and tenuous (weak) atmosphere, called an exosphere.

6. The moon has no moons.

7. The moon has no rings.

8. More than 100 spacecraft been launched to explore the moon. It is the only celestial body beyond Earth that has been visited by human beings.

9. The moon's weak atmosphere and its lack of liquid water cannot support life as we know it.

10. Surface features that create the face known as the "Man in the moon" are impact basins on the moon that are filled with dark basalt rocks.

–from nasa.gov

▶ **Fill in the blank with the word or words that best complete each statement.**

1. The moon always keeps the same _____ toward Earth.

2. The moon makes a complete rotation every

_____ days.

▶ **Circle the letter of the best answer.**

3. Which of the following can you infer from the information given about the moon?

A. The moon and the sun are about the same size.

B. Animals could survive on the moon if we brought them there.

C. At one time, many space rocks crashed into the moon.

D. The moon would be a good source of water if we run out of it on Earth.

4. According to the table on page 142, the diameter of Earth is 8,000 miles and the diameter of Jupiter is 89,000 miles. If the moon were the size of a green pea and Earth were the size of a nickel, Jupiter would be a little smaller than a

A. nickel

B. basketball

C. house

D. football stadium

▶ **Write your answer to each question.**

5. How is the moon similar to an artificial satellite, such as a weather satellite?

_____

_____

_____

6. Describe three ways that the moon is different from Earth.

_____

_____

_____

7. The last fact about the moon indicates that plants cannot live on the moon because of its weak atmosphere and lack of liquid water. Describe an experiment that would test whether plants could be kept alive on the moon in specially controlled greenhouses. State the hypothesis of the experiment, how the experiment would be conducted, and how scientists would know whether their hypothesis was supported. You can draw a diagram to help explain your answer.

_____

_____

_____

_____

_____

_____

_____

Check your answers on page 267.

THE UNIVERSE

Close your eyes and try to picture all the different kinds of organisms that live on Earth. Picture them all, from the tiny, single-celled organisms to the large elephants that roam the grasslands of Africa. Try to picture all the organisms that are yet to be discovered. It is not an easy task.

Now try to imagine everything that makes up the entire universe, from our home planet out to the very edges of space. Trying to understand what makes up our vast and largely unknown universe might just make picturing all the organisms on Earth seem easy after all!

Vocabulary

star

constellation

galaxy

universe

nebula

protostar

main sequence star

red giant

white dwarf

black dwarf

supernova

neutron star

black hole

big bang theory

dark energy

Relate to the Topic

This article describes the universe, which includes everything in existence. Think about what might be included in the universe.

What are three things very near to you and three distant things that you think make up the universe?

_____

_____

What discoveries about the universe do you think are yet to be made by scientists?

_____

_____

Reading Strategy

PREVIEWING DIAGRAMS   A diagram's title and labels provide important information about the visuals. The title tells you the subject of the diagram. The labels identify important details in the diagram. Look at the diagram on page 146. Then answer the questions.

1. What is the main idea of the diagram?

_____

Hint: Read the title.

2. What is the first phase in a star's development?

_____

Hint: Look for a label near the first arrow in the sequence.

Structures in the Universe

Recall that the solar system is made up of the sun and the objects that revolve around it, including the planets and their moons. Our sun is a **star**, a sphere of extremely hot, glowing gases that emits its own light. The gases that make a star are held together by gravity. A star gives off light as a result of nuclear reactions that happen deep in its core. Stars in the night sky form **constellations,** which are patterns of stars that ancient peoples developed to help them identify stars, navigate, and track the changing seasons.

If you traveled beyond our solar system, you would discover that our sun is just one of many stars that make up the Milky Way Galaxy. A **galaxy** is a massive system made up of gases and a very large number of stars held together by gravity. The Milky Way is so huge that even if you could travel at the speed of light, it would take 100,000 years to travel across it. It includes all the stars you can observe in the night sky, as well as millions of other stars too faint to be seen. In other words, it includes several hundred billion stars of all ages, sizes, and masses.

The **universe** is everything that exists, including all planets, stars, solar systems, and galaxies. You might wonder—just how big is the universe? Astronomers are still trying to answer that question. They know the universe is immense and contains too many structures to be counted, but they don't know if the universe is infinitely large, or even if our universe is the only universe in existence.

▶ Restating or Paraphrasing   When you paraphrase a passage, you restate it in a different way while keeping the same meaning. For example, the first sentence on this page can be paraphrased as: *The sun, the planets, and their moons are the parts of our solar system.* Which sentence paraphrases the first sentence of the third paragraph on this page?

A. Planets, stars, solar systems, galaxies, and everything that exists make up the universe.
B. Planets, stars, solar systems, and everything that exists make up the galaxies.

Age and Development of Stars

A star can exist for millions to billions of years. Our sun, for instance, is 4.6 billion years old. How a star lives and dies depends on its mass. The larger the mass of a star, the shorter the star's life will be. The most massive stars last only a few million years. Lower-mass stars like our sun burn up their fuel much more slowly, so they last billions, rather than millions, of years. The lowest mass stars burn fuel so slowly that they may last a hundred billion years or more.

A star starts out as a **nebula**, a giant cloud of gas and dust. Over time, gravity pulls the gas in the nebula together, and it starts to spin. As it spins faster, the nebula heats up and forms a dense cloud known as a **protostar**. The cloud becomes denser and hotter. At a certain point, nuclear fusion begins in the core of the cloud, which releases tremendous amounts of energy. The cloud starts to glow brightly. At this point, it becomes stable for millions or billions of years, and is called a **main sequence star**.

A star collapses and starts to die when it runs out of the fuel used for nuclear fusion. The core of the star contracts, while nuclear reactions outside the core cause the star itself to expand. The star becomes a **red giant**, or a large, cool star that glows red.

All stars go through similar initial phases and eventually collapse. However, the star's mass determines what happens to it after the red giant phase. If the star is low to average in mass (about the same mass as our sun), it will become a **white dwarf**, a very small and dense star. Eventually, a white dwarf becomes a **black dwarf**, a ball of gas that no longer emits light.

If the star has a large mass, it may release energy in a powerful explosion, called a **supernova,** and become a **neutron star**. The star may get swallowed by its own gravity after the supernova, imploding to form an infinite warp in space called a **black hole**. A black hole's gravity is so strong that not even light can escape it.

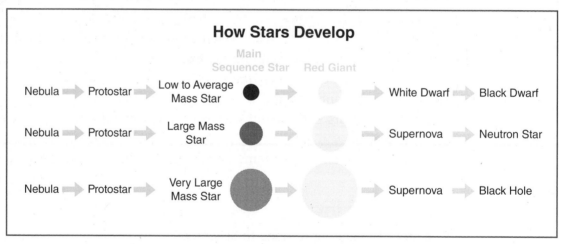

How a star develops after becoming a red giant depends on its mass.

Age and Development of the Universe

In the 1920s, astronomer Edwin Hubble made an incredible discovery while observing stars at California's Mount Wilson Observatory. The stars he observed were part of external galaxies far beyond the edge of our galaxy. Based on data, Hubble concluded that the universe is expanding.

The **big bang theory** is the most widely accepted model of how the universe began and developed. According to this theory, the observed expansion of the universe started about 13.7 billion years ago, when all energy and matter were contained in a single point in space. This tiny point was extremely hot and dense. Then, in a sudden event known as the "Big Bang," the universe was born. With time and expansion, the universe cooled and matter combined to form gas, dust, and structures such as planets, stars, and galaxies.

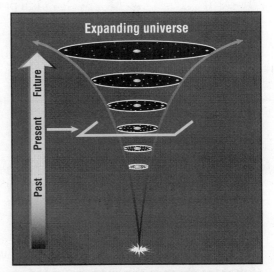

Astronomer Edwin Hubble discovered
that the universe is expanding.

Astronomers are still trying to accurately determine the eventual fate of the universe. Astronomers had predicted two possibilities: Either the universe would expand forever, but at a slower rate, or it would eventually collapse back on itself. Recent observations have shown that the rate of expansion is, in fact, accelerating. This unexpected finding has led scientists to search for new explanations. Scientists have called the force driving this accelerated expansion **dark energy**. Astronomers, with the help of space telescopes and probes, will continue Edwin Hubble's work of measuring the expansion of our vast universe and discovering new structures in it.

▶ Reading a Diagram   A diagram can help you see what an object looks like or how a process works. It also can help you better understand what an author is describing. The diagrams on pages 146 and 147 show how stars and the universe develop and change. The labels point out things that you should look at closely. The arrows show time or the order in which events occur.

1. In the diagram on page 146, which star phase comes immediately before the
   development of a neutron star? _____

2. In the diagram on page 147, how does the size of the universe in the future compare
   to the size in the present? _____

Check your answers on page 268.

Thinking About the Article

Practice Vocabulary

▶ The terms below are in the passage in bold type. Study the way each term is used. Then complete each sentence by writing the correct term.

black dwarf   **universe**   **constellation**   **galaxy**

1. A(n) _____ is a patterns of stars that ancient people identified long ago.

2. A(n) _____ is made up of gases and billions of stars held together by gravity.

3. A star that becomes a ball of gas that no longer emits light called a(n)

   _____ .

4. The _____ is everything that exists, including all planets, stars, solar systems, and galaxies.

Understand the Article

▶ Match each phase in a star's development with its description. Write the letter of the star phase in the space provided.

Description		Star Phase
_____	5. a large, cool star that glows red	A. black hole
_____	6. a giant gas and dust cloud at the start of a star	B. supernova
_____	7. an infinite warp from which light cannot escape	C. red giant
_____	8. a dense spinning cloud	D. nebula
_____	9. a powerful explosion	E. protostar

▶ Write the answer to each question.

10. What is the approximate age of the universe?

   _____

11. What is the big bang theory? Give a summary of the theory.

   _____

   _____

   _____

Apply Your Skills

▶ **Circle the letter of the best answer.**

12. According to the diagram on page 146, what does a low to average mass star become immediately after the red giant phase?

    A.   supernova

    B.   neutron star

    C.   black dwarf

    D.   white dwarf

13. According to the diagram on page 147, what will most likely happen to the universe during the next 1 billion years?

    A.   It will get bigger.

    B.   It will get smaller.

    C.   It will stay the same.

    D.   It will become a supernova.

14. Suppose an astronomer discovers what appears to be a ball of gases that gives off its own light. How should the astronomer classify the discovery?

    A.   as a universe

    B.   as a galaxy

    C.   as a star

    D.   as a nebula

Connect with the Article

▶ **Write your answer to each question.**

15. Describe a constellation that you have seen and how you could use it to help you.

_____

_____

_____

16. Why do you think it is important to understand how the universe began and developed? Explain your answer.

_____

_____

SCIENCE PRACTICE FOCUS

The International Space Station and the MAXI Camera

The International Space Station (ISS) is a spacecraft used by astronauts and scientists from all around the world to conduct scientific experiments and gather data about the universe. The ISS program is a joint project among the space agencies from the United States, Russia, Japan, Europe, and Canada.

In 2009, an X-ray camera, called the Monitor of All-sky X-ray Image (MAXI), was installed on the outside of one of the ISS modules. MAXI is operated by the Japan Aerospace Exploration Agency (JAXA). The camera is able to complete an entire scan of the sky during each of the 16 orbits the ISS makes around Earth each day, looking for X-rays. An X-ray is a very powerful form of energy thought to be connected to space phenomena such as the explosion of stars in deep space.

Although MAXI is operated by JAXA, the information gathered from it is made available to scientists from all over the world. Important information from MAXI has been used in several scientific studies and publications. In one study, the data MAXI gathered from the explosion of a star has helped scientists understand more about what might happen to the sun when it becomes a white dwarf star in about 5 billion years. In another study, MAXI observed a gamma-ray burst that occurs when a huge star collapses. The gamma-ray burst could be evidence of the formation of a black hole or neutron star. Scientists are hopeful that technology like MAXI can be used to help better understand the early history of the universe.

▶ **Circle the letter of the best answer.**

1. The sun will become a white dwarf in about

    A.   1 billion years

    B.   3 billion years

    C.   5 billion years

    D.   10 billion years

▶ **Fill in the blank with the word or words that best complete each statement**

2. The _____ is an X-ray camera installed on the outside of the ISS.

3. The ISS makes _____ orbits around Earth in one day.

▶ **Write the answer to each question.**

4. What kinds of data does MAXI gather?

_____

_____

_____

5. Why is it important that the data from MAXI is shared with scientists from all over the world?

_____

_____

_____

6. What are some of the ways that humans benefit from space exploration?

_____

_____

7. Peer review is a process often used by scientists after they have made conclusions about data, but before they have published those conclusions. Peer review is the evaluation of work by one or more people that have similar qualifications as the person or people who produced the work. Why is peer review important in the scientific studies that came from the data gathered by MAXI?

_____

_____

_____

8. Suppose that you are a scientist who has analyzed some of the data from MAXI. You are asked by another group of scientists to peer review their analysis. You find that they have drawn very different conclusions than you have about the data. What would you do next?

_____

_____

_____

_____

Check your answers on pages 268–269.

SCIENCE AT WORK

BUILDING TRADES:
CONSTRUCTION WORKER

As you walk or drive around your city or town, you will see construction workers. Construction workers work on a variety of projects. Some help build highways and roads. Others work on huge projects like skyscrapers or smaller projects like houses. Regardless of the size of the project, construction workers must be in good physical shape, have a good working knowledge of Earth's forces and materials, be able to read blueprints, and have strong measurement and visual skills.

Construction workers learn to use a wide variety of tools and machines. The equipment must be operated safely and correctly. Workers must also be concerned with the safety of others working at the job site. Dealing with the forces of nature and Earth materials such as sand, dirt, rock and water can be dangerous. Depending on the type of project on which they are working, construction workers must wear protective clothing such as hard hats, goggles, boots, and durable pants and shirts.

Look at the Some Careers in Building Trades chart.

● Do any of the careers interest you? If so, which ones?

● What information would you need to find out more about those careers? On a separate piece of paper, write some questions that you would like answered. You can find more information about those careers in the *Occupational Outlook Handbook* at your local library or online.

Carpet Installer removes any existing carpet and lays new padding and carpeting

Electrician installs and repairs electrical systems in buildings

Painter prepares walls for painting and applies paint to surface

Tilesetter prepares floors and walls for new tile; lays tiles in specific pattern

Construction workers must be able to follow directions to ensure that a project is done safely and correctly. They also need to apply their knowledge of Earth's forces and materials.

Building an In-ground Swimming Pool

1. **Pick and Prepare the Pool Site.** Pick a level area a good distance away from any structures. The pool site should be a little higher than the surrounding area to allow for proper drainage. Make sure the area directly around the pool is sloped away from the pool itself. Too much rain and splash water around the pool causes slipperiness, which is a safety hazard.

2. **Dig the Hole.** Plot out the area for the pool by connecting stakes one foot wider and one foot longer than the actual size of the pool itself. Dig the hole 2–4 inches deeper than the pool itself. Dig another 4-ft. x 6-ft. hole in the middle of the deep end of the pool. Make it one foot deep. This is where the pool's drainage equipment will be placed.

3. **Prepare the Hole to Receive the Pool Shell.** Fill and level the base of the hole with 2–4 inches of sand or rock dust, as they do not absorb much water. This bed will support the pool. A bed is needed for consistent, unchanging support and drainage underneath the pool. Do not use dirt because it absorbs too much water. If too much water collects beneath the pool, the shell may crack or shift.

▶ **Read the directions below for constructing a swimming pool. Then answer the questions.**

1. Which of the following materials are acceptable for making the pool shell's support base?

    A.   dirt and sand

    B.   dirt and rock dust

    C.   stakes and water

    D.   sand and rock dust

2. Why is it important to ensure proper drainage around the pool?

    A.   to make the pool look attractive and expensive

    B.   to make sure rain and splash water don't collect around the pool

    C.   to make sure the construction worker does his or her job correctly

    D.   to make sure that the pool can be drained for the winter

3. Have you seen construction workers on the job? Use a separate piece of paper to describe the job they were doing. What safety, weather, or pollution issues did they need to consider?

Weather Maps

A weather map uses symbols to indicate air masses, fronts, temperatures, and precipitation. The heavy lines show fronts. The symbols point in the direction in which the front is moving. The terms *warm front* and *cold front* describe the temperatures that are behind the front. Temperatures on U.S. weather maps are shown in degrees Fahrenheit. A stationary front is the area between two air masses that have stopped moving for awhile.

High Temperatures and Precipitation for July 22

> **Fill in the blank with the word or words that best complete each statement.**

1. According to the map, the high temperature in degrees Fahrenheit for

   Oklahoma City is in the _____ .

2. The type of precipitation for July 22 in the United States is _____ .

> **Circle the letter of the best answer.**

3. What is the weather like along the stationary front?

   A.   hot, with sunshine

   B.   hot, with showers

   C.   cold, with sunshine

   D.   cold, with snow flurries

The Ozone Hole

Ozone is a form of oxygen. A layer of ozone is found 6 to 30 miles above Earth's surface. Scientists have discovered that the ozone layer has become thinner since the 1970s. The area where the ozone layer is very thin is known as the ozone hole.

Gases called chlorofluorocarbons (CFCs) are the main cause of the ozone hole. CFCs were used in aerosol spray cans for many years. CFCs escape into the atmosphere and destroy ozone. The destruction of ozone is a serious problem because the ozone layer absorbs ultraviolet light from the sun. The energy from ultraviolet light, called **ultraviolet rays,** can cause sunburn and skin cancer. Thinning of the ozone layer allows more ultraviolet rays to get through to Earth's surface.

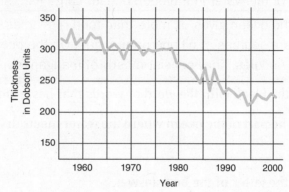

Average Thickness of Ozone Layer over Antarctica

▶ **Write the answer to the question.**

4. How much thicker was the ozone layer in 1965 than in 2000?

_____

▶ **Circle the letter of the best answer.**

5. Which sentence from the text supports the prediction that skin cancer will likely increase worldwide if the ozone layer continues to get thinner?

A. Thinning of the ozone layer allows more ultraviolet rays to get through to Earth's surface.

B. Ozone is a form of oxygen.

C. They have discovered that the ozone layer has become thinner since the 1970s.

D. Gases called chloroflourocarbons (CFCs) are the main cause of the ozone hole.

6. Based on the graph, what can you conclude about the ozone layer over Antarctica?

A. Since the 1950s, it has gradually increased in thickness.

B. It was thickest in the 1980s.

C. Its thickness decreased most rapidly between 1960 and 1976.

D. Its thickness decreased most rapidly between 1976 and 1992.

The Oceans

Oceans cover nearly three-fourths of Earth's surface. The water is relatively shallow where the oceans meet the continents. The bottom of the ocean has a gentle slope in this area. It is called the **continental shelf** because the ocean bottom is almost flat. Since the water is shallow, sunlight can reach the bottom. There are many plants here. There are also many animals. We get shellfish, such as clams and lobsters, from the continental shelf. This is also the richest part of the sea for fishing.

Along the world's coastlines, the continental shelf can extend from just a few miles to as much as a thousand miles from the shore. Then the bottom slopes more steeply. This is the **continental slope.** The slope levels out to form the **ocean basin,** the bottom of the sea. The resources from these regions come mostly from the upper layers of the water in the open ocean. Large fish, such as tuna, are caught here.

The ocean gives us more than food resources. The rock layers of the continental shelf are sources of oil and natural gas. On the ocean basin are lumps of minerals, called nodules. They consist mostly of manganese, iron, copper, and nickel.

▶ **Fill in the blank with the word or words that best complete the statement.**

7. The part of the ocean where the water meets dry land is the

_____ .

▶ **Circle the letter of the best answer.**

8. Most of the food resources in the ocean are found in

    A.   nodules on the ocean basin

    B.   waters of the open ocean

    C.   waters of the continental-shelf region

    D.   waters of the continental-slope region

9. If you sailed away from a continent, in which order would you pass over the different areas of the ocean bottom?

    A.   ocean basin, continental shelf, continental slope

    B.   ocean basin, continental slope, continental shelf

    C.   continental slope, continental shelf, ocean basin

    D.   continental shelf, continental slope, ocean basin

10. Polluting the water over the continental shelf has negative economic consequences. Which statement supports this conclusion?

    A.   The continental shelf has a gentle slope.

    B.   The water over the continental shelf is shallow.

    C.   Sunlight can reach the bottom of the continental shelf.

    D.   Shellfish are harvested from the continental shelf.

The Sun

The sun is not especially large or bright when compared to other stars. The sun appears large and bright because it is so much closer to Earth than any other star. The next nearest star is more than 250,000 times farther away.

Huge amounts of heat energy and light energy are given off by the sun. The energy comes from nuclear reactions in the sun. These reactions take place in the **core,** which is the center of the sun. The temperature there is believed to be about 27 million degrees Fahrenheit. A large portion of the heat energy is changed into light energy on the surface of the sun. As a result, the temperature of the surface is only about 10,000 degrees Fahrenheit.

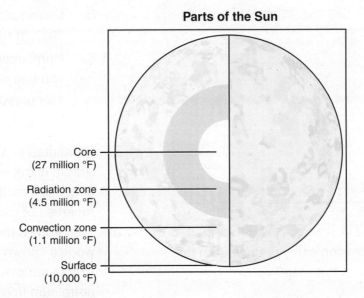

Parts of the Sun

Core
(27 million °F)

Radiation zone
(4.5 million °F)

Convection zone
(1.1 million °F)

Surface
(10,000 °F)

▶ **Write the answer to the question.**

11. What is the cause of the intense energy given off by the sun?

_____

▶ **Circle the letter of the best answer.**

12. Altair is a star similar in size and age to the sun. Based on the diagram, which part of Altair would you expect to have the lowest temperatures?

    A.   the core

    B.   the convection zone

    C.   the surface

    D.   Not enough information is given.

SCIENCE
EXTENSION

Select one natural disaster or type of bad weather that your area sometimes experiences. Then make a list of things you could do to prepare yourself and your family for such an event.

MINI-TEST

This is a 15-minute practice test. After 15 minutes, mark the last number you finished. Then complete the test and check your answers. If most of your answers were correct but you did not finish, try to work faster next time.

▶ **Directions: Choose the <u>one best answer</u> to each question.**

Questions 1 and 2 refer to the following map.

Average Annual Precipitation in Oregon

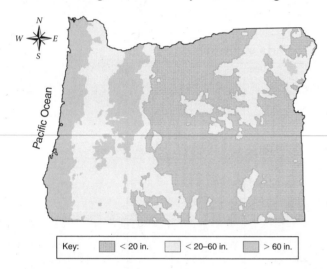

Key: ▨ < 20 in.   ☐ < 20–60 in.   ▨ > 60 in.

1. Which conclusion can you draw from the information on this map?

   Annual precipitation is

   A. greater in the southern half of Oregon than in the northern half of Oregon

   B. greater in the western half of Oregon than in the eastern half of Oregon

   C. highest in the southeastern part of Oregon

   D. lowest along the coast of Oregon

2. What inference can you make from the information on this map?

   A. Northwestern Oregon has more sunny days than other parts of the state.

   B. Desert plants are found mostly in the eastern half of Oregon.

   C. Hurricanes are common in the southeastern part of Oregon.

   D. The temperature is nearly the same in all parts of Oregon.

3. Petroleum is a valuable resource. Saudi Arabia is the world's largest exporter of petroleum. It has known petroleum reserves of more than 260 billion barrels. That equals more than one-quarter of the world's known petroleum. In 1996, Saudi Arabia removed three billion barrels of petroleum from the ground.

   Which of the following statements supports the prediction that Saudi petroleum reserves will be depleted within a century?

   A. Saudi Arabia is too close to the equator.

   B. Every year Saudi Arabia removes about one-ninetieth of its petroleum reserves.

   C. Saudi Arabia has known petroleum reserves of less than 300 billion barrels.

   D. Saudi Arabia has about one-quarter of the world's known petroleum.

4. A geologist is studying two fossils. The first fossil comes from a rock layer that is lower than the rock layer containing the second fossil. Which of the following conclusions is the geologist most likely to draw?

A. The second fossil is older than the first fossil.

B. The first fossil is older than the second fossil.

C. The fossils are the same age.

D. The geologist cannot draw a conclusion because there is not enough information.

5. A scientist releases a balloon into the atmosphere. The balloon carries instruments that measure altitude and temperature. As the balloon rises, it sends data back to the scientist on the ground. The scientist analyzes the data and concludes that the temperature of the atmosphere decreases as the altitude increases.

Which data would support this conclusion?

A. 25 °F at 1,000 feet, 29 °F at 2,000 feet, and 32 °F at 3,000 feet

B. 32 °F at 1,000 feet, 29 °F at 2,000 feet, and 32 °F at 3,000 feet

C. 32 °F at 1,000 feet, 35 °F at 2,000 feet, and 32 °F at 3,000 feet

D. 32 °F at 1,000 feet, 29 °F at 2,000 feet, and 25 °F at 3,000 feet

Questions 6–8 refer to the following table.

The Inner Planets				
Planet	Diameter (in miles)	Mass (compared to Earth's mass)	Distance from Sun (in millions of miles)	Time of Rotation (in Earth days)
Mercury	3,000	0.06	36.5	58.7
Venus	7,600	0.82	67.3	243
Earth	8,000	1	93.5	1
Mars	4,200	0.11	142	1

6. Which statement about the inner planets is an opinion?

A. Mercury has the smallest diameter.

B. Venus has the longest time of rotation.

C. Earth is the most beautiful planet.

D. Mars is the farthest from the sun.

7. Imagine you could travel to one of the inner planets. If you wanted to experience a day-night cycle least like Earth's, which planet should you visit?

A. Venus

B. Mars

C. All of the inner planets have a day-night cycle very similar to that of Earth.

D. All of the inner planets have a day-night cycle very different from that of Earth.

8. What is the difference between the diameters of Earth and Mars?

A. 400 miles

B. 3,800 miles

C. 4,800 miles

D. 5,000 miles

Physical science includes the branches of chemistry and physics. **Chemistry** is the study of matter, or any substance that takes up space. When you study chemistry, you learn about the building blocks of matter and the ways that matter can change. **Physics** is the study of the basic things that make up the universe and what happens when they exert forces on one another. Heat, sound, and motion are some of the phenomena that are studied in physics. Chemistry and physics are involved in all the processes that involve matter, such as cooking.

Describe how you cooked something recently.

_____

Describe what happens when you knock a jar off the kitchen counter.

_____

Thinking About Physical Science

You may not realize how often you use chemistry and physics as you go about your daily life. Think about your recent activities.

Check the box for each activity you have done recently.

- ☐ Did you clean your house or car?
- ☐ Did you do the laundry?
- ☐ Did you ride in a car, truck, bus, or other motorized vehicle?
- ☐ Did you cook on a stovetop, oven, or grill?
- ☐ Did you turn a doorknob?
- ☐ Did you lift something?
- ☐ Did you play a sport?
- ☐ Did you listen to music?

Write some other activities in which you used chemistry or physics.

_____

_____

_____

Previewing the Unit

In this unit, you will learn:

- what matter is and how it behaves

- how substances can combine to form new substances

- how different kinds of matter can mix together

- how thermal energy, heat, and temperature are related

- how machines make it easier to do work

- what happens when moving objects collide

- how sound waves produce music

Lesson 17	Matter	**Lesson 21**	Heat Transfer
Lesson 18	Changes in Matter	**Lesson 22**	Machines
Lesson 19	Mixtures and Solutions	**Lesson 23**	Momentum
Lesson 20	Combustion	**Lesson 24**	Sound Waves

MATTER

Supermarkets usually have an entire aisle full of different kinds of cleaning products. There are cleaners for the kitchen and cleaners for the bathroom. There are cleaners for white laundry and cleaners for colored laundry.

Many of these cleaners contain the same few chemicals in different combinations. They work in similar ways to clean. It's interesting to look at some basic ideas about matter, using cleaning products and processes as examples.

Vocabulary

substance

mixture

element

compound

atom

molecule

chemical symbol

chemical formula

chemical reaction

reactants

products

chemical equation

Relate to the Topic

This lesson describes the types of matter in some common cleaning products. Think about the different kinds of cleaning products in your home.

List some household cleaning products that your family uses.

_____

_____

Do you dilute any of the products with water before using them? Why?

_____

_____

Reading Strategy

PREVIEWING A TABLE   A table organizes information into rows and columns. A table usually has a title and headings. The title tells you the general topic of the table. The headings tell you the kind of information each column in the table contains. Skim the table on page 163. Then answer the questions.

1. What is the topic of the table?

_____

Hint: Look at the title.

2. What kind of information does each column in the table contain?

_____

Hint: Look at the headings above each column.

The Chemistry of Cleaning

Almost everyone has run into the laundry problems of "ring around the collar" or stubborn yellow stains. Makers of detergents and bleaches claim their products can remove the toughest stains. Detergents can remove many stains. But recently scientists figured out why some oily yellow stains won't go away.

If the clothing is washed right away, the oily stain can be removed. But what happens if the stain sits for a week? The aging oil can combine with oxygen from the air. This process changes the colorless oil to a yellow substance. The yellow substance reacts with the fabric. In effect, the clothing is dyed yellow.

The sooner stained clothing is washed, the easier it is to clean.

Substances and Mixtures

Solving laundry problems is just one practical application of chemistry. Knowing about chemistry can help you make better use of the products you buy for cleaning and other jobs around the house.

Everything is made up of matter. Matter can be divided into two groups—substances and mixtures. All the matter in a **substance** is the same. A **mixture** is a combination of two or more substances that can be separated by physical means.

There are two kinds of substances. An **element** is a substance that cannot be broken into other substances by ordinary means. Two or more elements can combine chemically to form a **compound,** another type of substance. The smallest unit of an element is an **atom.** The smallest unit of a compound is a **molecule.** Each molecule in a compound is made up of atoms from each of the elements in the compound.

Forms of Matter

Mixtures	Substances	
	Compounds	Elements
lemonade	salt	oxygen
granola	sugar	carbon
salad	water	iron
soil	ammonia	gold
cement	bleach	nitrogen

Chemical Symbols and Formulas

When they write about matter and its changes, chemists use a kind of code. A **chemical symbol** of one or two letters stands for each element. The symbols for some common elements are shown in the table on this page. When elements combine to form a compound, the symbols are grouped together in a **chemical formula.** For example, H_2O is the chemical formula for water. The formula shows that the elements hydrogen (H) and oxygen (O) make up the compound water. The formula also shows there are two atoms of hydrogen for each atom of oxygen in the compound. Another chemical formula is NH_3, which is the formula for ammonia.

Symbols of Common Elements

Element	Symbol
Hydrogen	H
Carbon	C
Nitrogen	N
Oxygen	O
Sodium	Na
Magnesium	Mg
Sulfur	S
Chlorine	Cl
Iron	Fe
Calcium	Ca

▶ **Understanding Chemical Formulas** Chemical formulas can tell you a great deal if you know how to decode them. They tell what elements are in a compound. Formulas also show how many atoms of each element make up each molecule of the compound. For example, the formula for sugar is $C_{12}H_{22}O_{11}$. This means that each molecule of sugar has 12 atoms of carbon, 22 atoms of hydrogen, and 11 atoms of oxygen. Reread the first paragraph on this page, and refer to the table above. Then answer the questions.

1. Name the elements in NH_3 (the compound ammonia).

   _____

2. How many atoms of each element are in each molecule of ammonia?

   _____

Chemical Reactions

In a **chemical reaction,** elements are combined into compounds or compounds are changed into other substances. For example, iron is a gray solid. Oxygen is a colorless gas. When iron and oxygen combine, they form a new substance. This substance is iron oxide, or rust. It is a brownish red or orange solid. In a chemical reaction, the substances that you start with are called the **reactants.** In this example, iron and oxygen are the reactants. The substances that result from the reaction are called the **products.** In this example, there is one product—iron oxide.

Scientists use equations to describe reactions. A **chemical equation** shows the reactants and products of a reaction. This equation shows how rust forms:

iron + oxygen = iron oxide

Rust stains are hard to remove from clothing. However, you can remove the stain if you reverse the chemical reaction. The acid in lemon juice reacts with rust to form a water-soluble iron compound. When you rinse the treated stain, the iron washes away.

Compounds in Household Cleaners

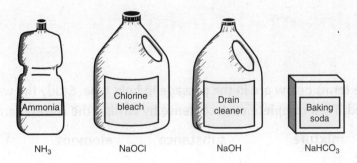

Ammonia — NH_3
Chlorine bleach — NaOCl
Drain cleaner — NaOH
Baking soda — $NaHCO_3$

Another example of a chemical reaction is the effect of bleach on clothing. The formula for chlorine bleach is NaOCl. In water, this compound produces salt and oxygen. The release of oxygen causes the whitening of the fabric. Nonchlorine bleaches use other sources of oxygen. One source is hydrogen peroxide, H_2O_2. Another source is calcium carbonate, $CaCO_3$.

▶ **Understanding Chemistry Roots, Suffixes, and Prefixes** The name of a compound tells you what's in it. The root names of the elements are in the name of the compound. For example, table salt, NaCl, is called sodium chloride. It consists of sodium (Na) and chlorine (Cl). But why is it called sodium chlor*ide* and not sodium chlorine? When the suffix -*ide* is added to the end of the root name of the second element of a compound, it has a special meaning. It means the compound consists of just two elements. Another special suffix in chemistry is -*ate*. For example, calcium carbon*ate* is $CaCO_3$. The suffix -*ate* is used when the second element of a compound has the element oxygen with it.

1. What elements are in the compound barium chloride? Circle the letter of each correct answer.

   A. barium   B. calcium   C. chlorine   D. oxygen

2. What elements are in the compound calcium chlorate? Circle the letter of each correct answer.

   A. barium   B. calcium   C. chlorine   D. oxygen

Prefixes are used when more than one compound can be made from the same elements. For example, CO and CO_2 are both made from carbon and oxygen. Prefixes are used to distinguish the two compounds. So CO is carbon *mono*xide. *Mon*- means "one," and it tells you there is one atom of oxygen in each molecule of carbon monoxide. CO_2 is carbon *di*oxide. *Di*- means "two," and it tells you there are two atoms of oxygen in each molecule of carbon dioxide. Some common prefixes are shown in the table at the right.

Prefix	Meaning
mono-	one
di-	two
tri-	three
tetra-	four

3. How many chlorine atoms are in the compound carbon tetrachloride? _____

4. What is the name of the compound that has one aluminum atom and three oxygen atoms? Circle the letter.

   A. aluminum monoxide   B. aluminum dioxide   C. aluminum trioxide

Check your answers on page 271.

Thinking About the Article

Practice Vocabulary

▶ The terms below are in the passage in bold type. Study the way each term is used. Then complete each sentence by writing the correct term.

mixture	substance	element
compound	atom	chemical reaction

1. A(n) _____ such as iron or oxygen is a pure substance that cannot be broken down into other substances by ordinary means.

2. Salad dressing is a(n) _____ , a combination of two or more kinds of matter that can be separated by physical means.

3. When elements or compounds change into one or more different substances, a(n) _____ takes place.

4. All the matter in a(n) _____ is the same.

5. The smallest particle of an element is a(n) _____ .

6. The elements sodium and chlorine combine chemically to form a(n) _____ commonly called table salt.

Understand the Article

▶ Circle the letter of the correct answer.

7. The chemical symbol for the element calcium is
   A. C   B. Ca

8. The chemical formula for the compound called chlorine bleach is
   A. NaOCl   B. Cl

9. Chemists show the reactants and products in a chemical reaction by writing a
   A. chemical symbol   B. chemical equation

10. Which two elements combine to form rust?
    A. oxygen and iron
    B. hydrogen and oxygen
    C. iron and calcium

11. The products of a chemical reaction have
    A. the same characteristics as the reactants
    B. different characteristics than the reactants

Apply Your Skills

▶ **Circle the letter of the best answer for each question.**

12. Which of the following elements are in hydrogen peroxide (H_2O_2)?

A. helium and potassium

B. helium and boron

C. hydrogen and oxygen

D. hydrogen and phosphorus

13. What is the name of the compound MgS?

A. magnesium sulfur

B. magnesium sulfide

C. magnesium disulfide

D. sulfur magnesiate

14. The compound calcium carbonate has the elements calcium and carbon. The suffix *-ate* tells you that the compound also has which element?

A. chlorine

B. nitrogen

C. oxygen

D. hydrogen

Connect with the Article

▶ **Write your answer to each question.**

15. The body of an automobile is made mostly of steel, which contains iron. Paint protects these steel parts from rusting. If the paint wears away, the auto body may start to rust. How does painting the steel help prevent it from rusting?

_____

_____

_____

16. Name a common household cleaning compound and describe how you or someone you know uses it.

_____

_____

_____

SCIENCE PRACTICE FOCUS

What's the Matter?

Elements are the building blocks of all matter. Everything on our planet, from Earth itself to the living things that exist on it, is composed of elements.

An organic compound is a compound that contains carbon, often chemically bonded with hydrogen. Organic compounds, such as sugars, proteins, fats, and nucleic acids, are found in living things. Inorganic compounds do not contain any significant amounts of carbon. Inorganic compounds are found in the rock and other materials that make up Earth.

The table below shows the occurrence of some common elements in the human body and Earth's crust. Study the table and then answer the questions that follow.

Element	Human Body (Percent)	Earth's Crust (Percent)
Oxygen	65	47
Carbon	18	0.05
Hydrogen	10	0.15
Nitrogen	3	0.005
Calcium	1	4
Phosphorus	1	0.1
Potassium	0.25	3
Silicon	0.002	28

▶ **Write the answer to each question.**

1. What are the four most commonly found elements in the human body?

_____

_____

2. What are the four most commonly found elements in Earth's crust?

_____

_____

3. Compare and contrast the four most commonly found elements in the human body and in Earth's crust.

_____

_____

_____

_____

4. Most of the silicon and oxygen in Earth's crust occurs in the form of SiO_2, or silicon dioxide. Do you think SiO_2 is an organic compound or an inorganic compound? Explain.

_____

_____

_____

_____

5. Suppose you are examining a sample and want to determine whether it is organic or inorganic. Explain how you could use data about the level of hydrogen in the sample to make your determination.

_____

_____

_____

_____

▶ **Circle the letter of the best answer.**

6. About how many times more abundant is nitrogen in the human body than in Earth's crust?

   A. 6

   B. 60

   C. 600

   D. 6,000

7. Which of the following conclusions is supported by the data in the table?

   A.   Nitrogen and silicon make up the greatest percentage of elements in Earth's crust.

   B.   Calcium is found in roughly the same percentage in the human body and Earth's crust.

   C.   Potassium is found only in the human body, not in Earth's crust.

   D.   Phosphorus is found in abundant quantities in the human body and Earth's crust.

CHANGES IN MATTER

All cooks use chemistry, even cooks who can only boil water or fry an egg. When you cook, you often change matter from one state to another. For example, heating water changes it from a liquid to a gas—steam—if you leave it boiling long enough. This is one kind of a physical change.

You also change matter when you cook. One example is cooking an egg. Adding heat to an egg causes chemical changes in the proteins the egg contains. You can see that a chemical change has occurred by observing how a scrambled egg is different from a raw egg. The properties of the egg have changed.

Vocabulary

solid

liquid

gas

melting

freezing

boiling

evaporation

condensation

physical change

chemical change

oxidation

Relate to the Topic

This lesson explains the difference between physical and chemical changes. Think about your favorite cooked food.

What is the food like when it is raw? _____

_____

What is it like when it is cooked? _____

_____

Reading Strategy

PREVIEWING PHOTOS   Science articles often have photos that show real-life examples to illustrate scientific concepts. A photo can help you understand a concept that might otherwise take many words to explain. A photo usually has a caption that tells you how the photo relates to the rest of the article. Look at the photos on pages 171 and 173. Then answer the questions.

1. What do the photos on page 171 show? _____

_____

    Hint: Look at the photos and caption.

2. What does the photo on page 173 show? _____

_____

    Hint: Look at the caption under the photo.

Cooking with Chemistry

Ice cubes, water, and steam are used by cooks. Ice cubes are used to chill liquids. Water is used to boil food and as an ingredient in many recipes. Steam, which is actually water vapor, is used to cook vegetables. What do ice, water, and steam have in common? They are three forms, or states, of the same compound, H_2O.

Each state of matter has its own properties, or characteristics. A **solid** has a definite shape and takes up a definite amount of space. A **liquid** takes up a definite amount of space, but it doesn't have a definite shape. A liquid flows and takes the shape of its container. A **gas** does not have a definite size or shape. It expands to fill its container. If you remove the lid from a pot of steaming vegetables, water vapor escapes and spreads throughout the kitchen.

Changes of State

Matter changes state when energy, in the form of heat, is added to or removed from a substance. When you leave an ice cube tray on the counter, the ice absorbs heat from the air. Eventually the ice cubes melt. **Melting** is the change from a solid to a liquid. If you put the tray back in the freezer, the water will change back into ice. **Freezing** changes a liquid to a solid by removing the heat from it.

When you heat water, bubbles of gas form. They rise and burst on the surface of the water. **Boiling** is the rapid change from a liquid to a gas. A liquid can also change to a gas slowly through **evaporation.** If a glass of water is left out for a long time, the water evaporates from its surface. The reverse of boiling or evaporation is **condensation.** This is the change from a gas to a liquid. If a soft drink bottle is taken from the refrigerator, water vapor in the air will condense on the cold surface of the bottle.

Boiling and melting are two changes in state.

Physical Changes and Chemical Changes

A **physical change** is one in which the appearance of matter changes but its make-up and most of its properties stay the same. The boiling of water, the melting of butter, the dissolving of sugar in tea, and the smashing of a plate are physical changes. No new substances are formed. Matter is changed from one state to another in boiling and melting. When sugar dissolves, matter is mixed. When a plate breaks, it changes size and shape.

Unlike a physical change, a **chemical change** causes new substances to form. Some people make a beverage called a lemon fizz with baking soda and lemonade. This involves a chemical change. Baking soda mixed with an acid, like lemonade, gives off the gas carbon dioxide. This is a new product.

Many activities involve both physical and chemical changes. Making an omelet is an example. Breaking and beating the eggs cause physical changes. The chemical make-up of the eggs has not changed. You have just mixed the parts together. Cooking the eggs causes a chemical change. The heat changes the chemical make-up of the proteins in the eggs and makes them harden.

▶ Finding the Main Idea The main idea of a paragraph tells what the paragraph is about in general. It is often stated in a topic sentence. The main idea of the first paragraph on this page is that the chemical make-up of matter stays the same during physical change. The main idea is stated in the first sentence of the paragraph, the topic sentence. Reread the second paragraph on this page. Look for the main idea and topic sentence.

What is the main idea of the second paragraph on this page?
A. A chemical change causes new substances to form.
B. Making a lemon fizz involves a chemical change.

Cooking a Hamburger

Cooking and eating a hamburger involves both physical and chemical changes. When a butcher grinds beef to make hamburger meat, the meat is ground into small pieces. No new substances are made, so grinding beef is a physical change.

Until the meat is packaged in plastic, the surface of the meat reacts with oxygen in the air. Myoglobin, a chemical in the beef, combines with oxygen. This chemical change is called **oxidation.** This change turns the surface of the meat bright red.

The next step is to form hamburger patties. In this step, you are changing the shape of the ground beef. There aren't any chemical changes, just a physical change.

Cooking hamburgers and hot dogs involves both physical and chemical changes.

Now the hamburgers are ready for cooking. Many cooks quickly sear one side and then the other on a very hot surface. Searing causes a chemical change in the surface proteins, and they form a crust. The crust keeps too much water from evaporating. It also keeps some of the fat from melting and seeping out of the hamburger. By preventing these physical changes, the crust keeps the hamburger from becoming dry.

▶ **Applying Knowledge to Other Contexts** Information becomes more valuable when you use it. This article describes the physical and chemical changes in a hamburger as it is prepared and cooked. You can apply your knowledge of physical and chemical changes to other foods. For example, baking brownies causes a chemical change. The proteins in the liquid batter undergo chemical changes and become firm. On the other hand, cutting up brownies is a physical change. You are just changing the shape of the brownies when you cut them. Label each of the following as a *chemical change* or a *physical change*.

1. A piece of apple turns brown when it is exposed to the oxygen in air.

_____

2. A tray of ice cubes melts when left outside of the freezer.

_____

As a hamburger cooks, the inside loses its red color. This is caused by another chemical change in myoglobin. At the same time, chemical changes in the proteins make the meat become firmer.

When you eat the hamburger, more physical and chemical changes occur. Your teeth cut and grind the hamburger. This is a physical change. The hamburger is broken down chemically by substances in your digestive system. Digestion is another series of physical and chemical changes.

© Houghton Mifflin Harcourt • Image Credits: ©Photodisc/Getty Images

 Check your answers on page 272.

Thinking About the Article

Practice Vocabulary

▶ The terms below are in the passage in bold type. Study the way each term is used. Then complete each sentence by writing the correct term.

gas	chemical change	solid
physical change	liquid	

1. A _____ is a state of matter that has a definite shape and takes up a definite amount of space.

2. A _____ is a state of matter that takes up a definite amount of space but doesn't have a definite shape.

3. A _____ is a state of matter that will spread out to fill all the available space.

4. A _____ is one in which the appearance of matter changes, but its make-up and most of its properties remain the same.

5. A _____ causes new substances to form that were not present before the change.

Understand the Article

▶ Write the answer to the question.

6. Name the three states of matter of H_2O.

    _____

▶ Match the process with its description.

_____	**7.** boiling	A. change from liquid to solid
_____	**8.** evaporation	B. rapid change from liquid to gas
_____	**9.** freezing	C. change from gas to liquid
_____	**10.** condensation	D. slow change from liquid to gas

▶ Identify each of the following as a *chemical change* or *physical change.*

11. Chopping onions _____

12. Baking cookies _____

Apply Your Skills

▶ **Circle the letter of the best answer for each question.**

13. Which title <u>best</u> describes the main idea of this article?

   A.   Chemical Changes

   B.   Physical Changes

   C.   Chemical Changes in Cooking

   D.   Chemical and Physical Changes in Cooking

14. Jason leaves a bar of chocolate on the dashboard of his car. When he comes back, he finds it has melted in the sun. This is an example of

   A.   a chemical reaction

   B.   condensation

   C.   a chemical change

   D.   a physical change

15. Which of the following is an example of a chemical change?

   A.   melting a bowl of ice cream

   B.   freezing a popsicle

   C.   mixing a milk shake

   D.   baking a cake

Connect with the Article

▶ **Write your answer to each question.**

16. Think about one of the changes of state, such as freezing or evaporating. What is an example of it from everyday life?

_____

_____

_____

17. Describe an experience you or someone you know has had while cooking a meal or snack. What physical or chemical changes occurred in the food as it was cooked?

_____

_____

_____

_____

SCIENCE PRACTICE FOCUS

Design an Investigation About Physical Changes in Water

Suppose you are asked to design an investigation about one the following topics:

A. the thickness of pond ice in relation to the number of days the air temperature is below freezing

B. whether adding salt to water affects the time it takes for the water to boil

C. the time it takes for boiling water and cold water to freeze

Remember that an investigation is designed to answer a question related to something you've observed in nature. You must develop a hypothesis, or possible answer to the question, that the investigation will test.

You also must decide what variables, or factors, the investigation will test. The independent variable is the factor you will change in your investigation. The dependent variable is the factor that changes as a result of changes made to the independent variable.

▶ **Write the answer to each question.**

1. Write a hypothesis for each of the three possible investigations.

A. _____

_____

_____

B. _____

_____

_____

C. _____

_____

_____

2. Identify the independent variable and dependent variable for each investigation.

    A.   independent variable: _____

          _____

          dependent variable: _____

          _____

    B.   independent variable: _____

          _____

          dependent variable: _____

          _____

    C.   independent variable: _____

          _____

          dependent variable: _____

          _____

3. Now think of your own question related to physical or chemical changes in matter. State your question and describe how you could attempt to answer your question.

_____

_____

_____

_____

_____

4. Write a possible hypothesis for the investigation you chose for **Question 3**.

_____

_____

5. Identify the independent and dependent variables for your investigation.

_____

_____

_____

_____

      Check your answers on page 273.

LESSON 19

MIXTURES AND SOLUTIONS

Vocabulary

mixture

distillation

solution

solvent

solute

solubility

Most of the foods we eat are mixtures of two or more substances. Chocolate chip cookies and tossed salad are two examples. You can actually see the different parts of these mixtures. This is not the case for all mixtures.

For example, have you ever added sugar to a cup of tea? As you stir the sugar and tea, the sugar disappears—it dissolves in the tea. This type of mixture is called a solution. The sugar is evenly distributed in the tea. Orange soda and hot chocolate drinks are also solutions.

Relate to the Topic

This lesson is about common types of substances called mixtures and solutions. Most of the beverages we drink are mixtures. Think about the beverages you drink.

List two beverages you like to drink.

....

Do you think these beverages are mixtures? Why or why not?

....

....

Reading Strategy

PREVIEWING A LINE GRAPH   A **line graph** shows how one thing changes as a second thing changes. Instead of telling you in words, the graph shows you with a line. The title and labels help you read the line graph. The title tells you the main idea. The labels along the side and bottom tell you what two things are being compared. Skim the line graph on page 181. Then answer the questions.

1. What is the main idea of the line graph on page 181?

....

Hint: Look at the title.

2. What two things are being compared in the graph?

....

Hint: Look at the labels of the graph.

178   *Check your answers on page 273.*   UNIT 3   PHYSICAL SCIENCE

Mixing It Up

Mixtures are all around you. The paper in this book is a mixture of fibers. The inks with which it is printed are mixtures of colored substances. Even the air around you is a mixture. It contains nitrogen, oxygen, carbon dioxide, and other gases.

What is a mixture? A **mixture** is made up of two or more substances that can be separated by physical means. The properties of a mixture are the properties of its ingredients. That is why sugar water is sweet and wet. Neither the sugar nor the water loses its properties when they are mixed together. Another characteristic of a mixture is that the amounts of its ingredients can vary.

Mixtures can be solids, liquids, or gases. A penny is a solid mixture of the elements copper and zinc. Blood is a mixture of liquids, such as water; solids, such as cells, sugar, and proteins; and gases, such as oxygen and carbon dioxide. A soft drink is a mixture of flavored liquid and the gas carbon dioxide.

The substances in a mixture can be separated by physical means. A mixture of red and blue blocks can be sorted by hand. A filter can be used to separate sand from water. A magnet can separate a mixture of steel and plastic paper clips. Liquid mixtures can be separated by distillation. **Distillation** is the process of boiling a mixture of liquids so that they will separate from one another. Since the different liquids boil at different temperatures, the gases formed can be condensed and the condensed liquids collected as they boil out of the mixture one at a time. That's how alcohol is obtained from fermented juices and brewed grains.

Sterling silver is a mixture of silver and copper.

Milk is a mixture of water, proteins, fat, and sugar.

What Is a Solution?

A solution is a special type of mixture. In a **solution,** the ingredients are distributed evenly throughout. All samples taken from a solution have the same amount of each substance. That's why the first and last sip from a soft drink taste the same. Solutions can be made of solids, liquids, or gases. Brass is a solid solution. Tea is a liquid solution. Seltzer is a solution of carbon dioxide gas in water.

In a solution, the substance that is present in a greater amount is called the **solvent.** Water is the most common solvent. The substance present in a smaller amount is called the **solute.** The solvent and solute may be in different states before the solution is formed. However, the final state of the solution will be that of the solvent. So a solution of water and powdered fruit drink is a liquid, not a solid.

▶ Comparing and Contrasting When learning about things that are related, it is helpful to compare and contrast them. Comparing is pointing out how two things are alike. Contrasting is showing how two things are different. This article compares solutions and other mixtures. They are alike in that both can be separated by physical means. This article also contrasts solutions and other mixtures. One way they are different is that the ingredients of a solution are distributed evenly throughout. In other mixtures the ingredients can be mixed unevenly.

1. How are mixtures and solutions alike?
    A. Both are only liquids or gases.
    B. Both consist of two or more substances mixed together.

2. How are mixtures and solutions different?
    A. A solution is always liquid, and a mixture can be solid, liquid, or gas.
    B. A mixture can be in any state of matter, but a solution is always in the state of matter of the solvent.

How Solutions Form

When a solute dissolves, its particles spread evenly throughout the solution. How quickly the solute dissolves depends on several things. The smaller the particles of solute, the more quickly they dissolve. That's why instant coffee is made of small grains, not large chunks.

Stirring or shaking make a solute dissolve faster. The movement brings the solvent in contact with more of the solute. Stirring a cup of instant coffee makes the coffee dissolve more quickly.

Heat also makes a solute dissolve faster. Molecules move more quickly when they are hot. You can make instant coffee more quickly with boiling water than with cold water.

Solubility of Some Solids in Water

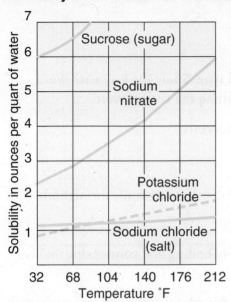

Solubility

The amount of a solute that will dissolve in a given amount of solvent at a given temperature is called its **solubility.** The effect of temperature on solubility is shown in the graph on this page. Each line on the graph is called a solubility curve. You can use this graph to find the solubility of substances in water at various temperatures.

The solubility of solids and liquids usually increases as the temperature rises. However, the opposite is true of gases. As the temperature rises, dissolved gas particles gain energy. They escape from the surface of the solution. That's why an opened bottle of soda goes flat more quickly at room temperature than in the refrigerator.

▶ **Reading a Line Graph** Line graphs show information instead of presenting it in words. The title tells you the main idea of the graph. This graph shows the solubility of some solids in water. The labels along the side show how many ounces of the solid will dissolve in one quart of water. The labels along the bottom show the temperature of the water. To find out how much sodium nitrate will dissolve in a quart of water heated to 176 °F, first find the line that shows sodium nitrate. Then find the point on that line that intersects with the grid line for 176 °F on the bottom temperature scale. From that point on the sodium nitrate line, look along the horizontal grid line to the left-hand scale. There you will see that about 5 ounces of sodium nitrate will dissolve in 1 quart of water heated to 176 °F.

1. How many ounces of salt will dissolve in one quart of boiling water (212 °F)?
   A. about 1.5   B. about 6

2. Which of the following substances is more soluble in water?
   A. potassium chloride   B. sugar

What happens if you add more solute than the solvent can hold? Extra solute settles to the bottom. That is why there is a limit to how sweet you can make iced tea. Once you reach the solubility limit of sugar, no more dissolves. The sugar on the bottom doesn't make the tea sweeter.

If the temperature of a sugar solution changes, the solubility of sugar changes. Suppose you dissolve all the sugar you can in hot water. Then you let the water cool. Sugar crystals will come out of the solution. If you let the water evaporate, the sugar crystals will be left behind. This is how rock candy is made.

Thinking About the Article

Practice Vocabulary

▶ **The words below are in the passage in bold type. Study the way each word is used. Then complete each sentence by writing the correct word.**

distillation   **solution**   **solvent**

solute   **solubility**

1. A mixture in which the substances are distributed evenly throughout

    is called a _____.

2. _____ is a process of boiling and condensing that is used to separate liquids in a mixture.

3. The _____ of liquids and solids usually increases with increases in temperature.

4. The substance present in the smaller amount in a solution is called the

    _____ .

5. Because so many substances dissolve in it, water is often called the

    universal _____ .

Understand the Article

▶ **All of the items listed below are mixtures. In each pair of items, however, one of the mixtures is a solution. For each pair, write the name of the solution.**

6. _____ chocolate chip cookie dough/hot chocolate

7. _____ instant coffee/chicken noodle soup

8. _____ brass/gravel

▶ **Circle the letter of the correct answer.**

9. Refer to the line graph on page 181. The solubility of which of the following solids is <u>less</u> affected by changes in temperature?

    A. sodium chloride   B. sodium nitrate

10. Why does adding heat make a solid or liquid solute dissolve more quickly?

    A. The heat melts the solute.

    B. The heat makes the molecules move more quickly so they mix together faster.

Apply Your Skills

▶ **Circle the letter of the best answer for each question.**

11. What is the difference between a solvent and a solute?

A.   A solvent is part of a mixture, and a solute is part of a solution.

B.   A solvent is always a gas, and a solute is always a liquid.

C.   A solvent is present in a greater amount in a solution, and a solute in a lesser amount.

D.   A solvent can be separated out by chemical means, and a solute can be separated out by physical means.

12. How are soil, cement, and air alike?

A.   They are all solutions.

B.   They are all mixtures.

C.   They are all elements.

D.   They are all compounds.

13. Refer to the line graph on page 181. Approximately how much sugar will dissolve in 1 quart of water at 32°F?

A.   2 ounces

B.   4 ounces

C.   6 ounces

D.   7 ounces

Connect with the Article

▶ **Write your answer to each question.**

14. Suppose you mixed a fruit drink from grape-flavored powder, sugar, and water. Identify the solvent and the solutes. What happens when you combine them?

_____

_____

_____

15. What is an experience you or someone you know has had with a mixture or solution?

_____

_____

_____

SCIENCE PRACTICE FOCUS

Earth: A Giant Mixture

Few things on Earth occur naturally as pure substances. Clouds are mixtures of the gases in the atmosphere, as well as water vapor droplets and pollution particles. Rocks usually are mixtures of different minerals. Even fresh water is a solution. H_2O is the solvent and calcium, iron, sodium, and potassium are some of the typical solutes. Ocean water is a solution of almost all 92 naturally-occurring elements!

A homogeneous mixture is another name for a solution. Homogeneous mixtures are the same throughout. Adding fluoride to tap water creates a homogeneous solution. A heterogeneous mixture is not uniform throughout. In a sample of sand, for example, you can see that the grains are made of different materials.

▶ **Fill in the blank with the word or words that best complete each statement.**

1. A solution is made up of solutes dissolved in a _____ .

2. Vegetable soup is an example of a(n) _____ mixture.

Write your answer to each question.

3. Look at the satellite photograph of Earth. Describe three different mixtures you can see in the photograph.

4. Explain how, over time, ocean water could become a mixture of nearly every naturally occurring element on Earth.

5. The label on a bottle of apple juice states that it contains "100% Pure Juice." Does this mean that the juice is a pure substance, or could it still be a mixture? Explain your reasoning.

6. Think about the last meal or two that you ate. List some examples of heterogeneous and homogeneous mixtures in your food and drinks.

Circle the letter of the best answer.

7. Which of the following drinks is a heterogeneous mixture?

A. sweetened tea

B. unsweetened tea

C. orange juice with pulp

D. filtered orange juice

Check your answers on page 274.

COMBUSTION

You may not be familiar with the word *combustion*. But you rely on this process every day. Combustion refers to chemical reactions that involve burning, or fire.

You may use combustion to heat your home in the winter by burning wood, gas, or oil. These are examples of combustion reactions. You also use a combustion reaction to get to work every day if you travel by car or bus.

Vocabulary

combustion

hydrocarbons

activation energy

kindling
    temperature

Relate to the Topic

This lesson is about combustion. Think about your experiences with an accidental fire or a fire that could have become dangerous.

Describe an experience you've had with fire. _____

_____

_____

_____

How did you put the fire out? _____

_____

_____

_____

Reading Strategy

SCANNING BOLDFACED WORDS Science materials often highlight technical terms in bold type. Words are highlighted this way in order to draw attention to terms that are likely to be new to the reader. Look at the boldfaced terms on page 187. Then answer the questions.

1. What are hydrocarbons made of?

_____

Hint: Scan the second paragraph.

2. What is a kindling temperature?

_____

Hint: Scan the last paragraph.

The By-Products of Burning

Humans first used fire in prehistoric times. Ever since then, people have been burning fuels to produce heat. At first, people burned wood for warmth and then for cooking. During the 1700s, the first engines were invented. In an engine, a fuel is burned and heat energy is produced. This energy is then captured and used to produce motion. Today, fuels are used to provide heat and to power engines.

Combustion Reactions

Burning is a chemical change that chemists call **combustion.** In combustion, oxygen reacts with a fuel. Heat and light energy are released. An example of combustion is the burning of a fuel such as kerosene, oil, or gas. These fuels are **hydrocarbons,** or compounds made only of hydrogen and carbon. When they burn, the hydrogen and carbon combine with oxygen from the air. Carbon dioxide and water vapor are produced.

Combustion reactions need a little energy to get them started. This energy is called **activation energy.** To start a twig burning, you must light a match to it. Once combustion starts, no additional energy is needed.

Each substance has its own **kindling temperature.** That's the temperature to which the substance must be heated before it will burn. The form of a substance affects its kindling temperature. For example, sawdust catches fire faster than a log. Vaporized gasoline ignites more easily than liquid gasoline.

The burning of gasoline in this motorcycle's engine is an example of combustion.

How a Combustion Heater Works

A small kerosene or natural gas heater can be used to warm one or two rooms. A kerosene heater has a small built-in fuel tank. Some natural gas heaters have fuel tanks, too. Other gas heaters are connected to the gas lines of the house. The fuel is piped to the burners. Most heaters use an electric spark to start the combustion reaction. Cool air from the room enters at the base of the heater. The heat from combustion warms the

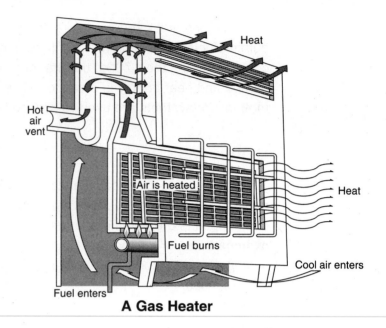

A Gas Heater

air. Warmed air then flows into the room. With a gas heater, the waste products of combustion leave the house through a vent. With a kerosene heater, all of the hot air flows into the room.

Kerosene heaters have many advantages. A kerosene heater is not very expensive. It does not have to be attached to a chimney, so it can be moved from room to room. These heaters warm up quickly and provide heat for up to 30 hours without refueling.

Kerosene heaters also have some disadvantages. If not used properly, they can be unsafe. If the heater is close to drapes, they may catch fire. The outside of the heater is very hot and can cause burns. The heater may tip over, causing injury or a fire. These are all obvious hazards. Less obvious is the hazard caused by the release of pollutants into the air.

▶ Making Predictions Active readers think about what they read. They make predictions about what will come next. Sometimes the predictions are based only on what they have just read. Sometimes they look ahead for clues about what's coming. Reread the second and third paragraphs above. The second paragraph discusses the advantages of kerosene heaters. When you read that, you can predict that the next paragraph will discuss the disadvantages of kerosene heaters. Based on what you have read about the advantages and disadvantages of kerosene heaters, which of the following topics is more likely to come next? Circle the letter of your prediction.

A. The low cost of running combustion heaters.

B. The hazards of pollutants produced by combustion heaters.

Check your answers on page 274.   UNIT 3 PHYSICAL SCIENCE

Indoor Air Pollution

Complete combustion produces carbon dioxide and water vapor. Combustion is complete only if the fuel is pure and there is plenty of oxygen. Often the fuel is not pure. Also, there may be too little oxygen. Then combustion is incomplete. When combustion is incomplete, other substances are released along with carbon dioxide and water vapor. These substances pollute the air.

Incomplete combustion can cause a high level of pollutants to develop in the air. These may include carbon monoxide, nitric oxide, nitrogen dioxide, or sulfur dioxide. These substances can harm the eyes, throat, and lungs. Carbon monoxide is especially dangerous. You can't smell it or see it. Yet high levels of carbon monoxide can cause death.

▶ **Understanding the Implied Main Idea** Sometimes a writer does not actually state the main idea of a paragraph in a topic sentence. You have to "read between the lines" and add up the details to figure out the main idea. The first paragraph above has no topic sentence. Instead, it describes complete combustion and incomplete combustion. The main idea is that complete combustion produces harmless products, and incomplete combustion produces pollutants. Reread the second paragraph above. Circle the letter of its implied main idea.

   A. Indoor air pollutants can be harmful to health and can even cause death.

   B. Indoor air pollutants can collect even when a room is not airtight.

Both natural gas and kerosene heaters can give off pollutants. Natural gas burns more cleanly than kerosene. But makers of kerosene heaters claim that these heaters can burn cleanly, too. If high-quality kerosene is used, the combustion reaction is 99.5 percent complete, meaning that only 0.5 percent of the reaction is incomplete.

Kerosene and natural gas heaters are not the only producers of indoor air pollution. Wood stoves, fireplaces, gas stoves, and tobacco smoke are other sources. Leaking chimneys and furnaces also produce indoor air pollution.

Safety Precautions

People using kerosene heaters or other types of combustion devices indoors should always follow the manufacturer's instructions. The heater should always be in a safe place. It should be placed away from materials that might burn and away from places where children play.

To reduce indoor pollution, use only high-quality kerosene in a kerosene heater. Keep the doors to other rooms open for ventilation. Remember that combustion uses oxygen from the air. It is a good idea to open a window slightly to let more oxygen in and allow pollutants to escape.

Thinking About the Article

Practice Vocabulary

▶ The terms below are in the passage in bold type. Study the way each term is used. Then complete each sentence by writing the correct term.

combustion   kindling temperature

activation energy   hydrocarbon

1. Chemists call burning _____ .

2. A(n) _____ is a compound, such as kerosene or natural gas, made only of hydrogen and carbon.

3. The energy required to start a combustion reaction is called

_____ .

4. Before it will burn, a substance must be heated to its

_____ .

Understand the Article

▶ Write or circle the answer to each question.

5. Which gas from the air is needed for combustion?

_____

6. What happens during a combustion reaction?

A. Oxygen reacts with a fuel, producing heat, light, carbon dioxide, and water vapor.

B. Carbon dioxide, water vapor, and carbon monoxide combine to form heat, oxygen, and carbon by-products.

7. Which pollutants can be produced when combustion is incomplete? Circle the letter of each correct answer.

A. sulfur dioxide and nitrogen dioxide

B. carbon monoxide

C. oxygen and kerosene

D. nitric oxide

8. Why is it important to provide oxygen to a kerosene or gas heater?

A. Without enough oxygen, combustion is incomplete, producing pollutants.

B. Without enough oxygen, the heater costs more to run.

Apply Your Skills

▶ **Circle the letter of the best answer for each question.**

9. On the basis of the information in the article, which of the following can you predict about small kerosene and gas heaters?

    A. Wood-burning stoves produce more air pollution than do small heaters.

    B. Sales of small heaters have increased since the fuel shortages of the 1970s.

    C. High-quality kerosene produces more pollutants than low-quality kerosene.

    D. More fires are caused by small heaters than by built-in heating systems.

10. Which of the following would you predict might happen if kerosene were used in a small heater in an airtight room?

    A. Only carbon dioxide and water vapor would be produced, making the room warm and damp.

    B. The pollutants released by incomplete combustion would eventually overcome the people in the room.

    C. Oxygen from outdoors would be used to keep the combustion reaction going to heat the room.

    D. The combustion reaction would speed up, eventually causing the heater to explode.

11. What is the implied main idea of the first paragraph on page 187?

    A. The first fuel was wood, used to provide heat.

    B. Over time, people have burned fuels for many purposes.

    C. Engines change heat energy into the energy of motion.

    D. Air pollution is caused by burning fuels.

Connect with the Article

▶ **Write your answer to each question.**

12. How can the hazards of using a kerosene or gas heater be reduced?

13. Describe something you have that uses combustion. What type of fuel is used? Do you think it is producing any air pollutants?

SCIENCE PRACTICE FOCUS

Wildfires

A wildfire is the uncontrolled combustion of plants in a wilderness area. The fuel for a wildfire could be grass, trees, roots, desert plants, or dead plant materials. Needed oxygen comes from the air. Activation energy can be supplied by lightning, a neglected campfire, or a lit cigarette tossed from a car window. Many wildfires are intentionally started by people.

Some wildfires creep along at ground level, while others send flames towering into the sky. Wildfires can jump over streams if a spark is carried by the wind to the fresh fuel on the other side. Plants and animals that live in fire-prone areas have adaptations that help them survive the heat. Burrowing underground and producing heat-activated seeds are two strategies that allow fire and life to coexist.

▶ **Fill in the blank with the word or words that best completes the statement.**

   1. Plant material provides the _____ for a wildfire.

▶ **Write your answer to each question.**

   2. What provides the activation energy for combustion as a wildfire spreads to new plant material?

_____

_____

          UNIT 3 PHYSICAL SCIENCE

3. How does wind help a fire to move across a stream?

_____

_____

4. Look at the photograph of the wildfire. Is this fire an example of complete or incomplete combustion? Explain your answer using evidence from the picture.

_____

_____

_____

5. Plants are mostly cellulose, which contains carbon, oxygen, and hydrogen. Predict the main products of plant combustion.

_____

6. Using what you know about the requirements for a combustion reaction, describe three possible strategies for putting out a wildfire.

_____

_____

_____

_____

_____

7. Millions of Americans live in areas where wildfires are an annual threat. Describe three strategies homeowners could use to prevent their houses from burning in a wildfire.

_____

_____

_____

_____

8. How is a wildfire similar to the reaction that takes place in a kerosene heater? How are they different?

_____

_____

_____

 Check your answers on page 275.

HEAT TRANSFER

It's a hot summer day at the pool and you've worked up a powerful thirst. You are just about to take your first sip from an ice-filled glass of lemonade when your friend calls to you from the water. She convinces you to put down your drink and join her for a swim.

When you return to your lemonade a while later, what's happened? The ice has long since melted, and the lemonade is warm. How did this happen? Energy from the air transferred to the ice and lemonade, warming them up. In other words, heat transfer struck again!

Vocabulary

kinetic energy

temperature

thermal energy

heat

conduction

convection

convection currents

radiation

work

heat engine

Relate to the Topic

This article describes heat and how it moves. Think about the ways in which heat affects your life and the world around you.

What are some ways you used heat today?

_____

_____

How did heat affect what you wore today?

_____

_____

Reading Strategy

USING HEADINGS TO ASK QUESTIONS   When you come to a heading, think about it for a moment before reading the information that follows it. Think of a question that might be answered in that section. As you continue reading, look for answer to your question. Read the headings on pages 195 through 197. Then answer the questions.

1. What is one question that is likely to be answered on page 195?

_____

Hint: Read the heading.

2. What is one question that is likely to be answered on page 197?

_____

Hint: Read the heading.

Energy and Temperature

Matter is made up of particles that are constantly moving. The energy of motion is known as **kinetic energy**. Fast moving particles have more kinetic energy than slow moving particles. **Temperature** is the measure of the average kinetic energy of the particles in a substance. The tool used to measure temperature is the thermometer. Scientists often measure the temperature of matter in units of degrees Celsius (°C), but in the United States, weather forecasters usually measure air temperature in degrees Fahrenheit (°F). Another unit of measure for temperature used in science is the kelvin (K).

The temperature of a substance changes when the motion of the particles that make up the object changes. As the speed of the particles in an object increases, the temperature of the substance increases. Think again about an ice-filled glass of lemonade. As the warm air around it heats the ice and lemonade, the particles making up these substances have more energy and increase in speed. As the particles move faster, the temperatures of the ice and lemonade increase.

Temperature also is an indicator of a substance's thermal energy. **Thermal energy** is the total energy of moving particles that make up matter.

The Flow of Heat

Heat is the flow of thermal energy. Heat always flows from a warmer object to a cooler object, or from part of a substance with a higher temperature to another part with a lower temperature. Another name for the flow of heat is heat transfer. Heat continues to flow, or be transferred, until all objects or parts of a substance have the same temperature.

Suppose you have a glass of cold lemonade, and the temperature of that lemonade is 5 °C. The temperature of the surrounding air is 26 °C. What will happen to that cold liquid and the warmer air around it over time? Heat will flow from the warmer air to the cooler lemonade. Heat flows out of the warmer air, so the air loses thermal energy and decreases in temperature. Heat flows into the lemonade, which gains thermal energy and increases in temperature. Heat will continue to transfer from the warmer air to the cooler lemonade until the surrounding air and lemonade have the same temperature.

▶ **Applying Knowledge to Other Contexts** General knowledge can be put to use in new situations. Scientists and others apply their knowledge to understand new observations, predict events, and solve problems. For example, meteorologists use their knowledge of heat and temperature to understand air masses.

Which of the following most likely describes how tropical air becomes warm?
A. Heat flows from the warm tropical ocean below to the cooler air mass above.
B. Heat flows to the warm tropical ocean below from the cooler air mass above.

There are three main ways in which heat is transferred: conduction, convection, and radiation.

Conduction is the transfer of heat from one particle of matter to another. This transfer happens within a substance or between substances when particles come in contact, but it does not involve a flow of matter. If you have ever walked barefoot on hot sand at the beach, then you have experienced conduction. The hot sand has a greater temperature than your feet, so heat moves from the particles of sand to the particles of your feet touching the sand. Your feet gain thermal energy from the hot sand, and the particles in your feet increase in speed. As a result, the temperature of your feet increases—that's why your bare feet suddenly feel scorching hot!

In contrast, **convection** is the transfer of heat through the movement of a fluid. Fluids are liquids and gases, such as water or air. Fluid particles move freely, making it possible for currents to flow within them. Imagine a pot of water heating on a stove. The stove burner heats the metal pot, and then heat transfers by conduction from the hot metal of the pot bottom to the water particles in contact with the metal. As the water at the bottom of the pot gets heated, its particles spread apart, or expand, and the water becomes less dense than at the top of the pot. The cooler and denser water near the top of the pot sinks, forcing the warmer and less dense water at the bottom of the pot to rise. As the cooler water gets heated at the bottom of the pot, it also rises, setting up circular patterns of rising and sinking fluid movement called **convection currents**. Convection currents occur naturally in Earth's atmosphere and mantle, helping to transfer heat throughout the air and drive the motion of tectonic plates.

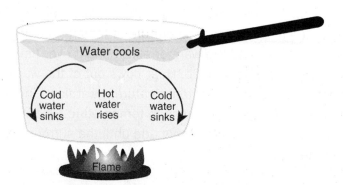

When you heat water on a stove, convection currents transfer heat throughout the water in the pot.

▶ **Understanding Sequence** The order in which things happen is called sequence. Understanding sequence helps you understand how processes like heat transfer occur. For example, the paragraph above explains the sequence of events that leads to the development of convection currents. The diagram helps you visualize this sequence. The first step involves the stove burner heating the metal pot. What happens immediately after the metal of the pot gets heated?

    A. The cooler and denser water near the top of the pot sinks.

    B. Heat transfers from the metal to the water particles in contact with it.

Radiation is the transfer of heat by electromagnetic waves. Radiation can transfer heat through empty space, known as a vacuum, unlike conduction and convection, which need matter to transfer heat. The sun is Earth's main source of energy, and radiation is the process by which this energy flows from the sun to Earth. When you face the sun on a sunny day, radiation transfers heat to your face and warms it. And when you stand near a burning campfire, radiation transfers heat from the fire to your body and warms it.

Heat and Work

The transfer of heat can result in work being done. **Work** is done when a force acting on an object causes the object to move. A device that uses heat to do work is called a **heat engine**.

One example of a heat engine is the engine of a car or truck, called an internal combustion engine. When a fuel (in this case gasoline) is burned in the engine, energy stored in the fuel is released and converted to thermal energy. This energy gets transferred to the surrounding air, and this heat transfer does work on the engine's piston, causing it to move. This motion eventually leads to the car's motion.

This internal combustion engine uses heat to do work.

          Check your answers on page 276.

Thinking About the Article

Practice Vocabulary

▶ **The terms below are in the passage in bold type. Study the way each term is used. Then complete each sentence by writing the correct term.**

heat	convection	temperature
radiation	kinetic energy	

1. The energy of motion is known as _____ .

2. _____ is a measure of the average kinetic energy of the particles in a substance.

3. The transfer of heat by electromagnetic waves is called

   _____ .

4. _____ is the transfer of heat through the movement of a fluid.

5. The flow of thermal energy is called _____ .

Understand the Article

▶ **Write or circle the answer to each question.**

6. Name three main ways in which heat is transferred.

   _____

   _____

   _____

7. Which of the following is a tool used to measure temperature?
   A. heat engine
   B. thermometer

8. How are heat and work related? Give an example.

   _____

   _____

   _____

Apply Your Skills

▶ **Circle the letter of the best answer.**

9. Which of the following describes an effect of heat radiation?

   A.   Soup gets hot when you heat it in a metal pot on the stove.

   B.   Your finger gets warmer when you hold it near a candle flame.

   C.   An ice cube melts when you place it in a bowl of warm water.

   D.   Your hand gets hot when you touch a cup of hot tea.

10. Which of the following will most likely happen when a warm block of copper is place on top of a cooler block of iron?

   A.   Heat will not flow between the blocks.

   B.   Heat will flow from the iron block to the copper block.

   C.   Heat will flow from the copper block to the iron block.

   D.   Heat will flow back and forth between the blocks.

11. Suppose you blow up a balloon and tie the end. Then you use a blow dryer to heat one end of the balloon. How does heat get transferred throughout the air inside the balloon?

   A.   conduction

   B.   convection

   C.   heat engine

   D.   radiation

Connect with the Article

▶ **Write your answer to each question.**

12. How would you explain the difference between thermal energy and heat to a friend?

   _____

   _____

   _____

13. Describe an example of conduction that you experienced.

   _____

   _____

   _____

SCIENCE PRACTICE FOCUS

Measuring Calories in Food

A calorie is a unit of heat energy. The Calorie you see on a food label is actually a kilocalorie (1,000 calories). A Calorie (kcal) is the amount of heat energy it takes to raise the temperature of one kilogram of water by one degree Celsius.

A device called a bomb calorimeter can be used to measure the amount of Calories a food product contains. The food is placed in a sealed container surrounded by water. Electrodes in the lid of the calorimeter ignite the food and it is allowed to burn completely. The heat inside the calorimeter is transfers into the water that surrounds it. The rise in water temperature is measured to determine the number of Calories the food contains. The diagram below shows a bomb calorimeter.

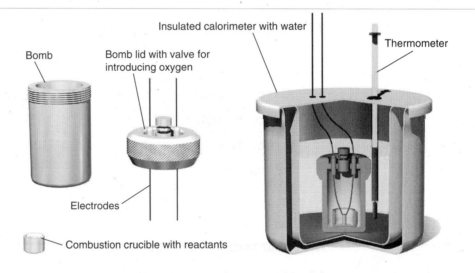

Another method, the Atwater system, determines the amount of protein, carbohydrate, fat and alcohol a food contains. It uses an average value of 4 Cal/g for protein, 4 Cal/g for carbohydrate and 9 Cal/g for fat. Using the Atwater system, a food containing 5 g of protein, 10 g of carbohydrate, and 3 g of fat would contain 87 Calories.

▷ **Circle the letter of the best answer.**

1. A kilocalorie is equivalent to

    A. 10 calories

    B. 100 calories

    C. 1,000 calories

    D. 10,000 calories

▶ **Write your answer to the question.**

2. Use the Atwater system to determine the amount of calories in a food that contains 6 g of protein, 6 g of carbohydrate, and 5 g of fat. Show your work.

_____

_____

▶ **The table below shows some of the information found on the food label of an individual-sized bag of potato chips. Use the data to answer the questions below.**

Nutrition Facts	Cholesterol 0mg
Serving Size 1 oz (28g)	Sodium 250mg
Servings Per Container About 2.5	Total Carbohydrate 13g
Amount Per Serving	Dietary Fiber less than 1g
Calories 150 Calories From Fat 90	Sugars 1g
Total Fat 10g	Protein 2g
Saturated Fat 1.5g	Calcium 0mg
Trans Fat 0g	Vitamin C 0mg

3. Does this product contain a high percentage of fat? Explain your answer.

_____

_____

4. It is important to your health to read food labels carefully. About how many calories will you take in if you eat the whole bag of chips?

_____

5. Is this food a good source of dietary fiber? Explain your answer.

_____

_____

6. Would eating this food help to build healthy bones? Explain your answer.

_____

_____

7. A raw potato contains about 30 mg of vitamin C. What happens to the amount of vitamin C when raw potatoes are made into potato chips?

_____

_____

MACHINES

Walk into a bicycle store and you'll see an amazing assortment of bikes. There are racing bikes, mountain bikes, and bikes with training wheels. There are one-speed bikes and 21-speed bikes. There are even bikes that let you pedal while you lie on your back.

Despite their differences, all bicycles have certain things in common. They all let you get around more quickly than you can by walking or running. And all bikes—even ones with many complicated parts—are really just a collection of simple machines that work together.

Relate to the Topic

This lesson is about force and work. It describes some simple machines, which are devices that help us do work. It also describes a more complex machine—the bicycle. Think about the last time you rode a bicycle.

Why did you ride the bicycle? _____

_____

How many speeds did the bicycle have? _____

_____

Reading Strategy

RELATING TO WHAT YOU KNOW   When you read, think about what you already know about the topic. The topic of this lesson is machines, including levers and gears. Think about what you already know about levers and gears. Then answer the questions.

1. When would you use a lever? _____

_____

Hint: Picture a lever and think about how you would use it.

_____

2. Where are you likely to find gears? _____

_____

Hint: Think about where you have seen gears or a gearshift.

Vocabulary

force

gravity

friction

work

effort

resistance

simple machine

lever

pivot

mechanical advantage

wheel and axle

gear

compound machine

How a Bicycle Works

In many large cities, businesses use messengers to carry documents across town. These messengers can be seen speeding past clogged traffic. Are they running? Are they driving? No, they're riding bicycles.

A bicycle is a good way to get around. You don't have to be very strong to go at a moderate speed. If you have a bicycle with 3, 10, or 21 speeds, it can help you ride easily up most hills. By riding a bicycle, you can get your exercise on the way to work.

A bicycle is a good means of transportation.

Force and Work

When you push down on the pedal of a bicycle, you are applying a force to it. A **force** is a push or a pull. There are many kinds of forces. The pull of one magnet on another is a force. The pull that Earth has on you and all other objects is the force of **gravity**. A force between surfaces that touch each other is known as **friction.** Friction between the brake pads and the wheel of a bicycle or automobile stops the wheel from turning.

Work is done when a force causes an object to move. Lifting a bag of groceries is work. Your upward force of lifting overcomes the downward force of gravity. The force you exert is called the **effort.** The force you overcome is the **resistance.**

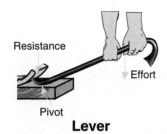

Resistance

Effort

Pivot

Lever

Wheel

Axle

Wheel and Axle

Gears

Simple Machines

Sometimes your effort cannot overcome the resistance. Then you need the help of a machine. If you have ever used a screwdriver to pry the lid off a paint can, you have used a machine. A **simple machine** is a device used to do work. There are several kinds of simple machines. A bicycle has three of them: a lever, a wheel and axle, and gears.

A **lever** is a bar that turns on a pivot. A **pivot** is an object on which another object turns. When you open the paint can, you are using the screwdriver as a lever. The lever transfers the force from your hand to the lid. The lever also multiplies your effort. The greater force overcomes the friction holding the lid on the can.

The number of times a machine multiplies your effort is the **mechanical advantage** of the machine. You may have noticed that a longer screwdriver is a better lever than a shorter screwdriver. That is because a longer lever gives a greater mechanical advantage.

A **wheel and axle** is another type of simple machine. It is made of two objects that turn in a circular motion on the same center. A wheel and axle doesn't always look like a wheel. A crank handle is a wheel and axle.

Gears are wheels with teeth. Unlike a wheel and axle, gears do not turn on the same center. The gears are arranged so that the teeth meet, and each gear turns on its own center. If you turn one gear, then you cause any gear it touches to turn.

▶ **Understanding a Diagram** A diagram is a picture that shows how something is put together or explains how something works. Some diagrams use arrows. To understand these diagrams, you have to look carefully at where the arrows point. In the diagram of a lever above, the arrow for the word *Resistance* shows the direction of the resistance force. The arrow for the word *Effort* shows that you have to push down on the lever to overcome the resistance.

1. The diagram of the lever indicates that when you push down on one end of a lever, the other end of the lever does what?
   A. also moves down   B. moves up to overcome the resistance

2. In the diagram of gears, the arrows show that the two gears turn
   A. in the same direction   B. in opposite directions

A Compound Machine

Sometimes it takes more than one machine to get a job done. A **compound machine** is made up of several simple machines. A bicycle is a compound machine. The brake handles and gearshifts are levers. The wheels and pedals are wheel and axle machines. Bicycles also contain gears. The number of "speeds" a bicycle has equals the number of front gears multiplied by the number of back gears. If a bike has many "speeds," you can get the mechanical advantage you need for any situation.

A bicycle is a compound machine.

A machine can multiply your effort. It can also multiply your speed. However, it cannot do both at once. When you ride a bicycle on a level path, you use the higher "speeds." The highest "speed" on a bicycle combines the largest front gear—at the pedals, which are a crank—with the smallest gear on the rear wheel. You have to pedal hard but not very quickly. Yet the bicycle moves quickly. The only resistance is friction, which is a small force. The bicycle is not multiplying your force. Instead, it is using your force to multiply your speed.

You use the lower "speeds" to climb hills. In the lowest "speed," you combine the smallest front gear at the pedals with the largest rear gear. You don't need to pedal hard. However, you do have to pedal quickly, even though the bike moves slowly. The bicycle is multiplying your effort to move you against a large force—gravity.

▶ Drawing Conclusions Conclusions are ideas that are based on facts. They follow logically from the facts. The previous paragraph describes pedaling a bicycle on a hill at the lowest gear speed. The low gear speed multiplies your effort. From the facts in the paragraph you can conclude that pedaling uphill is easier on a 21-speed bike than on a one-speed bike, because the 21-speed bike multiplies your effort much more.

Based on the information in the first two paragraphs on this page, which of the following conclusions are you likely to draw?

    A. Gravity exerts a larger force when you ride up a hill than friction does on level ground.

    B. Higher gear speeds result in more force on a level path than lower gear speeds do.

Check your answers on page 277.

Thinking About the Article

Practice Vocabulary

▶ The terms below are in the passage in bold type. Study the way each term is used. Then complete each sentence by writing the correct term.

force	**work**	**simple machine**
mechanical advantage	**compound machine**	

1. A _____ is a push or a pull.

2. A basic device used to do work is called a _____ .

3. A _____ like a bicycle contains several simple machines.

4. The number of times a machine multiplies your effort is the

   _____ of the machine.

5. In physics, _____ is done when a force causes an object to move.

Understand the Article

▶ Circle the letter of the answer to each question.

6. Gravity, magnetism, and friction are all examples of

   A. forces

   B. energy

7. When effort force is greater than resistance force, what happens?

   A. movement, or work

   B. nothing

8. Why does it take less effort to pry up the lid of a paint can with a longer screwdriver than with a shorter screwdriver?

   A. The longer screwdriver provides a greater mechanical advantage.

   B. The longer screwdriver fits better under the lid of the can.

▶ Match each simple machine with its example.

_____ 9. lever

_____ 10. wheel and axle

_____ 11. gears

A. a doorknob

B. a crowbar

C. the wheels that turn the blade of a can opener

Apply Your Skills

▶ **Circle the letter of the best answer for each question.**

12. Refer to the diagram of a wheel and axle on page 204. What do the arrows in the diagram show?

A. The wheel and the axle turn in opposite directions.

B. The wheel and the axle turn in the same direction.

C. The wheel turns but the axle does not turn.

D. The axle turns but the wheel does not turn.

13. When gears turn, the teeth rub on each other. This adds extra resistance. Which of the following forces is responsible for this extra resistance?

A. friction

B. gravity

C. magnetism

D. advantage

14. What happens when the resistance force is larger than the effort force?

A. The effort force will overcome the resistance force.

B. The effort force will continue.

C. The resistance force will decrease.

D. No work will be done.

Connect with the Article

▶ **Write your answer to each question.**

15. When you ride a bicycle up a hill, you can stand up as you pedal. How would this help you get up a hill?

_____

_____

_____

16. What is one experience you or someone you know has had riding or repairing a bicycle? Discuss simple machines, effort, resistance, or work in your description.

_____

_____

_____

Check your answers on page 277.

SCIENCE PRACTICE FOCUS

Simple Machines

In this lesson, you were introduced to three simple machines found in a bicycle: the lever, wheel and axle, and gear. The diagram below shows other types of simple machines.

Simple Machines

Wedge

Screw

Inclined plane

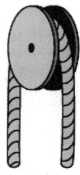

Pulley

A wedge is a movable inclined plane that thins out to a sharp edge, and it can be used to separate or lift up an object. A screw is an inclined plane wrapped around a cylinder. An inclined plane is a sloping surface used to move heavy loads with less effort. A pulley is a grooved wheel that holds a rope and also is used to lift loads with less effort.

▶ **Fill in the blank with the word or words that best complete each statement.**

1. A(n) _____ is a sloping surface.

2. A(n) _____ is an inclined plane wrapped around a cylinder.

3. A(n) _____ is a grooved wheel that holds a rope.

4. A(n) _____ thins out to a sharp edge.

▶ Use the information on page 208 to identify the type of simple machine represented by each everyday object below.

5. wheelchair ramp ....

6. knife blade ....

7. flagpole ....

8. nut and bolt ....

▶ The data table below shows the effect of the length of an inclined plane on the amount of effort force needed to move a 100-kg weight resistance force to a height of 1 meter. Use the data table to answer Questions 9–11.

Inclined Plane	Length (m)	Height (m)	Mechanical Advantage (Length/ Height)	Effort Force (kg)	Resistance Force (kg)
A	2	1	2	100	50
B	4	1	4	100	25
C	6	1	6	100	16.67
D	8	1	?	100	?

9. Do you agree or disagree with the following statement? Explain your answer.

It requires a greater amount of effort force to move a 100-kg resistance force to a height of 1 meter as the length of an inclined plane increases.

....

....

10. Use information from the data table to predict the mechanical advantage and resistance force for Inclined Plane D. Explain your answers.

....

....

....

11. Describe an example of how an inclined plane can make everyday work easier to do.

....

....

Check your answers on pages 277–278.   209

MOMENTUM

At a baseball game, the sound of a bat colliding with a ball is unmistakable. This collision sends the ball flying. A well-hit baseball has a lot of momentum. That means it will travel a long distance through the air before it hits the ground. If the ball has enough momentum and takes the right path, it could leave the field for a home run.

There are several ways that batters can give a baseball more momentum when they hit it. One way is to swing the bat faster. Another way is to use a heavier bat. Some baseball players break the rules to give the ball more momentum.

Vocabulary

energy

collision

momentum

elastic

Relate to the Topic

This lesson is about momentum. It explains what momentum is and how it is transferred when one object collides with another, such as when a bat hits a ball. Think about other sports you have played or watched.

When is momentum transferred in golf? _____

_____

When is momentum transferred in bowling? _____

_____

Reading Strategy

INTERPRETING PHOTO CAPTIONS   A **caption** is a short sentence that accompanies a photo or other illustration. The caption explains what is shown in the illustration or gives more information about it. Captions help you understand what is pictured and how it relates to the surrounding text. Read the caption beneath the photo on page 213. Then answer the questions.

1. What is shown in the photo?

_____

Hint: Look for a person's name in the caption.

2. Why does the article have a photo of that object?

_____

_____

Hint: Look for at the headings on pages 212 and 213.

Breaking the Rules

A major league pitcher can throw a fastball at more than 90 miles per hour. At this speed, the ball reaches the batter in less than half a second. The batter has only a bit more than one tenth of a second to decide if the pitch looks good. The batter must swing quickly. The swing cannot be early or late by more than a few thousandths of a second. If it is, what might have been a home run becomes a foul ball.

Even good batters get hits only about three out of ten times at bat. So batters are always looking for ways to improve their chances. Practice helps. Physical conditioning is also important. However, some batters look for ways that are outside the rules. Most of these ways involve changing the bat.

Collisions

A moving baseball has **energy,** the ability of matter to do work. A catcher can feel this energy as the pitched baseball slams into the mitt. In a **collision,** a moving object strikes another object. The second object may or may not be moving. A catcher's mitt is not moving at the time the ball collides with it. A bat, on the other hand, is moving as the ball collides with it.

This ball and the player's bat are about to collide.

All moving objects have momentum. **Momentum** is a measure of the motion of an object, and it depends on the object's weight and speed. When two objects collide, momentum is transferred from one object to the other. Suppose you stand still with your arm extended to the side. If someone throws a baseball into your hand, this collision will push your hand back. The ball transfers some of its momentum to your hand. The effect of the ball on your hand is greater if the ball has more momentum. This would be true if the ball were either heavier or moving faster.

The transfer of momentum is more complicated when both objects are moving. When the moving bat hits the moving ball, they are traveling in opposite directions. The bat is not moving as fast as the ball, but it is much heavier. Therefore, the bat has more momentum than the ball. When the two collide, the ball goes off in the direction in which the bat was moving.

The transfer of momentum also depends on how elastic the objects are. Something that is **elastic** can be stretched or compressed and will return to its original shape. In many collisions much of the momentum is lost. If the colliding objects are very elastic, only a little momentum is lost. If you drop a golf ball and a Super Ball, the Super Ball will bounce higher. This is because the Super Ball is more elastic than the golf ball, so it loses much less momentum.

▶ **Drawing Conclusions** A conclusion is an idea that follows logically from the information you have. Conclusions must be supported by facts. You have just read that a hit baseball moves in the direction in which the bat is swinging. You have also read that the bat has more momentum than the ball. From these facts, you can conclude that two colliding objects will move in the direction of the object that has more momentum.

Reread the third paragraph above. What can you conclude about the materials that Super Balls are made of?
   A.   Super Balls are made of materials that return to their original shape after being compressed.
   B.   Super Balls are made of materials that do not return to their original shape after being compressed.

Corking Bats

Some baseball players "cork" their bats. They cut off the top of the bat and hollow it out. They fill the space with cork, sawdust, or even Super Balls. Then they glue the top back on. Baseball players feel that this kind of change makes a bat springy. They think the bat becomes more elastic.

Corking bats is against the rules of professional baseball. If a player who hasn't been hitting well suddenly hits a string of home runs, the bat may be taken by the umpires. The bat is X-rayed or cut open. If the bat is corked, the player may be suspended from playing.

Players who cork their bats are cheating. Yet there is so much money in professional baseball that some players are willing to cheat in order to play better. After retiring, one player admitted to using a corked bat for years. He believed that it enabled him to hit a lot of home runs. The player who used Super Balls got caught when his bat cracked. The balls bounced out right in front of the umpire!

What Does Corking a Bat Do?

Scientists have analyzed what happens when a bat is corked. They have found that the bat gets lighter. A batter can swing a lighter bat more quickly. In the opinion of some scientists, this is the reason that the corked bat is better. If the batter can swing more quickly, the swing can be started a bit later. This gives the batter a little more time to decide whether or not to swing at the ball.

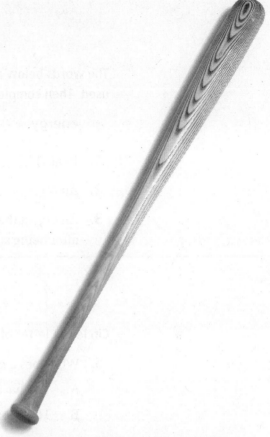

When Howard Johnson's hitting suddenly improved, he was accused of corking his bat. The bat was X-rayed and found to be solid wood.

▶ **Distinguishing Fact from Opinion** Facts can be proven true. Opinions, on the other hand, are what someone believes, thinks, or feels. They may or may not be true. When reading about science topics, it is important to distinguish fact from opinion. Reread the previous paragraph. One fact in the paragraph is that a corked bat is lighter than a solid wood bat. One opinion is that a corked bat is better because a lighter bat requires less time to swing, giving the player extra time to decide whether to swing.

Reread the first paragraph above. Write *fact* or *opinion* next to each statement.

1. The player who used Super Balls got caught when his bat cracked. _____

2. Using a corked bat is the best way to hit more home runs. _____

There may be one more advantage to the corked bat. This one is in the player's mind. If the batter thinks that the bat gives him an advantage, it may improve the batter's confidence. The batter steps up to the plate believing that he is about to hit a home run.

Check your answers on page 278.

Thinking About the Article

Practice Vocabulary

▶ The words below are in the passage in bold type. Study the way each word is used. Then complete each sentence by writing the correct word.

energy   collision   momentum   elastic

1. In a(n) _____, a moving object strikes another object.

2. An object's _____ depends on its weight and speed.

3. An object that is _____ returns to its original shape after being stretched or compressed.

4. _____ is the ability of matter to do work.

Understand the Article

▶ Circle the letter of the best answer.

5. Why does a moving baseball bat have more momentum than the ball?

   A.   The bat is much heavier than the ball.

   B.   The bat is moving much faster than the ball.

6. How can you increase an object's momentum? Circle the letter of each correct answer.

   A.   increase its weight

   B.   make it more elastic

   C.   increase its speed

   D.   decrease its speed

7. Why do some baseball players cork their bats?

   A.   They think it makes the bat more elastic, giving a hit ball more momentum.

   B.   They think solid wood bats are too heavy to swing properly.

8. Which of the following items is more elastic?

   A.   a golf ball

   B.   a Super Ball

9. When a moving object hits a standing one, what determines if the standing object moves? Circle the letter of each correct answer.

   A.   the speed of the moving object

   B.   the weight of the moving object

   C.   the weight of the standing object

Apply Your Skills

▶ **Circle the letter of the best answer for each question.**

10. Based on the information about collisions in the article, which of the following conclusions can you draw?

A. Collisions occur only when one object is moving.

B. All momentum is lost in collisions.

C. The momentum of a moving object increases after a collision.

D. A standing object will move if enough momentum is transferred.

11. Which of the following statements describes a <u>fact</u>?

A. A corked bat helps batters hit the ball better.

B. A corked bat can make a poor hitter into a good hitter.

C. A corked bat is lighter than a solid bat.

D. A corked bat is better than a solid bat.

12. From the appearance of a car after a collision, what can you conclude about cars?

A. Cars have more momentum than trucks.

B. Cars usually collide with moving objects.

C. Cars are not very elastic.

D. Cars return to their original shapes after a crash.

Connect with the Article

▶ **Write your answer to each question.**

13. Your friend is in a compact car and you are in a sport utility vehicle. Both vehicles are moving at the same speed along a highway. Which has more momentum? Explain your answer.

_____

_____

_____

14. Think about a time when you collided with something while riding in a car, walking, or playing a sport. What was the collision and the transfer of momentum like?

_____

_____

_____

Check your answers on page 278.

SCIENCE PRACTICE FOCUS

Mass and Momentum

Momentum is calculated by multiplying an object's mass by its velocity. The mass of an object is the amount of matter it contains and the velocity is the speed of the object in a certain direction. The standard metric unit of momentum is the kg x m/s.

Suppose your are given a small marble, large marble, grooved metric ruler, two textbooks, triple beam balance, and some masking tape. Your assignment is to design and conduct an experiment to determine how the mass of an object affects the its momentum.

1. Using the materials listed above, describe an investigation that determines the effect of an object's mass on the amount of momentum it has.

_____

_____

_____

_____

_____

_____

_____

_____

2. State a hypothesis that your investigation will test.

_____

_____

_____

▶ **Fill in the blank with the word or words that best complete each statement.**

3. The independent variable in this investigation is

_____ .

4. The dependent variable in this investigation is _____ .

▶ Circle the letter of the best answer.

5. What is the momentum of an object that has a mass of 15 kg and a velocity of 3 m/s?

A. 5 kg × m/s

B. 12 kg × m/s

C. 18 kg × m/s

D. 45 kg × m/s

▶ Use the sample data below to answer the questions.

Marble	Mass (g)	Distance Marble Traveled (cm)			
		Trial 1	Trial 2	Trial 3	Average
1	10	26.4	27.2	26.6	26.73
2	25	54.1	53.7	53.8	53.87

6. What conclusion can you draw from the sample data?

_____

_____

_____

7. How might this sample data affect your hypothesis?

_____

_____

_____

8. Why did the students conduct three trials and calculate an average distance for each marble instead of conducting only one trial with each marble?

_____

_____

_____

9. What would you expect to happen if you conducted a set of trials using a 50-g marble?

_____

_____

_____

SOUND WAVES

Vocabulary

sound

sound waves

pitch

pure tone

overtones

timbre

amplitude

resonance

Music is performed throughout the world for many different purposes. It's enjoyed as a source of entertainment. It is an important part of rituals in many cultures and religions. Music can be used to calm emotions, to rouse patriotism, and to stir people to action.

No matter why it is performed or how it is created, all music involves sound. Musical sounds have the same properties as other kinds of sound.

Relate to the Topic

This lesson is about music. It describes the basic features of musical sounds. It also explains why different instruments produce different sounds. Think about the music you listen to.

What kinds of music do you enjoy listening to most?

_____

_____

What instruments are usually played to make that music?

_____

_____

Reading Strategy

RELATING TO WHAT YOU KNOW   When you read, try to relate what you are reading to what you already know about the topic. The topic of this lesson is the physics of the sounds we call music. Then answer the questions.

1. How do the sounds of a foghorn and a referee's whistle differ?

   _____

   Hint: Think about times when you heard each sound.

2. How do the sounds of an exploding firecracker and a snapping twig differ?

   _____

   _____

   Hint: Think about how you reacted when you heard each sound.

The Physics of Music

Suppose someone asked you, "What is music?" What answer would you give? Everyone knows music when they hear it, but coming up with a definition of music is not an easy thing to do. Music usually involves an organized series of sounds with a definite pattern or rhythm. It may help to think of music as both art and physics. The art involves combining different sounds in a way that makes listeners feel a certain way—relaxed, excited, happy, or sad. The physics of music has to do with how the sounds are produced and controlled.

Sound is produced whenever an object, such as a guitar string, vibrates. A vibrating guitar string moves back and forth many times. Each time it moves out, it compresses the air in a small region next to it. Each time it moves back, it makes a small region of less compressed air. The alternating regions of compressed and less compressed air travel out from the string. These are the **sound waves** you hear when the guitar is strummed. You can imitate a sound wave by stretching a spring toy and then tapping one end of it. The tap will compress the coils near that end, and the compression will move through the coils to the other end.

When a sound wave reaches your ears, it makes your eardrums vibrate. The vibrations pass to your inner ear. Nerves in your inner ear convert the sound wave to an electrical impulse and send the impulse to your brain. In your brain, the electrical impulse is interpreted as sound. The type of sound that you hear depends mainly on three physical characteristics of the sound wave: its frequency, its harmonics, and its amplitude.

The faster an object vibrates, the more regions of compressed and decompressed air the object produces in a certain amount of time. A pair of alternating regions of compressed and decompressed air is called a cycle. The number of cycles produced each second is the frequency of the sound. Frequency is measured in hertz, abbreviated Hz. One hertz equals one cycle per second.

Most people with good hearing can hear sounds that have frequencies ranging from about 15 Hz to 20,000 Hz. A tuba can make sounds with frequencies as low as 40 Hz, and a piano can go as low as 30 Hz. At the high end, piccolos, violins, and some other instruments can make sounds with frequencies as high as 15,000 Hz. You perceive the frequency of a sound wave as its **pitch.** A high-pitched sound, such as one made by a piccolo, has a higher frequency than a low-pitched sound, such as one made by a tuba.

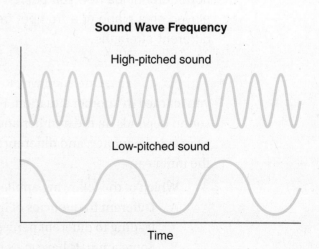

Sound Wave Frequency

High-pitched sound

Low-pitched sound

Time

Many factors affect the pitch of sounds made by an instrument. One factor is its size. Usually, larger instruments can make lower-pitched sounds than smaller instruments of the same type. For example, the lowest note on a violin has a frequency of 190 Hz. The lowest note on a cello, which is shaped like a violin but is much larger, has a frequency of 70 Hz. Another factor that affects pitch is the amount of tension, or stiffness, in the part that vibrates. On a stringed instrument, the tension in each string can be adjusted by turning a screw that the string is wrapped around. Turning the screw one way increases the tension in the string, raising the pitch. Turning the screw the other way decreases the tension, lowering the pitch.

Sound Wave Harmonics

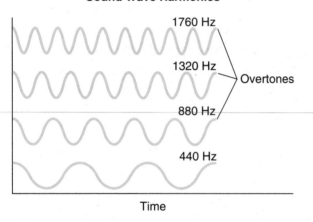

Time

Harmonics

A tuning fork produces a sound made up of a single frequency. Such a sound is known as a **pure tone.** In contrast, all musical instruments produce sounds that consist of more than one frequency, even when a single note is played. For instance, when the note A above middle C is played on a piano, the main frequency of the sound that is produced is 440 Hz, but other frequencies are produced at the same time. The other frequencies, called harmonics, or **overtones,** are exact multiples of 440 Hz: 880 Hz (two times 440), 1320 Hz (three times 440), 1760 Hz (four times 440), and so on.

The number and strength of overtones determines the quality, or **timbre,** of a note. That's because different sound frequencies stimulate different areas of the cochlea—a structure in your inner ear. When a particular point in the cochlea is stimulated, nerve signals are sent to the brain. The brain interprets the signal, and you perceive a certain pitch. The combination of signals caused by overtones of a note determines how you perceive that note. You can tell whether the note is being played on a piano or a trumpet because the overtones from each instrument have different strengths.

▶ Applying Ideas One good way to understand a new situation is to apply an idea that you learned in another situation. For example, you just read that your perception of a sound depends on the number and strength of overtones in the sound. Each overtone is a specific frequency, and different frequencies stimulate different areas of the cochlea in the inner ear.

Which of the following applies this model of perception to a new situation?
A. Different frequencies of light stimulate different light-sensitive cells in your eye, leading to different perceptions of color.
B. Some animals have eyes that are very sensitive to light, so they can see better at night than other animals can.

Amplitude

The more forcefully something vibrates, the more it compresses the air next to it. The extent to which the air is compressed in a sound wave is the called the **amplitude** of the wave. When a sound wave is drawn on a graph, the amplitude is shown by the height of the wave. The greater the amplitude of a sound wave, the harder the wave strikes your eardrums and the louder the sound that you hear. As a result, you perceive the amplitude of a sound wave as loudness. Loudness is measured in units called decibels.

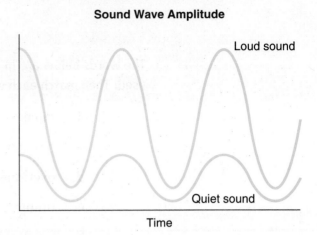

Sound Wave Amplitude

Loud sound

Quiet sound

Time

Loudness of Some Common Sounds

Sound	Decibels	Sound	Decibels
Quiet whisper	20	Lawn mower	85
Rustling leaves	40	Chain saw	115
Conversation	60	Rock concert	120
Hair dryer	75	Jet plane taking off	150

▶ Reading Charts A chart is a simple table that presents information in rows and columns. Information is often easier to find when it is listed this way than when it is written in a paragraph. In the chart above, different kinds of sounds are listed under the column headings "Sound." The loudness of each sound is listed to the right in the same row, under the column heading "Decibels." For example, the chart shows that the loudness of a quiet whisper is 20 decibels.

According to the chart, which is louder?

A. lawn mower   B. chain saw

Some small things that vibrate don't make very loud sounds by themselves because they don't compress much air. For example, if you strike a tuning fork, it will make a noise that you can barely hear unless you hold the tuning fork close to your ear. But if you strike the tuning fork again and touch the end to a hollow box of the right size, the noise will be louder. The vibrating tuning fork makes the box vibrate at the same frequency. This process is called **resonance.** Many musical instruments use resonance to make their sounds louder. For example, the body of an acoustic guitar, the bell of a trumpet, and the shell of a drum are all hollow structures that vibrate, or resonate, when another part of the instrument vibrates.

Thinking About the Article

Practice Vocabulary

▶ **The words below are in the passage in bold type. Study the way each word is used. Then match each word to its meaning. Write the letter.**

_____	**1.** pitch	**A.** the quality of a musical note based on the number and strength of overtones
_____	**2.** pure tone	
_____	**3.** overtone	**B.** how the frequency of a sound wave is perceived
_____	**4.** timbre	**C.** a measure of the height of a wave
_____	**5.** amplitude	**D.** when something that vibrates makes something else vibrate at the same frequency
_____	**6.** resonance	
		E. a frequency of sound that is an exact multiple of another frequency
		F. a sound that consists of a single frequency

Understand the Article

▶ **Write or circle the answer to each question.**

7. What creates a sound wave? _____

_____

8. What is the frequency of a sound wave?

A. the extent to which air is compressed in the wave

B. the number of alternating regions of compression and decompression (cycles) that occur each second

9. If two musical instruments are of the same type, which one can usually produce lower-pitched sounds?

A. the larger instrument　　B. the smaller instrument

10. Why does a note played on a harmonica sound different from the same note played on a clarinet?

A. The note lasts longer on the clarinet than on the harmonica.

B. The overtones of each instrument have different strengths.

11. What physical characteristic of sound waves is perceived as loudness?

_____

Apply Your Skills

▶ **Circle the letter of the best answer for each question.**

12. When you pluck a rubber band while stretching it, it will make a higher sound the farther you stretch it. Which of the following ideas does this illustrate?

   A.   Larger objects make lower-pitched sounds than smaller objects.

   B.   Pitch depends on the amount of tension in the part that vibrates.

   C.   Resonance enhances the sounds produced by many musical instruments.

   D.   Sound waves with greater amplitude strike your eardrums harder.

13. The sounds made by a music box will be louder if you set the music box on a table than if you hold it in the air. What causes this increase in loudness?

   A.   resonance

   B.   harmonics

   C.   timbre

   D.   frequency

14. Refer to the chart on page 221. According to the chart, which of the following sounds are both quieter than the sound of a hair dryer?

   A.   quiet whisper and lawn mower

   B.   chain saw and rustling leaves

   C.   conversation and rock concert

   D.   rustling leaves and conversation

Connect with the Article

▶ **Write your answer to each question.**

15. Why do most men have lower-pitched voices than most women?

   ....

   ....

16. A friend says that a note with a frequency of 370 Hz has an overtone with a frequency of 750 Hz. Is he correct? Explain.

   ....

   ....

   ....

SCIENCE PRACTICE FOCUS

Infrasonic and Ultrasonic Sound Waves

The normal hearing range for a human is about 15 Hz to 20,000 Hz. Sounds below 15 Hz have a frequency too low for humans to hear and are called infrasonic sound waves. Sounds above 20,000 Hz have a frequency too high for humans to hear and are called ultrasonic sound waves.

Infrasonic sound waves are produced in nature by volcanoes, earthquakes, tornadoes, avalanches, ocean waves, meteorites and auroras. Infrasound detectors are used to detect avalanches and send warning signals. These detectors also monitor the atmosphere for explosions. Scientists are working on making infrasound detectors that will help with the early detection of approaching natural disasters.

There are many everyday uses for ultrasonic sound waves. Ultrasound is used to get images of a developing fetus during a woman's pregnancy and images of internal organs such as the heart, liver, and kidney. Ultrasound can break up small stones found in the kidney and can remove plaque from teeth. It can also be used to detect cracks and other flaws in the metal of bridges, buildings and machines. Ultrasound also is used in the Sound Navigation and Ranging (SONAR) that ships use to measure the distance, speed, and direction of underwater objects.

▷ **Circle the letter of the best answer.**

1. Which of the following does NOT produce infrasonic sound waves?

    A. volcano

    B. SONAR

    C. earthquake

    D. tornado

▷ **Fill in the blank with the word or words that best complete each statement.**

2. The hearing range for a human is about _____ to 20,000 Hz.

3. Sounds above 20,000 Hz are called _____ sound waves.

4. An avalanche produces a(n) _____ sound wave.

▶ The data table below shows the approximate hearing ranges for some different animals. Use the data table to answer the questions below.

Animal	Hearing range (Hz)	Animal	Hearing range (Hz)
Human	15–20,000	Horse	55–33,5000
Bat	2000–110,000	Rat	200–76,000
Elephant	16–12,000	Snake	100–1000
Beluga Whale	1000–123,000	Fish	70–3,300
Dog	65–45,000	Moth	335–100,000
Cat	45–64,000	Bird	65–9,000
Dolphin	90–105,000	Porpoise	65–150,000

5. The keys on the left half of a piano will produce sounds with frequencies from 27.5 Hz to 330 Hz. According to the data table, which animals would not be able to hear the sounds produced by any of these keys?

6. Compare and contrast the hearing range of a human to the hearing range of a dolphin.

7. Researchers have developed devices that can record sounds above 20,000 Hz. How might these devices be useful to animal scientists?

8. Elephants have been observed screaming and moving to higher ground well before a tsunami hits a coastline. What is a possible explanation for this?

9. Some dog whistles used to train dogs have frequencies between 25,000 Hz to 50,000 Hz. What is the advantage of using one of these whistles to train a dog?

Check your answers on page 280.

SCIENCE AT WORK

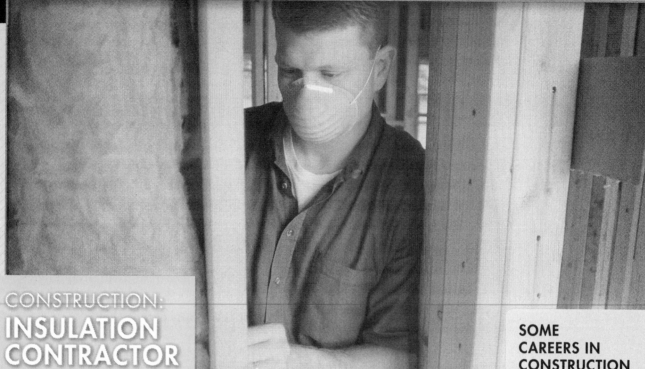

CONSTRUCTION:
INSULATION CONTRACTOR

SOME CAREERS IN CONSTRUCTION

Carpenter
frames, finishes, and remodels buildings and furniture

Drywall Installer
measures, installs, and finishes drywall or sheetrock surfaces in homes and buildings

Plumber
installs and repairs water pipes and drains

Roofer
repairs leaks and problems in roofs; removes old material and installs new roofs

Have you ever wondered what helps keep your home warm in the winter and cool in the summer? Through the use of insulation materials, homes and workplaces are kept at appropriate temperatures all year round. Selecting and installing the proper insulation materials are the responsibility of insulation contractors.

Insulation contractors pick the type of insulation material best suited for specific places in a building. Basements, walls, attics, water heaters, and ceilings are just some of the places where they apply their knowledge of insulation material selection and installation.

Insulation contractors must understand basic physics principles such as energy and heat transfer, condensation, and evaporation. They must also have good math and measurement skills and be able to read blueprints and other diagrams. The frequent introduction of new building materials and building safety codes requires that insulation contractors keep up to date about new developments in their field.

Look at the Some Careers in Construction chart.

- Do any of the careers interest you? If so, which ones?

- What information would you need to find out more about those careers? On a separate piece of paper, write some questions that you would like answered. You can find more information about those careers in the *Occupational Outlook Handbook* at your local library or online.

▶ **Use these guidelines to answer the questions that follow.**

Insulation Installation Guidelines

1. Before installing any insulation material, check for and seal any air leaks in the structure.

2. Check for sufficient ventilation and circulation of air in the building. Sufficient ventilation must be present to control moisture from condensation in heated areas of the building and to allow for circulation of clean air.

3. Select appropriate insulation material.

   A. Blanket insulation is laid in unfinished attic spaces, walls, and floors. Trim it to fit snugly in space.

   B. Loose-fill particles are blown into attic spaces or other unfinished, accessible building openings. Adhesive solutions may also be applied to help particles hold together if necessary.

   C. Spray foams are sprayed into hard-to-reach areas or between framing timbers. They must be applied with care, because the foam will expand to 30 times its original volume.

   D. Rigid insulation is used as exterior or interior protection. Some types may include a foil layer to prevent moisture buildup.

   E. Foil insulation is applied before finishing ceilings, walls, or floors. It is good at shielding against extreme summer heat and preventing winter heat loss.

1. Which would be the best insulation to put behind an existing interior brick wall?

   A. blanket insulation

   B. loose-fill particles

   C. spray foam

   D. foil insulation

2. Which of the following would be an effective insulation material for homes in desert environments?

   A. loose-fill particles

   B. spray foam

   C. rigid insulation

   D. foil insulation

3. Heat loss occurs when warm air moves from heated sections of a home to unheated sections. Using a separate piece of paper, explain why it would be important for the contractor to install insulation material under the floor of a room located above the home's garage.

Energy and Chemical Reactions

In a **chemical reaction,** one substance or set of substances is changed into another substance or set of substances. In this process, energy may be given off or taken in. An **exothermic reaction** gives off energy. Burning, or **combustion,** is an example of an exothermic reaction. When wood is burned, energy is given off in the form of light and heat.

Photosynthesis is a chemical reaction that takes place in plants. In this reaction, plants use the energy in sunlight to turn carbon dioxide and water into glucose, a type of sugar, and oxygen. This is an example of an **endothermic reaction,** or one that takes in energy.

You may have used an instant hot pack for first aid. These plastic pouches contain chemicals. When you break the seal inside the pouch, the chemicals come together and react. The reaction is exothermic and gives off heat. Once the reaction is finished, no additional heat is given off.

There are also instant cold packs used for first aid. When the chemicals in these pouches react, they do not give off heat. Instead, they take in heat. Because the reaction absorbs heat, the pouch feels cold when placed against the skin.

▷ **Fill in the blank with the word or words that best complete each statement.**

1. A(n) _____ gives off energy.

2. A(n) _____ takes in energy.

3. In a(n) _____ , substances are changed into other substances.

▷ **Circle the letter of the best answer.**

4. What is the implied main idea of the last paragraph on this page?

    A.   Instant cold packs are more useful than instant hot packs.

    B.   Instant cold packs feel cold when placed against the skin.

    C.   The reaction in instant cold packs is exothermic.

    D.   The reaction in instant cold packs is endothermic.

5. Which chemical process produces the heat given off by a gas heater?

    A.   a physical reaction

    B.   combustion

    C.   an endothermic reaction

    D.   photosynthesis

Fusion Reactions

Nuclear reactions are changes in the nucleus, or center, of an atom. One kind of nuclear reaction that is being studied by many scientists is fusion. **Nuclear fusion** is the reaction in which two nuclei combine. In the process, the nucleus of a larger atom is formed.

In nuclear fusion, hydrogen nuclei fuse, or join, and form a helium nucleus. A huge amount of energy is released. This reaction takes place only under conditions of great pressure and high temperature. Such conditions are found on stars. Fusion reactions are the source of the energy that our sun gives off.

Hydrogen nucleus

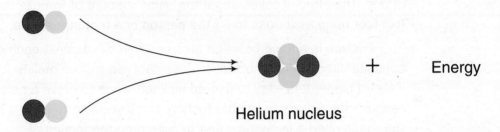

Helium nucleus

Hydrogen nucleus

There is no place on Earth as hot as the sun. Scientists are looking for ways to make fusion occur at lower temperatures. If scientists could make such "cold fusion" reactions work, then they would have a powerful energy source.

▶ **Fill in the blank with the word or words that best complete each statement.**

6. A nuclear reaction in which two nuclei combine is called a

   _____ .

7. Fusion reactions take place naturally on the _____ .

8. In a nuclear fusion reaction, hydrogen nuclei combine to form the

   nucleus of a(n) _____ atom.

▶ **Circle the letter of the best answer.**

9. Which of the following conclusions is supported by the text?

   A. Fusion reactions only take place on the sun.

   B. Very little energy is released in a fusion reaction.

   C. Fusion reactions do not take place naturally on Earth.

   D. Nuclear reactions do not involve any changes to atoms.

The Inclined Plane

A **simple machine** is a device used to do work. An inclined plane is one type of simple machine. An **inclined plane** is a long, sloping surface that helps raise an object that cannot be easily lifted. A ramp is an example of an inclined plane. Imagine trying to get a person in a wheelchair onto a porch that is one foot above the ground. Lifting the person and the wheelchair straight up would be difficult. You may not be able to exert a large enough force to do this. However, if the porch had a four-foot-long ramp, you could more easily get the person and the wheelchair onto the porch.

The amount of work done depends on the force needed and the distance moved. You would need less force to move the person up the ramp than to lift her straight up. However, you would have to move the person a longer distance, four feet instead of one. Therefore, it takes about the same amount of work to push the person up the four-foot ramp as it does to lift the person one foot straight up.

Friction is a force between surfaces that rub against each other. It acts in the opposite direction to an object's movement, so friction makes it harder to use an inclined plane. It is easy to use an inclined plane to move a person in a wheelchair because the wheels have little friction. But if you had to push a box up the same ramp, you would need a large force just to overcome the friction.

▷ **Write the word or words that best complete each statement.**

10. The amount of work done on an object depends on _____ and

_____ .

11. _____ is a force between surfaces that rub against each other.

▷ **Circle the letter of the best answer.**

12. In which situation would you need to exert the least force?

    A.   lifting a 120-pound box to a height of one foot

    B.   pushing a 75-pound box up a ramp three feet long

    C.   pushing a wheeled 75-pound cart up a ramp three feet long

    D.   lifting a wheeled 75-pound cart up to a height of one foot

13. Explain how the force of friction acts on a car as it moves down a road.

_____

_____

_____

Momentum

If an object is moving, it has momentum. The object's **momentum** depends on its weight and speed. The faster an object moves and the heavier it is, the more momentum it has. If an object is not moving, it has no momentum.

Momentum is involved in the game of pool, which is played with balls on a large table. All the balls weigh the same. Players use a heavy stick, called a cue, to hit a white ball, called the cue ball. When the cue collides with the cue ball, momentum is transferred to the cue ball. The cue ball rolls along the table until it collides with one or more of the other balls.

If the cue ball hits one other ball dead on, the cue ball will stop and transfer all its momentum to the other ball. The other ball will move away as fast as the cue ball was moving before the collision. If the cue ball hits two other balls at the same time, both of the other balls will move after the collision. Part of the cue ball's momentum will be transferred to each of the other balls.

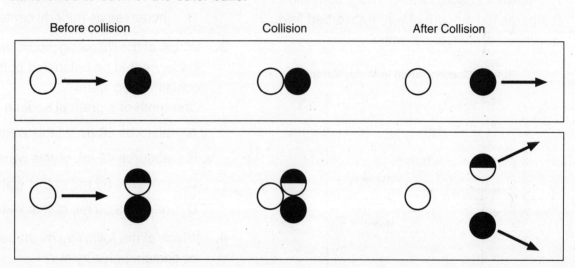

| Before collision | Collision | After Collision |

▶ **Circle the letter of the best answer.**

14. Which statement about the situation shown in the bottom diagram is correct?

    A.   The cue ball has more momentum before the collision than after.

    B.   The other balls have more momentum before the collision than after.

    C.   The other balls have the same momentum before and after the collision.

    D.   The cue ball moves at the same speed before and after the collision.

SCIENCE EXTENSION

Simple machines are all around us. Look in your home for examples of simple machines. (They may be part of a compound machine.) Make a table. In one column list these simple machines: inclined plane, lever, wheel and axle, wedge, gears, and screw. In the second column, list all the examples you find. Here's one to get you started: Lever—bottle opener.

MINI-TEST

This is a 15-minute practice test. After 15 minutes, mark the last number you finished. Then complete the test and check your answers. If most of your answers were correct but you did not finish, try to work faster next time.

▶ **Directions: Choose the one best answer to each question.**

Questions 1 through 4 refer to the following information and graph.

Some types of bottled water contain minerals and some do not. One way to measure the amount of minerals in water is to add a known amount of water to a known amount of a white powder called sodium polyacrylate. This powder absorbs water. The graph below compares the amount of water absorbed from four different samples of water.

Mineral Concentration in Water Samples

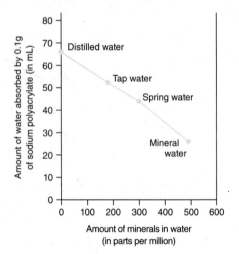

1. Compare the samples of water tested. Based on the graph, which sample contained the least amount of minerals?

   A. distilled water

   B. tap water

   C. spring water

   D. mineral water

2. You can infer from the graph that the amount of water absorbed by sodium polyacrylate

   A. is the same for all types of water

   B. is lowest for tap water

   C. decreases as mineral content increases

   D. increases as mineral content increases

3. Which of the following would provide evidence that an unlabeled bottle of water contained tap water?
   One-tenth of a gram of sodium polyacrylate

   A. absorbs 50 mL of this water

   B. absorbs 42 mL of this water

   C. releases 65 mL of this water

   D releases 50 mL of this water

4. Which of the following might be a good use for sodium polyacrylate?

   A. to flavor mineral water

   B. to purify distilled water

   C. to clean up polluted water

   D. to soak up urine in disposable diapers

5. The law of conservation of momentum states that the total momentum of a system does not change. For example, imagine a bowling ball rolling toward bowling pins. The ball has momentum because it is moving. The pins have no momentum because they are stationary. If the ball strikes some of the pins, it will slow slightly, losing some of its momentum. The pins will move, gaining momentum. The total momentum of the ball and the pins does not change.

Which sentence below restates information in the paragraph above?

A. Bowling pins and bowling balls have the same momentum.

B. A bowling ball gains momentum when it strikes some of the pins.

C. Bowling pins do not have momentum unless they are moving.

D. Momentum is not conserved if a bowling ball misses all of the pins.

6. Humans can detect sounds because of specialized cells in the inner ear that sense the vibrations produced by sound waves. All these cells develop before birth. Loud sounds can damage or kill some of the cells. The cells that die cannot be replaced. Which of the following statements supports the conclusion that earplugs should be worn in noisy places?

A. Sound waves produce vibrations.

B. Humans can hear well before birth.

C. Specialized cells in the ear aid hearing.

D. Loud sounds can kill cells in the inner ear.

Question 7 refers to the following information and graph.

A company that manufactures windows tested different window designs to determine which design was best at reducing the transmission of sound. The results of the testing are graphed below.

Sound Transmission Through Windows

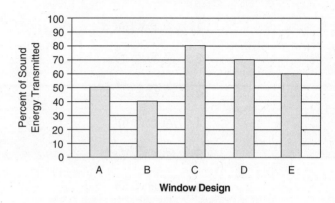

7. Which of the following conclusions is supported by the information presented in the graph?

A. Design C blocks more outside noise than any of the other designs.

B. Design B is the best choice for buildings in noisy neighborhoods.

C. Design E is the most expensive of the windows.

D. Design A allows the most light to pass through.

ANSWER SHEET

Posttest
Science

Name: _____ Class: _____ Date: _____

1 Ⓐ Ⓑ Ⓒ Ⓓ

2 Ⓐ Ⓑ Ⓒ Ⓓ

3 Ⓐ Ⓑ Ⓒ Ⓓ

4 Ⓐ Ⓑ Ⓒ Ⓓ

5 Ⓐ Ⓑ Ⓒ Ⓓ

6 Ⓐ Ⓑ Ⓒ Ⓓ

7 Ⓐ Ⓑ Ⓒ Ⓓ

8 Ⓐ Ⓑ Ⓒ Ⓓ

9 Ⓐ Ⓑ Ⓒ Ⓓ

10 Ⓐ Ⓑ Ⓒ Ⓓ

11 Ⓐ Ⓑ Ⓒ Ⓓ

12 Ⓐ Ⓑ Ⓒ Ⓓ

13 Ⓐ Ⓑ Ⓒ Ⓓ

14 Ⓐ Ⓑ Ⓒ Ⓓ

15 Ⓐ Ⓑ Ⓒ Ⓓ

16 Ⓐ Ⓑ Ⓒ Ⓓ

17 Ⓐ Ⓑ Ⓒ Ⓓ

18 Ⓐ Ⓑ Ⓒ Ⓓ

19 Ⓐ Ⓑ Ⓒ Ⓓ

20 Ⓐ Ⓑ Ⓒ Ⓓ

21 Ⓐ Ⓑ Ⓒ Ⓓ

22 Ⓐ Ⓑ Ⓒ Ⓓ

23 Ⓐ Ⓑ Ⓒ Ⓓ

24 Ⓐ Ⓑ Ⓒ Ⓓ

25 Ⓐ Ⓑ Ⓒ Ⓓ

Directions

This is a 40-minute practice test. After 40 minutes, mark the last number you finished. Then complete the test and check your answers. If most of your answers were correct but you did not finish, try to work faster next time.

The Pre GED® Science Posttest consists of multiple-choice questions that measure general science concepts. The questions are based on short readings and/or illustrations, including maps, graphs, charts, diagrams, or other figures. Study the information given and then answer the question(s) following it. Refer to the information as often as necessary in answering the questions.

Record your answers on the answer sheet on page 234. You may make a photocopy of this page. To record your answer, fill in the numbered circle on the answer sheet that corresponds to the answer you select for each question in the Posttest.

After you complete the Posttest, check your answers on pages 282–284. Then use the chart on page 245 to identify the science skills and content areas that you need to practice more. Fill in the lettered circle on the answer sheet that corresponds to the answer that you select for each test question.

EXAMPLE

Which object in the solar system has the greatest mass?

A. the sun
B. Earth
C. the moon
D. an asteroid

(On Answer Sheet)

● Ⓑ Ⓒ Ⓓ

The correct answer is "the sun"; therefore, answer space 1 would be marked on the answer sheet.

If you do not use the answer sheet provided, mark your answers on each test page by circling or writing the correct answer for each question.

▶ **Directions: Choose the <u>one best answer</u> to each question.**

Questions 1 and 2 refer to the following information and diagram.

There are three types of ants involved in an ant colony: workers, males, and the queen. Workers take care of the anthill and its queen. In the spring, newly hatched males and queens fly out of the anthill and mate. The new queens fly away, to set up new colonies.

Worker   Male   New Queen

1. What is one of the main differences between a male ant and a worker ant?

   A. A male ant has wings and a worker ant does not.

   B. A male ant has antennae and a worker ant does not.

   C. A male ant has six legs and a worker ant has four legs.

   D. A male ant is smaller than a worker ant.

2. After the mating flight, a queen loses her wings.

Which of the following can you infer from this information?

   A. The males lose their wings, too.

   B. The workers grow wings instead.

   C. The queen lays fertilized eggs under the wings.

   D. The queen does not mate again.

Questions 3 and 4 refer to the following data table and information below.

Temperature (°C)	Amount of Substance That Dissolves in 50 mL Water (g)		
	Substance 1	Substance 2	Substance 3
60	14	29	42
50	12	31	31
40	7	35	25
30	4	38	20

3. Students conduct an experiment to determine how decreasing the temperature of water will affect the amount of a substance that will dissolve in the water. Some students hypothesize that decreasing the water temperature will always result in less of a substance dissolving in the water. The data table above shows the results of the investigation. The students' hypothesis is weakened by the results from which substance?

   A. Substance 1

   B. Substance 2

   C. Substance 3

   D. None of the substances.

4. What is the independent variable in this investigation?

   A. the amount of water

   B. the amount of substance that dissolves in the water

   C. the water temperature

   D. the amount of time it takes for the substance to dissolve

---

Question 5 refers to the following bar graph.

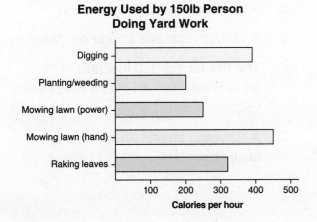

Energy Used by 150lb Person Doing Yard Work

5. Althea needs to do yard work, but she wants to take it easy. Which task should she do?

   A. digging

   B. planting or weeding

   C. mowing grass with a power mower

   D. mowing grass with a hand mower

Go on to the next page.

Questions 6 and 7 refer to the following graph.

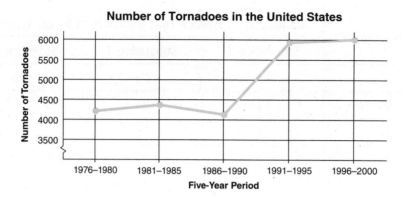

Number of Tornadoes in the United States

6. Approximately how many tornadoes occurred between1986 and1990?

   A. 3,500

   B. 4,100

   C. 4,700

   D. 5,300

7. Which generalization is best supported by the information in the graph?

   A. The number of tornadoes has increased during every five-year period since 1976.

   B. The number of tornadoes has decreased during every five-year period since 1976.

   C. Tornadoes have become more destructive over the past three decades.

   D. There were more tornadoes during the 1990s than during the 1980s.

Question 8 refers to the following information.

   The momentum of a baseball is affected by air resistance. As the ball travels through the air, it must push the molecules of gas aside. Thus, the ball loses energy and speed. A ball batted at 110 miles per hour would travel 750 feet in a vacuum before falling to the ground. At Shea Stadium in New York, it would go about 400 feet.

8. Which of the following facts supports the conclusion that air resistance slows a baseball's momentum?

   A. Air is made up of gas molecules.

   B. A vacuum contains little or no matter.

   C. The ball travels 350 feet less in the air at Shea Stadium than it would in a vacuum.

   D. A curveball travels slower than a fastball.

Question 9 refers to the following nutrition labels.

Cereal A	
Calories	116
Calories from Fat	0
Total fat	0 g
Sodium	210 mg
Potassium	50 mg
Total Carbohydrates	21 g
Sugars	3 g
Other Carbohydrates	17 g
Protein	8 g

Cereal B	
Calories	160
Calories from Fat	36
Total fat	4 g
Sodium	320 mg
Potassium	50 mg
Total Carbohydrates	28 g
Sugars	7 g
Other Carbohydrates	21 g
Protein	3 g

9. You and your friend read the nutrition labels from the two boxes of cereal. Your friend concludes that Cereal B is healthier. What information could you provide to convince your friend that Cereal A is actually healthier than Cereal B?

   A. Cereal A has less sodium and sugar than Cereal B.

   B. Cereal A has more sugar and potassium than Cereal B.

   C. Cereal A has more total fat than Cereal B.

   D. Cereal A has more calories than cereal B.

10. The chemical formula for ferric oxide (rust) is Fe_2O_3. How many different elements are in the compound Fe_2O_3?

    A. 1

    B. 2

    C. 3

    D. 5

11. Matter cannot be destroyed or created. When you burn something, however, you may notice there is usually less solid matter afterwards. For example, a piece of wood before burning weighs more than the resulting ash does. Which of the following would be evidence that no matter has been destroyed during combustion?

    A. Oxygen is required for combustion to occur.

    B. Dryness of the wood effects how quickly it burns.

    C. Wood tends to turn black during combustion due to oxidation.

    D. Combustion changes some solid matter to gas and energy.

Go on to the next page.

Questions 12 through 14 refer to the following information.

Conventional farming uses chemical fertilizers and pesticides, while organic farming does not. Ruth wanted to test the difference in taste between organically grown vegetables and conventionally grown vegetables. She set up an experiment by placing two groups of tomatoes, carrots, and broccoli, and a questionnaire on a table. Group A was the conventionally grown vegetables, and Group B was the organically grown ones. Ruth's questionnaire asked whether the taster liked Group A or B best. Ruth put the results from 25 tasters in the following chart:

Taste-Test Results

Vegetable	Number who Preferred Group A	Number who Preferred Group B
Tomatoes	7	18
Carrots	4	21
Broccoli	10	15

Ruth decided that organically grown vegetables do taste better than conventionally grown vegetables.

The three questions in the next column ask you to classify statements about the experiment based on the following categories:

- the problem—the question being tested in the study
- the hypothesis—a testable statement that explains something related to the problem
- the experiment—a way of testing whether the hypothesis is correct
- data—information gathered through testing and/or observation during the experiment
- conclusion—a summary statement supported by the data from the experiment

12. People will prefer the taste of organically grown vegetables to the taste of conventionally grown vegetables.

   This statement is an example of which category?

   A. hypothesis

   B. experiment

   C. data

   D. conclusion

13. Organically grown carrots were preferred by 21 people.

   This statement is an example of which category?

   A. hypothesis

   B. experiment

   C. data

   D. conclusion

14. Based on the taste-test results, organically grown vegetables taste better than conventionally grown vegetables.

   This statement is an example of which category?

   A. problem

   B. hypothesis

   C. data

   D. conclusion

Question 15 refers to the following graph.

Location of Bones in an Adult Human

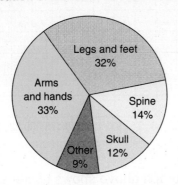

Question 16 refers to the following diagram.

A Yeast Cell Budding

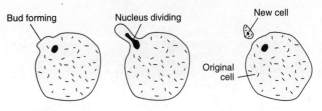

15. How does the number of bones in the arms and hands compare with the number of bones in the legs and feet?

   A. There are three times as many bones in the arms and hands as in the legs and feet.

   B. There are twice as many bones in the arms and hands as in the legs and feet.

   C. There are about the same number of bones in the arms and hands as in the legs and feet.

   D. There are half as many bones in the arms and hands as in the legs and feet.

16. Which of the following best summarizes what is shown in the diagram?

   A. Yeast cells reproduce by growing a bud that splits off the parent cell.

   B. The original cell bulges outward, producing a small bud.

   C. The nucleus of a yeast cell divides during budding.

   D. Right after budding, the new cell is smaller than the original cell.

17. Some DNA paternity tests are done with samples of cells from the child and the alleged father. A cell sample from the mother is not necessary. Other DNA paternity tests are done with cells from the child, the mother, and the parents of the alleged father.

   What conclusion can you draw from this information?

   A. A child and his or her parents have identical DNA.

   B. A child and its grandparents have a identical DNA.

   C. The mother's cells are always needed for DNA paternity tests.

   D. DNA paternity tests can be done with or without cells from the alleged father.

Go on to the next page.

Question 18 refers to the following map.

Range of the Bald Eagle

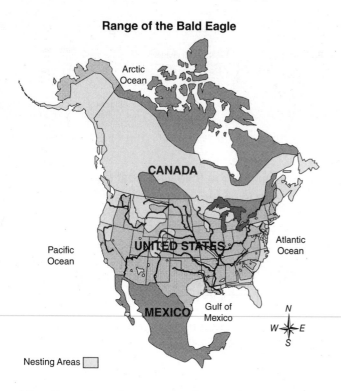

Nesting Areas ☐

18. Based on the map, which of the following could cause the most harm to bald eagles nesting in the United States?

    A.   increased pollution of arctic islands

    B.   increased pollution of the Mississippi River basin and the Great Lakes

    C.   increased farm size in the Midwest

    D.   decreased forestland in New England

Question 19 refers to the following graph.

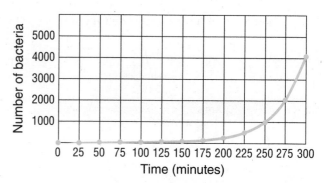

19. The graph above shows bacterial growth in a Petri dish over a 300-minute period of time. If the bacteria continue to grow at the same rate, how many bacteria do you predict will be present at a time of 325 minutes?

    A.   about 4,500

    B.   about 5,000

    C.   about 5,500

    D.   about 8,000

Question 20 refers to the following chart.

Common Air Pollutants

Pollutant	Source
Carbon monoxide	Burning fuel in motor vehicles
Lead	Smelting and manufacturing plants
Nitrogen oxides	Burning fuel in power plants, boilers, and motor vehicles
Particulate matter	Solid particles in smoke, dust, vehicle exhaust
Sulfur oxides	Emissions from factories, power plants, and refineries

20. Which statement best summarizes the chart?

   A. Air pollution comes from transportation and industry.

   B. Lead is a byproduct of smelting.

   C. Burning fuel releases nitrogen oxides.

   D. Sulfur oxides are industrial emissions.

21. Hector is designing an experiment to determine if the amount of salt added to water affects the water's boiling point. Hector plans on adding different amounts of salt to four pots containing different amounts of water. Which of the following identifies a possible source of error in Hector's design?

   A. Hector should use the same amount of salt in each pot of water.

   B. Hector should use fewer pots of water.

   C. Hector should use the same amount of water in each of the four pots.

   D. There are no possible sources of error.

Question 22 refers to the following diagrams.

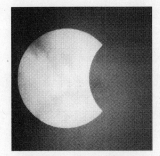
Partial solar eclipse

Total solar eclipse

22. A solar eclipse occurs when the moon passes in front of the sun, blocking it. What is the difference between a total solar eclipse and a partial solar eclipse?

   In a total eclipse of the sun, the moon

   A. blocks the sun except for a rim of light

   B. blocks half of the sun

   C. is farther away than in a partial eclipse

   D. is on the far side of the sun

Go on to the next page.

Question 23 refers to the following graph.

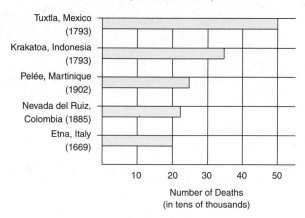

Some Deadly Volcanic Eruptions

Number of Deaths
(in tens of thousands)

23. What can you conclude based on the information in the graph?

A. Volcanic eruptions can be predicted.

B. The first volcanic eruption causing more than 1,000 deaths occurred in Italy in 1669.

C. Of the volcanic eruptions listed in the graph, Tuxtla, in Mexico, caused the most known deaths.

D. More people died in volcanic eruptions in prehistoric times than in ancient or modern times.

24. A group of students creates a model of a sodium bicarbonate ($NaHCO_3$) molecule using medium-sized foam balls to represent the atoms in the molecule and sticks to represent the chemical bonds between the atoms. Which of the following is a disadvantage of using these materials for this model?

A. The model is not three-dimensional.

B. The model does not show the number of atoms in the molecule.

C. The model does not show the sizes of the different types of atoms in the molecule.

D. The model does not show the number of chemical bonds in the molecule.

25. In a certain breed of chickens, black feathers (B) are dominant over white feathers (b). A black female chicken with the genotype Bb is crossed with a black male chicken with the genotype Bb. Predict the percentage of offspring that will have white feathers.

A. 0%

B. 25%

C. 75%

D. 100%

Posttest Evaluation Chart

The chart will help you determine your strengths and weaknesses in science content and thinking skills.

Directions

Check your answers on pages 282–284. In the first box below, circle the number of each item that you answered correctly on the Posttest. Count and write the number of items you answered correctly in each row. For example, in the Life Science row, write the number correct in the blank before /12, which means *out of 12.*

Complete this process for the remaining rows. Then add the 3 totals to get your *Total Correct* for the whole Posttest.

- If you answered fewer than 20 items correct, determine the areas in which you need more practice. Go back and review the content in those areas. Page numbers for specific instruction appear in the left-hand column.

- If you answered 20 or more items correctly, your teacher may decide that you are ready to go on to Steck-Vaughn's Complete Test Preparation for the 2014 GED® Test.

Thinking Skill/ Content Area	Comprehension	Application	Analysis	Evaluation	Total Correct
Life Science (Pages 12–93)	**2, 16**	12, **13,** 14	**1, 15,** 17, **18, 19,** 25	10	____/12
Earth and Space Science (Pages 94–159)	**6, 20**		**22, 23**	7	____/5
Physical Science (Pages 160–233)	9	4, **5**	**3,** 21, 24	8, 11	____/8

Total Correct for Posttest _____ **out of 25**

Boldfaced numbers indicate questions based on charts, diagrams, graphs, and maps.

PRETEST

1. **nucleus** *(DOK Level: 1; Content Topic: L.d.2; Practice: SP.1.c)*

2. **cell wall** *(DOK Level: 1; Content Topic: L.d.2; Practice: SP.1.c)*

3. **C. vacuole is empty** *(DOK Level: 2; Content Topic: L.d.2; Practice: SP.1.c, SP.3.c)* According to the diagram, the vacuole stores water and minerals, so the plant would need more water if the vacuole were empty. The other options are incorrect because these structures have functions other than storing water.

4. **contracts** *(DOK Level: 1; Content Topic: L.a.1; Practice: SP.1.c)*

5. **relaxing** *(DOK Level: 1; Content Topic: L.a.1; Practice: SP.1.c)*

6. **B. at the front of the thigh** *(DOK Level: 2; Content Topic: L.a.1; Practice: SP.1.c, SP.3.b)* According to the diagram, the paired muscles in the arm are on opposite sides of the arm. From this, you can infer that muscles that do opposite jobs are in opposite positions. If the muscles at the back of the thigh bend the knee, muscles at the front of the thigh would straighten the knee. The first option is incorrect because these muscles bend the knee. The third and fourth options are incorrect because these muscles move the ankle joint.

7. **Lactic acid** *(DOK Level: 1; Content Topic: L.a.4; Practice: SP.1.a)*

8. **bacteria** *(DOK Level: 1; Content Topic: L.a.4; Practice: SP.1.a)*

9. **D. Once you open milk after pasteurizing, new bacteria may get in.** *(DOK Level: 3; Content Topic: L.a.4; Practice: SP.1.a, SP.5.a)* According to the article, bacteria are killed by the high temperatures involved in pasteurization. But new bacteria can get into milk once it is opened again. Since Alex and Ann both followed the same procedure, you can infer that they both killed the bacteria in the milk during pasteurization, so new bacteria getting in to one of their samples afterward is the only explanation for one sample having active bacteria. The first option is incorrect because Alex and Ann used the same temperature. The second option is incorrect because it does not explain why Alex observed active bacteria. The third option is incorrect because freezing is not involved in pasteurization.

10. **insects**   11. **insects**

12. **wind**   13. **wind**
    (DOK Level: 2; Content Topic: L.d.1; Practice: SP.1.a, SP.1.b, SP.1.c)

14. **D. Collect anthers and ovaries.** *(DOK Level: 3; Content Topic: L.a.1; Practice: SP.1.c, SP.2.d)* According to the article and diagram, these structures make the sperm and egg, which are needed for reproduction, so they both should be collected during the investigation. The first and second options are incorrect because both anthers and ovaries are necessary for reproduction. The third option is incorrect because petals are not necessary for reproduction, and the article states that some flowers have no petals.

15. **insulator** *(DOK Level: 2; Content Topic: P.a.1; Practice: SP.1.a, SP.3.b, SP.6.c, SP.7.a)*

16. **conductor** *(DOK Level: 2; Content Topic: P.a.1; Practice: SP.1.a, SP.3.b, SP.6.c, SP.7.a)*

17. **B. aluminum** *(DOK Level: 2; Content Topic: P.a.1; Practice: SP.1.a, SP.3.c, SP.7.a)* The article states that metals are good conductors that let heat flow through them easily, and the table states that the metal aluminum is a conductor. From this you can infer that aluminum would let the heat from a hot beverage escape easily. The other options are incorrect because, according to the table, they are insulators, so they would block heat from transferring and keep beverages hot better than a conductor would.

18. **A. test Ray's hypothesis, because cardboard is more likely to be the better insulator** *(DOK Level: 3; Content Topic: P.a.1; Practice: SP.1.a, SP.2.b, SP.2.c)* According to the article and table, paper is an insulator and copper is a

conductor of heat, and a conductor or an insulator of heat is likely to be a conductor or an insulator of electricity. Since cardboard is made of paper, you can infer it is more likely to be the better electrical insulator. The second and third options are incorrect because cardboard is more likely to be the better insulator. The last option is incorrect because copper is not likely to be a good insulator.

19. **C**   20. **A**   21. **B**   22. **D**
(*DOK Level: 2; Content Topic: ES.b.1; Practice: SP.1.a, SP.1.b, SP.1.c*)

23. **C. more than 50 percent** (*DOK Level: 3; Content Topic: ES.b.1; Practice: SP.1.a, SP.6.b, SP.8.c*) According to the article, water covers more than half of the planet. Half is the same as 50 percent. From this, you can infer that you have more than a 50 percent chance of landing on water. The other options are incorrect because more than 50 percent of Earth is covered by water, not 50 percent, less than 50 percent, or 100 percent.

24. **igneous rocks** (*DOK Level: 1; Content Topic: ES.b.3; Practice: SP.1.a, SP.1.b*)

25. **metamorphic rocks** (*DOK Level: 1; Content Topic: ES.b.3; Practice: SP.1.a, SP.1.b*)

26. **A. The rock contains layers of small pieces of granite.** (*DOK Level: 3; Content Topic: ES.b.3; Practice: SP.1.a, SP.3.a, SP.7.a*) According to the article, sedimentary rocks are made up of small pieces of the rocks that form layers. So, in a sedimentary rock you can expect to observe layers of small pieces of the rocks, even igneous rocks like granite. The second option is incorrect because, even though shale is a sedimentary rock, color is not mentioned in the article. The third option is incorrect because a gritty feel is not mentioned as a feature of sedimentary rocks. The fourth option is incorrect because, although limestone is a sedimentary rock, igneous and metamorphic rocks can be near limestone as well as sedimentary rocks.

27. **D. volcanoes** (*DOK Level: 2; Content Topic: ES.b.3; Practice: SP.1.a, SP.3.b*) According

to the article, volcanoes contain melted rock. When melted rock hardens, igneous rocks form. From this, you can infer that an area with many igneous rocks once had volcanoes. The first and second options are incorrect because rivers and sediment are associated with the formation of sedimentary rocks. The third option is incorrect because pressure is associated with the formation of metamorphic rocks.

28. **B**   29. **C**   30. **A**   31. **C**
(*DOK Level: 2; Content Topic: P.c.1; Practice: SP.1.a, SP.1.b, SP.1.c*)

32. **B. It has 5 electrons, 5 protons, and no charge.** (*DOK Level: 2; Content Topic: P.c.1; Practice: SP.1.c, SP.6.b, SP.7.a, SP.8.b*) According to the article and diagram, the number of electrons in the atom is equal to the number of protons, which means the amount of positive and negative electric charge is the same, so overall the atom has no charge. The first option lists the incorrect number of electrons. The third and fourth options list the incorrect number of protons.

33. **D. solid and liquid only** (*DOK Level: 2; Content Topic: P.c.2; Practice: SP.1.a, SP.3.b*) These states of matter have a definite volume that does not change. The first and second options are incorrect because they list only one of the states with a definite volume. The third option is incorrect because the volume of a gas changes as the gas expands to fill its container.

34. **A. Its shape will change from not definite to definite.** (*DOK Level: 2; Content Topic: P.c.2; Practice: SP.1.a, SP.3.c*) According to the table, a liquid does not have a definite shape, but a solid does. So you can predict that when alcohol changes from a liquid to a solid, its shape will become definite. The second option is incorrect because it is the opposite of what will happen. The third option is incorrect because both solids and liquids have definite volumes. The last option is incorrect because there is a change in a property.

35. **B. Pablo's conclusion is not supported because each substance changes state at a different temperature.** *(DOK Level: 3; Content Topic: P.c.2; Practice: SP.1.a, SP.1.c, SP.4.a)* According to the article, each substance changes state at different temperatures. Since the unknown substance changes to a gas at a different temperature than water does, it cannot be water and the conclusion is incorrect. The first and third options are incorrect because the conclusion is not supported. The fourth option is incorrect because, if both samples are liquids at room temperature, then they both have a definite volume.

36. **force** *(DOK Level: 1; Content Topic: P.b.2; Practice: SP.1.a, SP.1.b)*

37. **acceleration** *(DOK Level: 1; Content Topic: P.b.1; Practice: SP.1.a, SP.1.b)*

38. **A. acceleration** *(DOK Level: 2; Content Topic: P.b.1, P.b.2; Practice: SP.1.a, SP.3.b)* According to the article, when an unbalanced force acts on an object, the movement of the object changes. This is acceleration. All other options are examples of forces, not effects of forces.

39. **C.** ↓ *(DOK Level: 2; Content Topic: P.b.2; Practice: SP.1.a, SP.1.b, SP.6.a)* According to the article, gravity pulls down, so it can be shown with an arrow that points down. The other options are incorrect because they show arrows pointing in other directions.

UNIT 1: LIFE SCIENCE

LESSON 1

PAGE 14

Relate to the Topic
Many answers are possible. Sample answer: I got a sunburn at the beach. Now I wear sunscreen and a hat when I'm in the sun. *(DOK Level: 1; Content Topic: L.a.2, L.a.4)*

Reading Strategy
1. **a type of light given off by the sun and tanning lamps** *(DOK Level: 1; Content Topic: P.a.5; Practice: SP.1.b)*

2. **basal cell skin cancer, squamous cell skin cancer** *(DOK Level: 1; Content Topic: L.a.2; Practice: SP.1.b)*

PAGE 16

A *(DOK Level: 1; Content Topic: L.d.1; Practice: SP.1.a)*

PAGE 17

B *(DOK Level: 2; Content Topic: L.d.1; Practice: SP.1.c)*

PAGES 18–19

1. **A**   2. **D**   3. **C**
4. **B**   5. **F**   6. **E**
(DOK Level: 1; Content Topic: L.d.1; Practice: SP.1.b)

7. **Basal cell skin cancer looks like an open sore, mole, or shiny bump; this type of cancer rarely spreads to other parts of the body and usually can be cured. Squamous cell skin cancer looks like raised pink spots; it grows faster and can spread to other parts of the body. Melanomas are oddly shaped blotches that can grow and spread quickly.** *(DOK Level: 1; Content Topic: L.a.4; Practice: SP.1.a)*

8. **B** *(DOK Level: 2; Content Topic: L.a.2; Practice: SP.1.a)*

9. **A** *(DOK Level: 2: Content Topic: L.a.4; Practice: SP.1.a)*

10. **Cells are organized into tissues, organs, and organ systems.** *(DOK Lesson: 1; Content Topic: L.d.2; Practice: SP.1.a)*

11. **C. Sunlight can cause skin cancer.** *(DOK Level: 1; Content Topic: L.a.2, L.a.4; Practice: SP.1.a)* This sentence sums up the main point of the paragraph.

12. **C. in the cytoplasm** *(DOK Level: 2; Content Topic: L.d.1; Practice: SP.1.c)* The diagram on page 16 shows the mitochondria in the cytoplasm.

13. **D. Preventing Skin Cancer** *(DOK Level: 1; Content Topic: L.a.4; Practice: SP.1.a)* This section deals with ways to avoid getting skin cancer.

14. **The doctor can check the moles for changes in size or color that might indicate**

skin cancer. *(DOK Level: 3; Content Topic: L.a.4; Practice: SP.1.a, SP.3.b)*

15. **Many answers are possible. Sample answer: I will sit in the shade, wear sunscreen, and avoid the midday sun.** *(DOK Level: 3; Content Topic: L.a.4; Practice: SP.1.a, SP.3.b)*

PAGES 20–21

1. **C. stomach lining** *(DOK Level: 1; Content Topic: L.d.2; Practice: SP.3.b)* According to the table, the lifespan of a stomach-lining cell is 2 days. The lifespans of the other cells are much longer.

2. **D. bone** *(DOK Level: 1; Content Topic: L.d.2; Practice: SP.3.b)* According to the table, bone cells have a lifespan of 25–30 years. The other cells have lifespans that are measured in days.

3. **B. A cell's lifespan is related to its job or function in the body.** *(DOK Level: 2; Content Topic: L.d.2; Practice: SP.4.a)* The table shows that different cells have average lifespans, so you can reasonably conclude that a cell's lifespan is related to its function. The other options are not supported by the data in the table.

4. ***Other cells may never be replaced.*** **You can infer from this sentence that some cells will never reproduce.** *(DOK Level: 2; Content Topic: L.d.2; Practice: SP.3.a)*

5. **Sample answer: These cells have a short lifespan because of the harsh conditions they are exposed to inside the body. The stomach contains acid and other substances needed to digest food, and the colon is where waste is eliminated from the body.** *(DOK Level: 2; Content Topic: L.a.1, L.d.2; Practice: SP.3.b)*

6. **Sample answer: It is important to protect nerve cells from damage because they are not replaced.** *(DOK Level: 2; Content Topic: L.d.2; Practice: SP.3.b)*

7. **Sample answer: I think a skin cell has a short lifespan, because the skin is the protective outer layer of the body that must**

constantly be replaced due to constant contact with objects in the environment. (In fact, the average lifespan of a skin cell is 1–34 days.) *(DOK Level: 3; Content Topic: L.d.2; Practice: SP.3.b)*

8. **Sample answer: By self-destructing when they are damaged or infected, an unhealthy cell will not be able to reproduce, which can also reproduce the damage or infection. This way, only healthy cells can reproduce to replace older cells.** *(DOK Level: 2; Content Topic: L.d.2; Practice: SP.3.b)*

LESSON 2
PAGE 22

Relate to the Topic

Many answers are possible. Sample answer: I like chips, chocolate, and ice cream. These foods probably aren't good for my heart because they have a lot of fat and calories. *(DOK Level: 2; Content Topic: L.a.3; Practice: SP.3.b)*

Reading Strategy

1. the percent of total calories provided by various nutrients in tortilla chips *(DOK Level: 2; Content Topic: L.a.3; Practice: SP.1.c)*

2. left graph: nutrient percentages for regular tortilla chips; right graph: nutrient percentages for low-fat tortilla chips *(DOK Level: 2; Content Topic: L.a.3; Practice: SP.1.c)*

PAGE 24

A *(DOK Level: 1; Content Topic: L.a.3; Practice: SP.3.b)*

PAGE 25

1. A *(DOK Level: 2; Content Topic: L.a.3; Practice: SP.1.c, SP.8.a)*

2. three *(DOK Level: 2; Content Topic: L.a.3; Practice: SP.1.c, SP.8.a)*

PAGES 26–27

1. D   2. B   3. A   4. E   5. C
   (DOK Level: 1; Content Topic: L.a.3; Practice: SP.1.b)

6. A *(DOK Level: 1; Content Topic: L.a.3, L.b.1; Practice: SP.1.a, SP.1.b)*

7. **Extra cholesterol is deposited on the inside walls of arteries and clogs them.** *(DOK Level: 1; Content Topic: L.a.3; Practice: SP.1.a)*

8. A *(DOK Level: 1; Content Topic: L.a.1; Practice: SP.1.a)*

9. B, C, D *(DOK Level: 1; Content Topic: L.a.3, L.a.4; Practice: SP.3.b)*

10. **C. Eat foods low in saturated fat.** *(DOK Level: 1; Content Topic: L.a.4; Practice: SP.1.a, SP.3.b)*

11. **B. saturated fat** *(DOK Level: 2; Content Topic: L.a.3; Practice: SP.1.c)* There is no wedge representing saturated fat in the circle graph for low-fat tortilla chips.

12. **D. You cannot tell because the graphs do not show the salt content.** *(DOK Level: 2, Content Topic: L.a.3; Practice: SP.3.b)* The graphs only show fat, carbohydrates, and protein, so you cannot tell how much salt is in either type of chip.

13. **Many answers are possible. Sample answer: He or she will want to still read the labels because these foods may still contain high amounts of saturated fat and cholesterol.** *(DOK Level: 3; Content Topic: L.a.3, L.a.4; Practice: SP.1.a, SP.3.b)*

14. **Many answers are possible. Sample answer: If he doesn't reduce the amount of cheese and bacon he eats, then he may develop heart disease and have a heart attack.** *(DOK Level: 3; Content Topic: L.a.4; Practice: SP.3.b, SP.3.c)*

PAGES 28–29

1. **Sample answer: Allow all subjects to rest for 2 minutes. Take and record the blood pressure measurements. Have the first subject look at the red colored card for 2 minutes and measure and record the blood pressure. Have the subject rest for 2 minutes. Repeat this procedure with the other colored cards. Repeat these steps with the subjects.** *(DOK Level: 2; Content Topic: L.a.2; Practice: SP.2.d)*

2. **Sample answer: Brighter colors like red and yellow increase blood pressure more than calmer colors like blue and green.** *(DOK Level: 2; Content Topic: L.a.2; Practice: SP.2.b)*

3. **the subject's blood pressure after viewing a color** *(DOK Level: 2; Content Topic: L.a.2; Practice: SP.2.e)*

4. **the color of the card** *(DOK Level: 2; Content Topic: L.a.2; Practice: SP.2.e)*

5. **Sample answer: The colors red and yellow are associated with higher blood pressures than the colors blue and green.** *(DOK Level: 2; Content Topic: L.a.2; Practice: SP.3.b)*

6. **Sample answer: If Kyle did not test each subject under the exact same conditions, then the blood pressure measurements may not provide reliable data.** *(DOK Level: 2; Content Topic: L.a.2; Practice: SP.2.a)*

7. **C. Each subject's normal blood pressure was not measured and recorded.** *(DOK Level: 2; Content Topic: L.a.2; Practice: SP.2.c)* Kyle did not record the blood pressure of each subject under normal circumstances. It is a weakness in the design that makes it difficult to analyze how the colors affected each subject's blood pressure.

LESSON 3

PAGE 30

Relate to the Topic

Many answers are possible. Sample answer: I would recommend walking because it's safe, easy, and cheap. It's important to exercise regularly to stay healthy, keep weight down, and look good. *(DOK Level: 1; Content Topic: L.a.1, L.a.4; Practice: SP.1.a)*

Reading Strategy

1. **how muscles work in pairs** *(DOK Level: 1; Content Topic: L.a.1, L.d.2; Practice: SP.1.c)*

2. **the joints of the body** *(DOK Level: 1; Content Topic: L.a.1, L.d.2; Practice: SP.1.c)*

PAGE 32

B *(DOK Level: 1; Content Topic: L.a.1; Practice: SP.1.a)*

PAGE 33

B *(DOK Level: 2; Content Topic: L.a.1; Practice: SP.1.a)*

PAGES 34–35

1. **joint** *(DOK Level: 1; Content Topic: L.a.1, L.a.2; Practice: SP.1.b)*

2. **ligament** *(DOK Level: 1; Content Topic: L.a.1, L.a.2; Practice: SP.1.b)*

3. **aerobic** *(DOK Level: 1; Content Topic: L.a.1, L.a.2; Practice: SP.1.b)*

4. **osteoporosis** *(DOK Level: 1; Content Topic: L.a.1, L.a.2; Practice: SP.1.b)*

5. **sprain** *(DOK Level: 1; Content Topic: L.a.1, L.a.2; Practice: SP.1.b)*

6. **healthier lungs and heart, stronger muscles, stronger bones** *(DOK Level: 1; Content Topic: L.a.2; Practice: SP.1.a)*

7. **When one muscle contracts, the bone moves one way. When the other muscle in the pair contracts, the bone moves the other way.** *(DOK Level: 2; Content Topic: L.a.1; Practice: SP.1.a, SP.1.c)*

8. **Your heart should be beating faster.** *(DOK Level: 1; Content Topic: L.a.2; Practice: SP.1.a)*

9. **B. It takes longer to walk a mile than to jog one.** *(DOK Level: 2; Content Topic: L.a.3; Practice: SP.1.a)* The other options are comparing, not contrasting. The other comparisons, while true, do not answer the question.

10. **C. Walking does not put a lot of stress on joints.** *(DOK Level: 1; Content Topic: L.a.1, L.a.2; Practice: SP.1.a)* According to the paragraph, joggers get stress injuries more than walkers do, and that implies that walking does not put a lot of stress on joints.

11. **B. The calf muscles are contracted.** *(DOK Level: 2; Content Topic: L.a.1; Practice: SP.1.c)* In the diagram, only the calf muscles are contracted in the leg on the left.

12. **Many answers are possible. Sample answer: A hinge joint works like a door hinge.** *(DOK Level: 2; Content Topic: L.a.1; Practice: SP.1.a, SP.1.c)*

13. **Many answers are possible. Sample answer: I would choose walking because it would place less stress on my joints and ligaments.** *(DOK Level: 3; Content Topic: L.a.2; Practice: SP.3.b)*

PAGES 36–37

1. **osteocyte** *(DOK Level: 2; Content Topic: L.a.1, L.d.2; Practice: SP.1.a, SP.6.a)*

2. **compact tissue** *(DOK Level: 2; Content Topic: L.a.1, L.d.2; Practice: SP.1.a, SP.6.a)*

3. **bone** *(DOK Level: 2; Content Topic: L.a.1, L.d.2; Practice: SP.1.a, SP.6.a)*

4. **skeletal system** *(DOK Level: 2; Content Topic: L.a.1, L.d.2; Practice: SP.1.a, SP.6.a)*

5. **B. The triceps muscle is contracted.** *(DOK Level: 2; Content Topic: L.a.1; Practice: SP.1.c, SP.7.a)* When the forearm is lowered, the triceps muscle is contracted and the biceps muscle is relaxed.

6. **A. The biceps muscle is contracted.** *(DOK Level: 2; Content Topic: L.a.1; Practice: SP.1.c, SP.7.a)* When the forearm is raised, the biceps muscle is contracted and the triceps muscle is relaxed.

7. **Sample answer: To raise the forearm, the biceps muscle contracts. This pulls on the bone in the forearm and causes the forearm to move upward. To lower the forearm, the triceps muscle contracts, which pulls down on the bone and causes the forearm to lower.** *(DOK Level: 2; Content Topic: L.a.1; Practice: SP.1.c, SP.7.a)*

LESSON 4

PAGE 38

Relate to the Topic

Many answers are possible. Sample answers: Alcohol, tobacco, and cocaine. I would tell her not to drink alcohol at all, because it could harm her developing baby. *(DOK Level: 3; Content Topic: L.a.2, L.a.4; Practice: SP.3.b)*

Reading Strategy

1. **Answers will vary. Sample answer: What types of things are hereditary?** *(DOK Level: 1; Content Topic: L.a.2, L.d.1; Practice: SP.1.a)*

2. **Answers will vary. Sample answer: How do a mother's activities affect an unborn child's health?** *(DOK Level: 1; Content Topic: L.a.2, L.d.1; Practice: SP.1.a)*

PAGE 40

A *(DOK Level: 3; Content Topic: L.a.1, L.d.1, L.d.2; Practice: SP.1.c)*

PAGE 41

A, C, D *(DOK Level: 1; Content Topic: L.a.2, L.a.4; Practice: SP.1.a)*

PAGES 42–43

1. **zygote, uterus** *(DOK Level: 1; Content Topic: L.d.1; Practice: SP.1.b)*

2. **embryo** *(DOK Level: 1; Content Topic: L.d.1; Practice: SP.1.b)*

3. **placenta** *(DOK Level: 2; Content Topic: L.a.1; Practice: SP.1.a, SP.1.c)*

4. **fetus** *(DOK Level: 1; Content Topic: L.a.4; Practice: SP.1.b)*

5. **Thalidomide and DES** *(DOK Level: 1; Content Topic: L.a.4; Practice: SP.1.a)*

6. **Tiny blood vessels separate the mother's and baby's bloodstreams and materials can pass between them.** *(DOK Level: 1, Content Topic: L.d.1; Practice: SP.1.a)*

7. **embryo** *(DOK Level: 1; Content Topic: L.a.4; Practice: SP.1.a)*

8. **any three of the following: Thalidomide, DES, cocaine, nicotine (cigarettes), alcohol** *(DOK Level: 1; Content Topic: L.a.4; Practice: SP.1.a)*

9. **A, B, D** *(DOK Level: 2; Content Topic: L.a.3; Practice: SP.1.a)*

10. **B. the embryo is connected to the placenta, which is connected to the mother** *(DOK Level: 2; Content Topic: L.d.1; Practice: SP.1.c)* The left side of the diagram gives you a view of the embryo, placenta, and mother's uterus and shows how they are connected to one another.

11. **A. all of the body organs have formed** *(DOK Level: 1; Content Topic: L.a.4; Practice: SP.1.a)* After the body organs have formed, any damage that occurs is more likely to be minor.

12. **D. do all of the above** *(DOK Level: 1; Content Topic: L.a.3; Practice: SP.1.a)* Diet, medical care, and no smoking or drinking will give a pregnant woman the best chance of having a healthy baby.

13. **Sample answer: Her baby might have FAS, which can result in low birth weight, physical abnormalities, and intellectual disabilities.** *(DOK Level: 2, Content Topic: L.a.4; Practice: SP.3.c)*

14. **I would explain that nicotine can cause the blood vessels in the placenta to contract, restricting the amount of oxygen and nutrients that reach the developing baby.** *(DOK Level: 2: Content Topic: L.a.4; Practice: SP.6.c)*

PAGES 44–45

1. **Sample answer: Meiosis is the process by which sex cells form. It involves two cell divisions and results in four cells that have half the number of chromosomes in the original cell.** *(DOK Level: 1; Content Topic: L.d.3; Practice: SP.1.a, SP.6.c)*

2. **Sample answer: Two sex cells, each with 23 chromosomes, will combine to form a cell with a full set of 46 chromosomes.** *(DOK Level: 2; Content Topic: L.d.3; Practice: SP.1.a, SP.6.c)*

3. **Sample answer: A gland releases hormones, which are chemicals. These chemicals probably communicate with organs to control their functions.** *(DOK Level: 2; Content Topic: L.a.2; Practice: SP.1.a, SP.6.c)*

4. **Sample answer: Estrogen is a hormone responsible for the growth and development of female sexual characteristics.** *(DOK Level: 1; Content Topic: L.a.2; Practice: SP.1.a, SP.6.c)*

5. **Sample answer: Estrogen rises to its highest level during the first half of the menstrual**

cycle, especially around Day 13. *(DOK Level: 2; Content Topic: L.a.1, L.a.2, L.d.1; Practice: SP.3.b)*

6. **Sample answer: Progesterone falls to its lowest level between Day 28 to Day 10.** *(DOK Level: 2; Content Topic: L.a.1, L.a.2, L.d.1; Practice: SP.3.b)*

7. **Sample answer: Estrogens drop sharply after Day 13 (ovulation) as progesterone rise slowly. After Day 16, levels of both estrogen and progesterone increase then decrease back to their lowest levels by Day 28.** *(DOK Level: 2; Content Topic: L.a.1, L.a.2, L.d.1; Practice: SP.3.b)*

8. **Sample answer: The progesterone level will be about 10 ng/ml on Day 21 of the menstrual cycle because it is 8 ng/ml on Day 19 and 11 ng/ml on Day 22.** *(DOK Level: 2; Content Topic: L.a.1, L.a.2, L.d.1; Practice: SP.3.b, SP.3.c)*

LESSON 5

PAGE 46

Relate to the Topic
Many answers are possible. Sample answer: Diabetes; I would take such a test so that I could prepare myself and my family, should I test positive for getting the disease. *(DOK Level: 1; Content Topic: L.e.2; Practice: SP.1.a)*

Reading Strategy
1. **Answers will vary. Sample answer: I have my mother's nose and cheekbones and my father's build.** *(DOK Level: 1; Content Topic: L.e.3; Practice: SP.1.a)*

2. **Answers will vary. Sample answer: I have my grandfather's curly hair.** *(DOK Level: 1; Content Topic: L.e.3; Practice: SP.1.a)*

PAGE 48

1. **no** *(DOK Level: 2; Content Topic: L.e.2; Practice: SP.1.a)*

2. **yes** *(DOK Level: 2; Content Topic: L.e.2; Practice: SP.1.a)*

PAGE 49

1. **fact** *(DOK Level: 2; Content Topic: L.e.2; Practice: SP.1.a)*

2. **opinion; circle the word** *feel* *(DOK Level: 2; Content Topic: L.e.2; Practice: SP.1.a)*

PAGES 50–51

1. **dominant trait** *(DOK Level: 2; Content Topic: L.e.1, L.e.2; Practice: SP.1.b)*

2. **Traits** *(DOK Level: 2; Content Topic: L.e.1, L.e.2; Practice: SP.1.b)*

3. **Genetics** *(DOK Level: 2; Content Topic: L.e.1, L.e.2; Practice: SP.1.b)*

4. **heredity** *(DOK Level: 2; Content Topic: L.e.1, L.e.2; Practice: SP.1.b)*

5. **recessive trait** *(DOK Level: 2; Content Topic: L.e.1, L.e.2; Practice: SP.1.b)*

6. **A** *(DOK Level: 1; Content Topic: L.e.1; Practice: SP.1.a)*

7. **dark hair; dark eyes** *(DOK Level: 1; Content Topic: L.e.2; Practice: SP.1.a)*

8. **Many answers are possible. Sample answer: sickle cell anemia** *(DOK Level: 2; Content Topic: L.e.3; Practice: SP.1.a)*

9. **Many answers are possible. Sample answer: Down syndrome** *(DOK Level: 2; Content Topic: L.e.3; Practice: SP.1.a)*

10. **Down syndrome is caused by the presence of an extra chromosome, so you cannot develop it later in life.** *(DOK Level: 2; Content Topic: L.e.2; Practice: SP.1.a)*

11. **B. amniocentesis** *(DOK Level: 1; Content Topic: L.a.4; Practice: SP.1.a)* According to the article, this is a test performed during pregnancy.

12. **C. two out of four** *(DOK Level: 2; Content Topic: L.e.2; Practice: SP.1.c, SP.8.c)* Two of the four boxes contain the dominant trait (H) for Huntington's.

13. **C. Some young people think it is better to be tested and know whether they will develop Huntington's in middle age.** *(DOK Level: 1; Content Topic: L.e.1; Practice: SP.4.a)* The word *think* signals an opinion.

14. **three out of four, because three combinations would include the dominant Huntington's trait, and one would not** *(DOK Level: 2; Content Topic: L.e.2; Practice: SP.3.b, SP.8.c)*

15. **The other parent has an HH trait for the disease.** *(DOK Level: 3; Content Topic: L.e.2; Practice: SP.7.a)*

PAGES 52–53

1. **5** *(DOK Level: 2; Content Topic: L.e.2; Practice: SP.1.b, SP.1.c, SP.3.b)*

2. **2** *(DOK Level: 2; Content Topic: L.e.2; Practice: SP.1.b, SP.1.c, SP.3.b)*

3. **1** *(DOK Level: 2; Content Topic: L.e.2; Practice: SP.1.b, SP.1.c, SP.3.b)*

4. **A. Individual 2** *(DOK Level: 2; Content Topic: L.e.2; Practice: SP.1.b, SP.1.c, SP.3.b)* In Generation III, the symbols for Individuals 1 and 2 are the only ones not partially or fully shaded.

5. **D. 6** *(DOK Level: 2; Content Topic: L.e.2; Practice: SP.1.b, SP.1.c, SP.3.b)* Six symbols on the pedigree chart are fully shaded.

6. **C. Individuals 2 and 4** *(DOK Level: 2; Content Topic: L.e.2; Practice: SP.1.b, SP.1.c, SP.3.b)* Individuals 1, 2, and 3 are siblings, as are Individuals 5 and 6.

7. **Sample answer: A pedigree chart can help dog breeders keep track of the lineage of their dogs. It can also help them keep track of good and bad genetic traits in their dogs.** *(DOK Level: 2; Content Topic: L.e.2; Practice: SP.3.b)*

8. **Sample answer: There is no chance. There is a two out of four chance the offspring will not carry the trait at all. There is also a two out of four chance that the offspring will carry the trait on one gene but not express it.** *(DOK Level: 3; Content Topic: L.e.2; Practice: SP.3.c, SP.8c)*

LESSON 6

PAGE 54

Relate to the Topic

Many answers are possible. Sample answer: I caught a bad cold from my son. My head was congested, my nose was running, and I had a headache. I took decongestants and rested. *(DOK Level: 2; Content Topic: L.a.4; Practice: SP.6.c)*

Reading Strategy

1. **germs** *(DOK Level: 2; Content Topic: L.a.4; Practice: SP.1.b)*

2. **colds, flu, tonsillitis, chicken pox** *(DOK Level: 2; Content Topic: L.a.4; Practice: SP.3.b)*

PAGE 56

cell wall, cell membrane, genetic material, cytoplasm *(DOK Level: 2; Content Topic: L.a.4; Practice: SP.1.c)*

PAGE 57

A *(DOK Level: 2; Content Topic: L.a.4; Practice: SP.3.b)*

PAGES 58–59

1. **E**   2. **C**   3. **B**   4. **A**   5. **D**
(DOK Level: 2; Content Topic: L.a.4; Practice: SP.1.b)

6. **B** *(DOK Level: 2; Content Topic: L.a.4; Practice: SP.5.a)*

7. **A. virus** *(DOK Level: 1; Content Topic: L.a.4; Practice: SP.1.a)*
   B. virus *(DOK Level: 1; Content Topic: L.a.4; Practice: SP.1.a)*
   C. virus, bacteria *(DOK Level: 1; Content Topic: L.a.4; Practice: SP.1.a)*

8. **B** *(DOK Level: 1; Content Topic: L.a.4; Practice: SP.1.a)*

9. **a dose of a dead or weakened disease-causing agent that causes the body to form antibodies against the disease** *(DOK Level: 1; Content Topic: L.a.4; Practice: SP.1.a, SP.1.b)*

10. **a substance the body makes to fight disease** *(DOK Level: 1; Content Topic: L.a.4; Practice: SP.1.a, SP.1.b)*

11. **C. genetic material** *(DOK Level: 2; Content Topic: L.a.4; Practice: SP.1.a)* According to the diagrams on pages 56 and 57, both a bacterial cell and a virus contain genetic material.

12. **C. Avoid people with colds.** *(DOK Level: 2; Content Topic: La.4; Practice: SP.3.b)* Since it's possible that colds are spread both by touch and by breathing air near people with

colds, the best way to avoid colds is to avoid sick people.

13. **A. Antibiotics do not fight viruses.** *(DOK Level: 2; Content Topic: La.4; Practice: SP.3.b)* According to the article, antibiotics fight bacteria, not viruses. Colds and the flu are caused by viruses.

14. **During the winter, people spend more time in small spaces indoors where it is easy to catch a cold or the flu from others.** *(DOK Level: 2; Content Topic: La.4; Practice: SP.3.b)*

15. **Many answers are possible. Sample answer: Try to stay away from people who are sick; wash hands frequently; avoid touching the face; eat well and exercise to improve fitness; get flu shots for older people in the family.** *(DOK Level: 2; Content Topic: La.4; Practice: SP.3.b)*

PAGES 60–61

1. **8,000** *(DOK Level: 1; Content Topic: L.d.2; Practice: SP.1.c)*

2. **32,000** *(DOK Level: 2; Content Topic: L.d.2; Practice: SP.3.c)*

3. **Sample answer: You have to kill all of the bacteria because they reproduce so fast. If you left a few alive, you would have thousands again in hours and they could make you sick.** *(DOK Level: 2; Content Topic: L.a.4, L.e.1; Practice: SP.3.b, SP.3.c, SP.6)*

4. **D. All of the above** *(DOK Level: 2; Content Topic: L.d.1; Practice: SP. 3.b, SP.3.c)* Preventing any step in the viral multiplication process would prevent illness.

5. **Sample answer: The text says that if the virus can't multiply, then it can't get people sick. The virus has to go through all of the steps to multiply. So attacking it at any of the steps would help.** *(DOK Level: 2; Content Topic: L.d.1; Practice: SP.3.a)*

LESSON 7

PAGE 62

Relate to the Topic

Many answers are possible. Sample answer: Baby: helpless, learned to walk and talk; child: learned a lot, played a lot; adolescent: grew up, understood more about the world; adult: became responsible for myself. *(DOK Level: 2; Content Topic: L.d.1; Practice: SP.1.a)*

Reading Strategy

1. **the gypsy moth's life cycle** *(DOK Level: 1; Content Topic: L.d.1; Practice: SP.1.c)*

2. **egg, caterpillar, pupa, adult** *(DOK Level: 1; Content Topic: L.d.1; Practice: SP.1.c)*

PAGE 64

1. **pupa** *(DOK Level: 1; Content Topic: L.d.1; Practice: SP.1.c)*

2. **egg, caterpillar, pupa** *(DOK Level: 1; Content Topic: L.d.1; Practice: SP.1.c)*

PAGE 65

1. **about a month and a half** *(DOK Level: 2; Content Topic: L.d.1; Practice: SP.1.c)*

2. **in late June or early July** *(DOK Level: 2; Content Topic: L.d.1; Practice: SP.1.c)*

PAGES 66–67

1. **egg** *(DOK Level: 1; Content Topic: L.d.1; Practice: SP.1.b)*

2. **pupa** *(DOK Level: 1; Content Topic: L.d.1; Practice: SP.1.b)*

3. **caterpillar** *(DOK Level: 1; Content Topic: L.d.1; Practice: SP.1.b)*

4. **adult** *(DOK Level: 1; Content Topic: L.d.1; Practice: SP.1.b)*

5. **life cycle** *(DOK Level: 1; Content Topic: L.d.1; Practice: SP.1.b)*

6. **A Frenchman brought gypsy moth eggs to the United States to use in the silk industry, and a few moths escaped.** *(DOK Level: 1; Content Topic: L.c.5; Practice: SP.1.a)*

7. **It eats the leaves of certain trees, such as oak.** *(DOK Level: 1; Content Topic: L.c.5; Practice: SP.1.a)*

8. **B**   9. **A**   10. **D**   11. **C**
(DOK Level: 2; Content Topic: L.c.5; Practice: SP.1.a)

12. **D. egg, caterpillar, pupa, adult** *(DOK Level: 2; Content Topic: L.d.1; Practice: SP.1.c)* According to the life cycle diagram and the article, this is the order in which the stages of the life cycle take place.

13. **A. egg** *(DOK Level: 2; Content Topic: L.d.1; Practice: SP.1.c)* The longest segment on the timeline is that of the egg stage.

14. **D. Soak the egg masses in kerosene, bleach, or ammonia.** *(DOK Level: 2; Content Topic: L.d.1; Practice: SP.1.c)* According to the timeline, in March the gypsy moths are in the egg stage. Soaking them in a toxic substance destroys them at that stage.

15. **Many answers are possible. Some animals that look different at different stages of the life cycle include butterflies, mosquitoes, mayflies, frogs, and toads.** *(DOK Level: 2; Content Topic: L.d.1; Practice: SP.6.c)*

16. **Many answers are possible. Sample answer: When we had ants in the house, we put an insecticide powder along doors and windows and in cupboards.** *(DOK Level: 2; Content Topic: L.d.1; Practice: SP.6.c)*

PAGES 68–69

1. **hatchling tadpole** *(DOK Level: 1; Content Topic: L.d.1; Practice: SP.1.c)*

2. **adult** *(DOK Level: 1; Content Topic: L.d.1; Practice: SP.1.c)*

3. **Sample answer: Both lay eggs and change a great deal from young to adult.** *(DOK Level: 2; Content Topic: L.d.1; Practice: SP.1.c, SP.7.a)*

4. **Sample answer: Moths create a cocoon and frogs do not. Tadpoles live in the water for a time and moths do not.** *(DOK Level: 2; Content Topic: L.d.1; Practice: SP.1.c, SP.7.a)*

5. **Sample answer: The frog populations would get smaller. There would be nowhere for the frogs to lay eggs, so they would leave or die out.** *(DOK Level: 2; Content Topic: L.c.5; Practice: SP.3.c)*

6. **Answers will vary. Diagrams should include the major life stages of the animal arranged in a line or a circle with arrows showing how one stage leads to the next.** *(DOK Level: 2; Content Topic: L.d.1; Practice: SP.6.a)*

7. **B. adults** *(DOK Level: 2; Content Topic: L.d.1; Practice: SP.1.a)* Adult animals carry on the species through reproduction and are a common life stage among animals.

LESSON 8

PAGE 70

Relate to the Topic
Many answers are possible. Sample answer: Tropical rain forests are green, wet, and full of plants and animals. If I were in a tropical rain forest, I might see many colorful plants, feel warm and sweaty, and hear birds calling. *(DOK Level: 2; Content Topic: ES.a.1; Practice: SP.6.c)*

Reading Strategy

1. **the world's tropical rain forests** *(DOK Level: 1; Content Topic: L.c.5, ES.a.1; Practice: SP.1.c)*

2. **Dark gray represents the area covered by rain forests today. Dark blue represents rain forests that have been damaged or destroyed.** *(DOK Level: 2; Content Topic: L.c.5, ES.a.1; Practice: SP.1.c)*

PAGE 72

B *(DOK Level: 2; Content Topic: L.c.5, ES.a.1; Practice: SP.1.a)*

PAGE 73

A *(DOK Level: 2; Content Topic: L.c.5, ES.a.1; Practice: SP.1.a)*

PAGES 74–75

1. **ecosystem** *(DOK Level: 1; Content Topic: L.c.2, ES.a.1; Practice: SP.1.b)*

2. **Respiration** *(DOK Level: 1; Content Topic: L.b.1, L.d.1; Practice: SP.1.b)*

3. **carbon dioxide–oxygen cycle** *(DOK Level: 1; Content Topic: L.c.1; Practice: SP.1.b)*

4. **Photosynthesis** *(DOK Level: 1; Content Topic: L.b.1, L.d.1; Practice: SP.1.b)*

5. tropical rain forests *(DOK Level: 1; Content Topic: L.c.5, ES.a.3; Practice: SP.1.b)*

6. The amount of space, food, and water can affect the number of animals that live there. *(DOK Level: 2; Content Topic: L.c.3; Practice: SP.1.a)*

7. A *(DOK Level: 1; Content Topic: L.b.1, L.c.1; Practice: SP.1.a)*

8. Farming, ranching, and logging; all three involve cutting down rain forest trees, which destroys the ecosystem. *(DOK Level: 1; Content Topic: L.c.5; Practice: SP.1.a)*

9. A. increased *(DOK Level: 2; Content Topic: L.c.5, ES.a.1; Practice: SP.1.a)* According to the article, burning fuel gives off carbon dioxide. So the increase in burning fuel has increased the amount of carbon dioxide in the air.

10. D. an increase in the amount of carbon dioxide in the atmosphere *(DOK Level: 2; Content Topic: L.c.5; Practice: SP.1.a)* According to the article, global warming may result from increased carbon dioxide in the atmosphere.

11. D. The monkey population would decrease. *(DOK Level: 2; Content Topic: L.c.3; Practice: SP.3.b)* With fewer trees for food and shelter, fewer monkeys would survive and the population would decrease.

12. Any three of the following reasons: Tropical rain forests have a wealth of plant and animal life. Tropical rain forests are the source of many medicines. Tropical rain forests are the source of many foods. Tropical rain forests help control the temperature of Earth. Tropical rain forests help add oxygen to the atmosphere. *(DOK Level: 2; Content Topic: ES.a.3; Practice: SP.3.b)*

13. Many answers are possible. Sample answer: I can buy rain forest products that are harvested without damaging the forest. I can refuse to buy furniture made from tropical woods. *(DOK Level: 2; Content Topic: L.c.5, ES.a.3; Practice: SP.3.b)*

PAGES 76–77

1. Sample answer: Does rainfall affect the number of species in an ecosystem? *(DOK Level: 1; Content Topic: L.c.3; Practice: SP.1.a)*

2. More rainfall will allow more kinds of animals and plants to live in the ecosystem. *(DOK Level: 1; Content Topic: L.c.3; Practice: SP.2.b)*

3. Sample answer: No, her results do not support her hypothesis. She predicted that there would be more species in the wet forest, but there were many more species in the dry grassland. *(DOK Level: 3; Content Topic: L.c.3; Practice: SP.3.a)*

4. Sample answer: No, her results are not accurate because the species weren't counted the same way. Chelsea spent a week counting in the forest, while the park may have trained naturalists observing for years. *(DOK Level: 2; Content Topic: L.c.3; Practice: SP.2.c)*

5. Sample answer: Chelsea could find an official list of species in the wet temperate forest, or she could do her own count in the grassland. *(DOK Level 2; Content Topic: L.c.3; Practice: SP.2.a)*

6. Sample answer: Yes, the new results support Chelsea's hypothesis. She found more species in the forest than the grassland, as she predicted. *(DOK Level: 2; Content Topic: L.c.3; Practice: SP.3.b)*

7. Sample answer: Not enough time, not enough training to identify all of the species, some species may only be present or active part of the year. *(DOK Level: 2; Content Topic: L.c.3; Practice: SP.3.b)*

LESSON 9

PAGE 78

Relate to the Topic

Many answers are possible. Sample answer: Birds have wings, feathers, beaks and claws. I recognize birds by their feathers and wings. *(DOK Level: 2; Content Topic: L.f.3; Practice: SP.6.c)*

Reading Strategy

1. a model of a feathered dinosaur called ***Caudipteryx*** *(DOK Level: 1; Content Topic: L.f.1; Practice: SP.1.c)*

2. **how birds might have evolved from dinosaurs** *(DOK Level: 1; Content Topic: L.f.1; Practice: SP.1.c)*

PAGE 80

B *(DOK Level: 2; Content Topic: L.f.3; Practice: SP.3.b)*

PAGE 81

A *(DOK Level: 2; Content Topic: L.f.1; Practice: SP.1.a)*

PAGES 82–83

1. **mutation** *(DOK Level: 1; Content Topic: L.e.3; Practice: SP.1.b)*

2. **adaptation** *(DOK Level: 1; Content Topic: L.f.3; Practice: SP.1.b)*

3. **Convergence** *(DOK Level: 1; Content Topic: L.f.3; Practice: SP.1.b)*

4. **Natural selection** *(DOK Level: 1; Content Topic: L.f.2; Practice: SP.1.b)*

5. **evolution** *(DOK Level: 1; Content Topic: L.f.1, L.f.2, L.f.3; Practice: SP.1.b)*

6. **They all had feathers.** *(DOK Level: 2; Content Topic: L.f.1; Practice: SP.1.a)*

7. **insulation; to attract females** *(DOK Level: 1; Content Topic: L.f.2; Practice: SP.1.a)*

8. **A** *(DOK Level: 1; Content Topic: L.f.3; Practice: SP.1.a)*

9. **A. are very different types of animals** *(DOK Level: 2; Content Topic: L.f.2; Practice: SP.3.b)* Birds have feathers and lay eggs, bats are mammals and have fur, and butterflies are insects; so you can infer they are not closely related.

10. **C. adaptation** *(DOK Level: 2; Content Topic: L.f.3; Practice: SP.1.a)* According to the article, an adaptation is a change that permits an organism to better survive in its environment. Bacteria that are resistant to antibiotics have a better chance of surviving.

11. **B. Humans would develop stronger legs.** *(DOK Level: 2; Content Topic: L.f.3; Practice: SP.3.b)* Through adaptation, as legs were used more, over generations of offspring they would become more important as a body part.

12. **Many answers are possible. Sample answer: I think birds evolved from dinosaurs because there are so many structural similarities between them, including feathers, flexible wrists, wishbones, and air-filled skulls.** *(DOK Level: 3; Content Topic: L.f.1, L.f.3; Practice: SP.3.a)*

13. **Many answers are possible. Sample answer: Before I read this article, I thought of dinosaurs as slow, heavy creatures; now I realize that some were light and some may have been very fast and even able to fly.** *(DOK Level: 2; Content Topic: L.f.2; Practice: SP.3.b)*

PAGES 84–85

1. **A. The population will gradually include more short-haired individuals again.** *(DOK Level: 2; Content Topic: L.f.2; Practice: SP.3.c, SP.7.a)* In a warm climate, natural selection will no longer favor thick-furred animals. Therefore, the proportion of thin-furred animals will probably increase.

2. **C. natural selection** *(DOK Level: 1; Content Topic: L.f.2; Practice: SP.1.b)* Natural selection means that the organisms best suited to their environments are most likely to survive. Thick fur helps to keep deer warm in a cold climate.

3. **D. adaptation** *(DOK Level: 1; Content Topic: L.f.3; Practice: SP.1.b)* An adaptation is a trait that makes an organism better able to survive in its environment.

4. **parasitism** *(DOK Level: 2; Content Topic: L.c.4; Practice: SP.1.a, SP.1.b)*

5. **commensalism** *(DOK Level 2; Content Topic: L.c.4; Practice: SP.1.a, SP.1.b)* Defined in passage above.

6. **Sample answer: Mutualism, because both benefit. Cats get food and a place to live, while humans get pest control and companionship.** *(DOK Level: 2; Content Topic: L.c.4; Practice: SP.3.b)*

7. Sample answer: Honeyguides that lead humans to beehives would get more food and be more likely to survive. Human who follow honeyguides would also get more food. Gradually, the trait to work together would become more common in both populations. *(DOK Level: 3; Content Topic: L.f.2; Practice: SP.3.b, SP.6.c)*

SCIENCE AT WORK
PAGE 87

1. **C. hand weights** *(DOK Level: 1; Content Topic: L.a.1; Practice: SP.1.a)*

2. **B. He might get hurt from too much exercising.** *(DOK Level: 1; Content Topic: L.a.1; Practice: SP.1.a)*

3. **C, A, B** *(DOK Level: 1; Content Topic: L.a.1; Practice: SP.1.a)*

UNIT 1 REVIEW
PAGES 88–91

1. **DNA** *(DOK Level: 1; Content Topic: L.d.1, L.e.1; Practice: SP.1.b)*

2. **mitosis** *(DOK Level: 1; Content Topic: L.d.1, L.d.3; Practice: SP.1.b)*

3. **D. An X-shaped chromosome consists of two copies of a parent chromosome.** *(DOK Level: 1; Content Topic: L.d.3, L.e.1; Practice: SP.1.c, SP.3.b)* According to the diagram, the DNA doubles in the parent cell before cell division. The X-shaped chromosomes appear in the diagram just after the doubling. Later in the diagram, the chromosomes split and each new cell gets only one-half of each X-shaped chromosome.

4. **artery** *(DOK Level: 1; Content Topic: L.a.1, L.d.2; Practice: SP.1.c)*

5. **left atrium** *(DOK Level: 1; Content Topic: L.a.1, L.d.2; Practice: SP.1.c)*

6. **A. right atrium, right ventricle, lungs, left atrium, left ventricle** *(DOK Level: 2; Content Topic: L.a.1, L.d.2; Practice: SP.1.c)* According to the arrows and labels in the diagram, the blood moves from the right atrium to the right ventricle. Then, the blood moves through an artery to the lungs. Next it flows to the left atrium of the heart through a vein. It moves from the left atrium to the left ventricle, which pumps the blood throughout the body.

7. **B**   8. **C**   9. **A** *(DOK Level: 2; Content Topic: L.a.3, L.c.2; Practice: SP.1.a, SP.1.c)*

10. **These animals get nitrogen by eating other animals that eat plants.** *(DOK Level: 2; Content Topic: L.a.3, L.c.2; Practice: SP.3.b)*

11. **protection** *(DOK Level: 1; Content Topic: L.c.4; Practice: SP.1.a)*

12. **scavengers** *(DOK Level: 1; Content Topic: L.c.1, L.c.2, L.c.4; Practice: SP.1.b)*

13. **A. A bird eats ticks that are on the back of an ox.** *(DOK Level: 2; Content Topic: L.c.4; Practice: SP.3.b)* The bird gets food from this relationship, and the ox gets rid of parasites. The second option incorrect because the only living species involved is the ant. The third option is incorrect because the lions don't get anything from the wild dog. The last option is incorrect because the two animals in the relationship are the same species, and mutualism is a relationship between two different species.

14. **Without food and shelter, the ant population will likely decrease or die out entirely.** *(DOK Level: 2; Content Topic: L.c.3, L.c.5; Practice: SP.3.c)*

Mini-Test Unit 1
PAGES 92–93

1. **B. The bird will get infected with the virus.** *(DOK Level: 2; Content Topic: L.a.4; Practice: SP.1.c, SP.3.c)* According to the diagram, infected mosquitoes can infect birds with the virus.

2. **C. unlikely** *(DOK Level: 2; Content Topic: L.a.4; Practice: SP.8.c)* If less than 1% of infected people get very sick, then it is unlikely you will get ill if bitten by an infected mosquito.

3. **A. not producing enough antibodies** *(DOK Level: 2; Content Topic: L.a.1, L.a.2, L.a.4; Practice: SP.3.b)* The white blood cells of a healthy person make enough antibodies to kill invading germs. So the person stays healthy. Therefore, you can infer that when someone gets an infection, his or her white blood cells are not producing enough antibodies to fight off invading germs.

4. **C. White blood cells protect the body.** *(DOK Level: 2; Content Topic: L.a.1, L.a.2, L.a.4; Practice: SP.1.a)* According to the information, white blood cells protect people from the numerous germs in the environment by producing germ-killing antibodies.

5. **B. Yes, if both parents have recessive genetic material for the handedness trait.** *(DOK Level: 2; Content Topic: L.e.2; Practice: SP.3.b, SP.7.a)* If both parents are right-handed, you can conclude that each parent has dominant genetic material for the trait of handedness. Each parent may also have recessive genetic material for the trait. In this case, the recessive form does not show up in the parents. However, both parents can pass recessive genetic material to their child, who would then be left-handed.

6. **A. not actively dividing** *(DOK Level: 2; Content Topic: L.d.3; Practice: SP.1.c, SP.4.a)* According to the graph, about 75% of the cells are in between cell divisions, and thus not actively dividing.

7. **B. more time in Phase 1 than in Phase 2** *(DOK Level: 2; Content Topic: L.d.3; Practice: SP.1.c, SP.4.a)* According to the graph, Phase 1 is much longer than Phase 2.

UNIT 2: EARTH AND SPACE SCIENCE

LESSON 10

PAGE 96

Relate to the Topic

Many answers are possible. Sample answer: being born, moving, traveling *(DOK Level: 2; Content Topic: ES.c.3; Practice: SP.1.a, SP.1.b)*

Many answers are possible. Sample answer: I was born in the month of May, 18 years ago. I traveled around the United States for 3 weeks last year. *(DOK Level: 2; Content Topic: ES.c.3; Practice: SP.1.a, SP.1.b, SP.6.b)*

Reading Strategy

1. **the geologic time scale** *(DOK Level: 2; Content Topic: ES.c.3; Practice: SP.1.a, SP.1.b)*

2. **millions of years** *(DOK Level: 2; Content Topic: ES.c.3; Practice: SP.1.a, SP.1.b)*

PAGE 98

A *(DOK Level: 3; Content Topic: ES.c.3; Practice: SP.1.a, SP.3.b)*

PAGE 99

B *(DOK Level: 2; Content Topic: ES.c.3; Practice: SP.1.a, SP.1.b, SP.6.b)*

PAGES 100–101

1. **relative age** *(DOK Level: 1; Content Topic: ES.c.3; Practice: SP.1.a, SP.1.b)*

2. **radioactive decay** *(DOK Level: 1; Content Topic: ES.c.34; Practice: SP.1.a, SP.1.b)*

3. **geology** *(DOK Level: 1; Content Topic: ES.c.3; Practice: SP.1.a, SP.1.b)*

4. **radiometric dating** *(DOK Level: 1; Content Topic: ES.c.3; Practice: SP.1.a, SP.1.b)*

5. **absolute age** *(DOK Level: 1; Content Topic: ES.c.3; Practice: SP.1.a, SP.1.b)*

6. **You can determine absolute age using radiometric dating and relative age using the principle of superposition or the principle of faunal succession.** *(DOK Level: 2; Content Topic: ES.c.3; Practice: SP.1.a, SP.6.c)*

7. **B** *(DOK Level: 1; Content Topic: ES.c.3; Practice: SP.1.c, SP.6.b)*

8. **The geologic time scale is a record of the major events in Earth's history.** *(DOK Level: 1; Content Topic: ES.c.3; Practice: SP.1.a, SP.1.b, SP.6.c)*

9. **D. when rock layers formed** *(DOK Level: 2; Content Topic: ES.c.3; Practice: SP.1.a, SP.1.b)* A geologist is a scientists who studies Earth and its history.

10. **D. She used the principle of faunal succession to determine relative age.** *(DOK Level: 2; Content Topic: ES.c.3; Practice: SP.1.a, SP.3.b)* The scientist is using the fossils to identify the relative age of the rocks.

11. **B. Hadean Eon** *(DOK Level: 2; Content Topic: ES.c.3; Practice: SP.1.b, SP.1.c)* The text states that the Acasta Gneiss has an absolute age of 4.03 billion years. According to the chart, that falls in the Hadean Eon.

12. **Phanerozoic Eon, Cenozoic Era, Quaternary Period, Holocene Epoch** *(DOK Level: 2; Content Topic: ES.c.3; Practice: SP.1.a, SP.1.b)*

13. **Many answers are possible. Sample answer: My friend Juan's absolute age is 19 years old and his relative age is older than me.** *(DOK Level: 2; Content Topic: ES.c.3; Practice: SP.1.a, SP.6.b, SP.6.c)*

PAGES 102–103

1. **D. Oligocene** *(DOK Level: 1; Content Topic: ES.c.3; Practice: SP.1.c)* According to the chart, early humans developed during the Pleistocene Epoch, large carnivores and mammoths developed during the Pliocene Epoch, and pigs, cattle and deer developed during the Miocene Epoch.

2. **Holocene** *(DOK Level: 1; Content Topic: ES.c.3; Practice: SP.1.c)*

3. **Jurassic** *(DOK Level: 1; Content Topic: ES.c.3; Practice: SP.1.c)*

4. **Cenozoic** *(DOK Level: 1; Content Topic: ES.c.3; Practice: SP.1.c)*

5. **Sample answer: During the early Triassic Period, all of Earth's modern continent were combined into one supercontinent named Pangaea. The dinosaurs were able** to migrate across all of Earth's land areas without traveling across oceans. *(DOK Level: 2; Content Topic: ES.c.3; Practice: SP.1.c, SP.3.b)*

6. **Sample answer: The impact of the asteroid may have caused such widespread destruction that most dinosaurs could not survive.** *(DOK Level: 2; Content Topic: ES.c.3; Practice: SP.1.c, SP.3.b)*

7. **Sample answer: I would create a model where 1 millimeter represents 1 million years. I would measure the length of each time period and use the colored pencils to mark the length and label each time period.** *(DOK Level: 3; Content Topic: ES.c.3; Practice: SP.1.c, SP.6.b, SP.7.a, SP.8.b)*

8. **Sample answer: The United States has a very short history compared to that of Earth, so it would be difficult to show on a geologic time scale model.** *(DOK Level: 2; Content Topic: ES.c.3; Practice: SP.3.b, SP.6.c)*

9. **Sample answer: The Proterozoic Eon would be the longest at 1,957 million years. The Archeon Eon lasted for 1,300 million years, the Hadeon Eon lasted for 800 million years, and the Phanerozoic Eon is 543 million years old.** *(DOK Level: 2; Content Topic: ES.c.2; Practice: SP.1.c, SP.3.b, SP.6.b, SP.7.a, SP.8.b)*

LESSON 11

PAGE 104

Relate to the Topic

Many answers are possible. Sample answer: a volcano erupting *(DOK Level: 2; Content Topic: ES.b.4; Practice: SP.6.c)*

Many answers are possible. Sample answer: People's homes and food supplies were destroyed, and lives were lost. *(DOK Level: 2; Content Topic: ES.b.4; Practice: SP.1.a, SP.3.b)*

Reading Strategy

1. **a hard-boiled egg and what it looks like inside** *(DOK Level: 1; Content Topic: ES.b.4; Practice: SP.1.a)*

2. Many answers are possible. Sample answer: Forming a picture in my mind of something I already know, like the layers of an egg, might help me better understand Earth's layers. *(DOK Level: 2; Content Topic: ES.b.4; Practice: SP.3.b)*

PAGE 105

B *(DOK Level: 2; Content Topic: ES.b.4; Practice: SP.1.c)*

PAGE 106

A *(DOK Level: 2; Content Topic: ES.b.4; Practice: SP.3.b)*

PAGES 108–109

1. volcano *(DOK Level: 1; Content Topic: ES.b.4; Practice: SP.1.a, SP.1.b)*
2. earthquake *(DOK Level: 1; Content Topic: ES.b.4; Practice: SP.1.a, SP.1.b)*
3. plates *(DOK Level: 1; Content Topic: ES.b.4; Practice: SP.1.a, SP.1.b)*
4. landform *(DOK Level: 1; Content Topic: ES.b.4; Practice: SP.1.a, SP.1.b)*
5. B *(DOK Level: 1; Content Topic: ES.b.4; Practice: SP.1.b)*
6. D *(DOK Level: 1; Content Topic: ES.b.4; Practice: SP.1.b)*
7. E *(DOK Level: 1; Content Topic: ES.b.4; Practice: SP.1.b)*
8. A *(DOK Level: 1; Content Topic: ES.b.4; Practice: SP.1.b)*
9. C *(DOK Level: 1; Content Topic: ES.b.4; Practice: SP.1.b)*
10. the core *(DOK Level: 1; Content Topic: ES.b.4; Practice: SP.1.a)*
11. the idea that Earth's lithosphere consists of plates that slowly move as a result of currents in the mantle *(DOK Level: 1; Content Topic: ES.b.4; Practice: SP.1.a)*
12. D. core, mantle, crust *(DOK Level: 2; Content Topic: ES.b.4; Practice: SP.1.c)*
13. A. earthquakes *(DOK Level: 2; Content Topic: ES.b.4; Practice: SP.1.a, SP.7.a)*
14. C. the Juan de Fuca Plate sinking under the North American Plate *(DOK Level: 2; Content Topic: ES.b.4; Practice: SP.1.a, SP.7.a)*

15. Many answers are possible. Sample answer: The motion of tectonic plates is related to the building up of new crust and the building of landforms like mountains, volcanoes, and ocean basins. *(DOK Level: 3; Content Topic: ES.b.4; Practice: SP.1.a, SP.7.a)*
16. Many answers are possible. Sample answer: Earthquakes and volcanic eruptions commonly occur along plate boundaries, so people are at greater risk of getting hurt by these events. *(DOK Level: 3; Content Topic: ES.b.4; Practice: SP.3.b, SP.6.c)*

PAGES 110–111

1. continents *(DOK Level: 1; Content Topic: ES.b.4; Practice: SP.1.a)*
2. the theory of plate tectonics *(DOK Level: 1; Content Topic: ES.b.4; Practice: SP.1.b)*
3. Sample answer: Wegener studied rock formations and fossils at the edges of landmasses. *(DOK Level: 2; Content Topic: ES.b.4; Practice: SP.3.a)*
4. Geologists dismissed his ideas. *(DOK Level: 2; Content Topic: ES.b.4; Practice: SP.1.a)*
5. 1) Wegener was not a geologist; 2) Wegener didn't speak English well; 3) Wegener could not explain how the continents moved. *(DOK Level 2; Content Topic: ES.b.4; Practice: SP.1.a)*
6. Geologist began to accept Wegener's theory when they collected evidence of the spreading of the sea floor and continental movements. *(DOK Level: 2; Content Topic: ES.b.4; Practice: SP.3.a)*
7. Sample answer: He could not respond because he had died decades earlier. *(DOK Level: 2; Content Topic: ES.b.4; Practice: SP.1.a)*
8. Sample answer: I learned that the scientific community can be wrong about an idea and then reach a new conclusion with more data and time for research. *(DOK Level: 3; Content Topic: ES.b.4; Practice: SP.4.a)*
9. D. A world map of early Earth would look very different from a modern world map.

(DOK Level: 2; Content Topic: ES.b.4; Practice: SP.7.a) The theory of continental drift says that the continents are in constant motion.

LESSON 12

PAGE 112

Relate to the Topic

Many answers are possible. Sample answer: Yes, I heard about it on the radio. An ice storm covered everything with a layer of ice. The weight of the ice broke tree branches and brought down power lines. *(DOK Level: 1; Content Topic: ES.b.1; Practice: SP.6.c)*

Reading Strategy

1. **high temperatures and precipitation for the continental United States on June 28** *(DOK Level: 3; Content Topic: ES.b.1; Practice: SP.1.c)*

2. **a cold front** *(DOK Level: 3; Content Topic: ES.b.1; Practice: SP.1.c)*

PAGE 114

1. A   2. A   3. B
   (DOK Level: 3; Content Topic: ES.b.1; Practice: SP.1.b, SP.1.c)

PAGE 115

1. B   2. A
   (DOK Level: 3; Content Topic: ES.b.1; Practice: SP.1.c)

PAGES 116–117

1. air mass   2. front
3. forecast   4. meteorologists
5. weather map   6. stationary front
7. precipitation
8. A, C   9. B, C   10. A, D   11. B, D
   (DOK Level: 1; Content Topic: ES.b.1; Practice: SP.1.a, SP.1.b)
12. **from west to east** *(DOK Level: 1; Content Topic: ES.b.1; Practice: SP.1.a)*
13. **There are too many factors affecting the weather over a long period of time for accurate predictions to be possible.** *(DOK*

Level: 2; Content Topic: ES.b.1; Practice: SP.1.a, SP.2.c)

14. **C. stationary front** *(DOK Level: 2; Content Topic: ES.b.1; Practice: SP.1.b, SP.1.c)* The map key shows that alternating triangles and half circles pointing in opposite directions are the symbols for a stationary front.

15. **C. 90s** *(DOK Level: 3; Content Topic: ES.b.1; Practice: SP.1.c, SP.3b, SP.6.b)* Fargo's temperature is in the 80s on June 29, and a warm front is approaching from the south. The correct prediction is that Fargo's temperatures will rise, not fall.

16. **A. occasional showers, high temperature in the 60s** *(DOK Level: 3; Content Topic: ES.b.1; Practice: SP.1.b, SP.1.c, SP.3.c)* In Salt Lake City, temperatures are in the 60s and 70s, and there are showers. Even as the cold front moves to the east, Salt Lake City is likely to have this weather the next day.

17. **The cold air mass in the west is probably a maritime polar air mass. It is cool, indicating polar. And it is moist (showers), indicating maritime origins.** *(DOK Level: 3; Content Topic: ES.b.1; Practice: SP.1.b, SP.1.c)*

18. **Many answers are possible. Sample answer: The weather is cold and clear, so there is probably a continental polar air mass over the area.** *(DOK Level: 2; Content Topic: ES.b.1; Practice: SP.6.c)*

PAGES 118–119

1. **B. 100 kilometers** *(DOK Level: 2; Content Topic: ES.a.2; Practice: SP.1.c, SP.6.b, SP.8.b)* According to the diagram, the distance from the center of the eye to its left wall is 50 kilometers and the distance from the center of the eye to its right wall is 50 kilometers. The total distance across the eye is 100 kilometers.

2. **A. about 15,000 m** *(DOK Level: 1; Content Topic: ES.a.2; Practice: SP.1.c, SP.6.b)* The top of the highest clouds reach about 15,000 m on the diagram.

3. **A Category 3 hurricane is expected to have wind speeds between 111–130 mph, a storm surge between 9–12 ft, and extensive landfall damage.** *(DOK Level: 1; Content Topic: ES.a.2; Practice: SP.1.c, SP.3.b)*

4. **Category 2** *(DOK Level: 2; Content Topic: ES.a.2; Practice: SP.1.c, SP.3.b)*

5. **The greater the wind speed of a hurricane, the greater the storm surge.** *(DOK Level: 2; Content Topic: ES.a.2; Practice: SP.3.b, SP.6.c)*

6. **Sample answer: No; a hurricane that completely destroys some buildings and overturns other buildings has caused catastrophic damage and is most likely a Category 4 or 5 hurricane.** *(DOK Level: 2; Content Topic: ES.a.2; Practice: SP.3.b)*

LESSON 13

PAGE 120

Relate to the Topic

Many answers are possible. Sample answer: We use oil to heat the house, gas to cook, and gasoline in the car. We can turn the thermostat down in winter and carpool. *(DOK Level: 2; Content Topic: ES.a.1; Practice: SP.3.b)*

Reading Strategy

1. **Answers will vary. Sample answer: I watched a television program about how scientists use computer models to learn about climate change.** *(DOK Level: 2; Content Topic: ES.a.1; Practice: SP.6.c)*

2. **Answers will vary. Sample answer: More snow in the mountains and more ice at the poles might melt, raising water levels in rivers, lakes, and the oceans, and increasing the risk of severe floods.** *(DOK Level: 2; Content Topic: ES.a.1, ES.b.1; Practice: SP.3.c)*

PAGE 122

1. **A** *(DOK Level: 2; Content Topic: ES.a.1, ES.b.1; Practice: SP.3.b)*

2. **A** *(DOK Level: 2; Content Topic: ES.a.1, ES.b.1; Practice: SP.3.b)*

PAGE 123

1. **all over the world** *(DOK Level: 2; Content Topic: ES.b.1; Practice: SP.1.b)*

2. **a building (house) with plants (green)** *(DOK Level: 2; Content Topic: ES.b.1; Practice: SP.1.b)*

PAGES 124–125

1. **atmosphere** *(DOK Level: 1; Content Topic: ES.b.1; Practice: SP.1.b)*

2. **climate change** *(DOK Level: 1; Content Topic: ES.b.1; Practice: SP.1.b)*

3. **infrared radiation** *(DOK Level: 1; Content Topic: ES.b.1; Practice: SP.1.b)*

4. **greenhouse effect** *(DOK Level: 1; Content Topic: ES.b.1; Practice: SP.1.b)*

5. **fossil fuels** *(DOK Level: 1; Content Topic: ES.a.1; Practice: SP.1.b)*

6. **Radiant energy warms you when you sit out in the sun.** *(DOK Level: 1; Content Topic: ES.c.2, P.a.4; Practice: SP.1.a)*

7. **The greenhouse effect traps heat in the atmosphere the way a blanket traps heat.** *(DOK Level: 2; Content Topic: ES.b.1; Practice: SP.3.b)*

8. **carbon dioxide, ozone, chlorofluorocarbons (CFCs), methane, and nitrogen oxide** *(DOK Level: 1; Content Topic: ES.b.1; Practice: SP.1.b)*

9. **to reduce emissions of greenhouse gases** *(DOK Level: 1; Content Topic: ES.b.1; Practice: SP.1.a)*

10. **D. All of the above** *(DOK Level: 2; Content Topic: ES.a.1, ES.b.1; Practice: SP.3.c, SP.7.a)* All the options are possible effects of continued greenhouse emissions.

11. **A. Trees take in carbon dioxide during the process of photosynthesis.** *(DOK Level: 1; Content Topic: ES.a.3, ES.b.1; Practice: SP.3.b)* This statement explains how planting trees could reduce levels of greenhouse gases. The other options do not link the statements or are not true.

12. **C. The ice caps at the North and South poles melt.** *(DOK Level: 2; Content Topic: ES.a.1, ES.b.1; Practice: SP.3.b)* More water in the oceans would raise the sea level.

13. Industrialized nations have more factories, trucks, cars, and power plants, all of which produce greenhouse gases. *(DOK Level: 2; Content Topic: ES.a.1, ES.a.3; Practice: SP.3.b)*

14. Sample answer: Climate change has the potential to impact everyone on the planet. To be sure about the cause, many scientists and experts should agree and come to similar conclusions. *(DOK Level: 3; Content Topic: ES.a.1, ES.b.1; Practice: SP.3.b)*

PAGES 126–127

1. C. −55 degrees Celsius *(DOK Level: 1; Content Topic: ES.b.1; Practice: SP.1.c, SP.6.b)* According to the diagram, the temperature at the boundary between the troposphere and stratosphere is about −55 degrees Celsius.

2. −45 degrees Celsius *(DOK Level: 1; Content Topic: ES.b.1; Practice: SP.1.c, SP.6.b)*

3. As the altitude in the atmosphere increases, the air pressure decreases. *(DOK Level: 2; Content Topic: ES.b.1; Practice: SP.1.c, SP.3.b, SP.6.c)*

4. In the troposphere and the mesosphere, temperature decreases as altitude increases. In the stratosphere and thermosphere, temperature increases as altitude increases. *(DOK Level: 2; Content Topic: ES.b.1; Practice: SP.1.c, SP.3.b, SP.6.c)*

5. The concentration of carbon dioxide increased by 16 parts per million from 1990 to 2000. *(DOK Level: 1; Content Topic: ES.b.1; Practice: SP.1.c, SP.6.b)*

6. The carbon dioxide level has steadily increased from 1960 to 2010. *(DOK Level: 2; Content Topic: ES.b.1; Practice: SP.1.c, SP.3.b)*

7. Sample answer: The carbon dioxide level will be between 410–415 parts per million if levels continue to rise at the same rate. *(DOK Level: 2; Content Topic: ES.b.1; Practice: SP.1.c, SP.3.c)*

LESSON 14

PAGE 128

Relate to the Topic

Many answers are possible. Sample answer: My tap water comes from a reservoir. If I had no tap water, I would buy bottled water from a supermarket. *(DOK Level: 1; Content Topic: ES.a.3; Practice: SP.6.c)*

Reading Strategy

1. Glaciers are large masses of ice that form where more snow falls than melts. *(DOK Level: 1; Content Topic: ES.a.3; Practice: SP.1.a, SP.1.b)*

2. reservoir *(DOK Level: 1; Content Topic: ES.a.3; Practice: SP.1.a, SP.1.b)*

PAGE 130

A *(DOK Level: 2; Content Topic: ES.a.3; Practice: SP.1.a, SP.3.b)*

PAGE 131

B *(DOK Level: 2; Content Topic: ES.a.3; Practice: SP.1.c)*

PAGES 132–133

1. renewable resource *(DOK Level: 1; Content Topic: ES.a.3; Practice: SP.1.b)*

2. groundwater *DOK Level: 1; Content Topic: ES.a.3; Practice: SP.1.b*

3. resource *DOK Level: 1; Content Topic: ES.a.3; Practice: SP.1.b*

4. Glaciers *DOK Level: 1; Content Topic: ES.a.3; Practice: SP.1.b*

5. water cycle *DOK Level: 1; Content Topic: ES.a.1; Practice: SP.1.b*

6. from the mountains in the northern part of the state and from other states *(DOK Level: 1; Content Topic: ES.a.3; Practice: SP.1.a)*

7. rivers, lakes, precipitation, and groundwater *(DOK Level: 1; Content Topic: ES.a.3; Practice: SP.1.a)*

8. A drought occurs when not enough precipitation falls on an area. *(DOK Level: 1; Content Topic: ES.a.2, ES.b.3; Practice: SP.1.a)*

9. Any two of the following: take shorter showers; fix leaky faucets; install low-flow toilets; run the washing machine and dishwasher only with full loads; if doing dishes by hand, don't run the water continuously; turn off water when brushing teeth *(DOK Level: 2; Content Topic: ES.a.3; Practice: SP.1.a)*

10. A. There is too little precipitation in the northern part of the state. *(DOK Level: 2; Content Topic: ES.a.2, ES.b.3; Practice: SP.3.b)* Since California gets most of its water from the northern mountains, dry weather there will result in a statewide drought.

11. D. Some areas get too much precipitation, while others do not get enough. *(DOK Level: 2; Content Topic: ES.a.3; Practice: SP.3.b)* According to the article, water shortages are caused by the uneven distribution of rainfall in the United States. Even though there may be plenty of water on average, there is not enough in specific areas, depending in part on their population and water use.

12. B. It carries water from the Owens River to Los Angeles. *(DOK Level: 2; Content Topic: ES.a.3; Practice: SP.1.c)* The map shows that the Los Angeles Aqueduct carries water from the southern end of the Owens River to Los Angeles.

13. Many answers are possible. Sample answer: Taking the salt out of seawater is one alternative. *(DOK Level: 3; Content Topic: ES.a.3; Practice: SP.3.b)*

14. Many answers are possible. Sample answer: I turn off the water when brushing my teeth and I water the grass only once a week. *(DOK Level: 2; Content Topic: ES.a.3; Practice: SP.6.c)*

PAGES 134–135

1. Sample answers: coal, oil natural gas, nuclear fuel *(DOK Level: 1; Content Topic: ES.a.3; Practice: SP.1.a)*

2. sustainability *(DOK Level: 1; Content Topic: ES.a.3; Practice: SP.1.a)*

3. Sample answer; Wind is a renewable energy resource because it cannot be used up. There will always be more wind. *(DOK Level: 2; Content Topic: ES.a.3; Practice: SP.1.b)*

4. Garbage is renewable because people are always creating more garbage. *(DOK Level: 2; Content Topic: ES.a.3; Practice: SP.1.a, SP.3.b)*

5. Sample answer: Nonrenewable resources will get harder to find and more expensive. The price of electricity and goods will get higher and poor people won't be able to afford them. *(DOK Level 3; Content Topic: ES.a.3; Practice: SP.3.c)*

6. The solar power option is renewable but the coal power option is not. *(DOK Level: 2; Content Topic: ES.a.3; Practice: SP.1.a, SP.3.b)*

7. in favor of sustainable energy use *(DOK Level: 2; Content Topic: ES.a.3; Practice: SP.1.a)*

8. Responses may describe how their communities already use renewable energy resources or resources that are available to be used in the future (wind, solar, etc.) *(DOD Level: 3; Content Topic: ES.a.3; Practice: SP.6.c)*

LESSON 15

PAGE 136

Relate to the Topic

Many answers are possible. Sample answer: Yes, I would go because I enjoy having new experiences. I would hope to learn whether there is life on the planet. *(DOK Level: 1; Content Topic: ES.c.2; Practice: SP.6.c)*

Reading Strategy

1. Many answers are possible. Sample answer: When was the first space probe to an outer planet launched? *(DOK Level: 1; Content Topic: ES.c.2; Practice: SP.1.a)*

2. under the heading "Uranus and Neptune" *(DOK Level: 1; Content Topic: ES.c.2; Practice: SP.1.a)*

PAGE 138

1. **50** (*DOK Level: 2; Content Topic: ES.c.2; Practice: SP.1.a, SP.1.c*)

2. **84 years** (*DOK Level: 2; Content Topic: ES.c.2; Practice: SP.1.a, SP.1.c*)

PAGE 139

A (*DOK Level: 2; Content Topic: ES.c.2; Practice: SP.1.a, SP.1.c, SP.3.b*)

PAGES 140–141

1. **outer planets**   2. **Space probes**
3. **solar system**   4. **inner planets**
   (*DOK Level: 1; Content Topic: ES.c.2; Practice: SP.1.b*)

5. **C**   6. **B**   7. **E**   8. **A**   9. **D**
   (*DOK Level: 1; Content Topic: ES.c.2; Practice: SP.1.b*)

10. **Mercury, Venus, Earth, Mars, Jupiter, Saturn, Uranus, and Neptune** (*DOK Level: 1; Content Topic: ES.c.2; Practice: SP.1.b*)

11. **We must use space probes because the outer planets are so far away.** (*DOK Level: 1; Content Topic: ES.c.2; Practice: SP.1.a*)

12. **its rings** (*DOK Level: 1; Content Topic: ES.c.2; Practice: SP.1.b*)

13. **C. Uranus** (*DOK Level: 2; Content Topic: ES.c.2; Practice: SP.1.a, SP.1.c, SP.3.a*) According to the table, Saturn is 892 million miles from the sun. Uranus is 1,790 million miles from the sun. This distance is about twice as far from the sun as Saturn's distance.

14. **B. Saturn** (*DOK Level: 2; Content Topic: ES.c.2; Practice: SP.1.a, SP.1.c*) According to the table, Saturn has the most moons, 53.

15. **C. Jupiter** (*DOK Level: 1; Content Topic: ES.c.2; Practice: SP.1.a, SP.6.c*) Jupiter is the only option that is a gas giant like Saturn. Titan is a moon of Saturn and not a planet, and Earth and Mars are rocky inner planets.

16. **Sample answer: Since conglomerate is formed by a process that involves water, I can conclude that water once existed on the surface of Mars.** (*DOK Level: 3; Content Topic: ES.c.2; Practice: SP.1.a, SP.3.b*)

17. **Sample answer: Our knowledge of the solar system would be limited to observations from Earth. For example, Galileo space probe showed that Saturn's rings were in fact made up of thousands of narrow rings, instead of a few very wide rings.** (*DOK Level: 3; Content Topic: ES.c.2; Practice: SP.1.a, SP.3.a, SP.3.b*)

PAGES 142–143

1. **side or face** (*DOK Level: 1; Content Topic: ES.c.2; Practice: SP.1.a*)

2. **27** (*DOK Level: 1; Content Topic: ES.c.2; Practice: SP.1.a*)

3. **C. At one time, many space rocks crashed into the moon.** (*DOK Level: 2; Content Topic: ES.c.2; Practice: SP.3.b*) Facts #4 and #10 describe the effects of many impacts from space objects.

4. **B. basketball** (*DOK Level: 2; Content Topic: ES.c.2; Practice: SP.3.b*) Jupiter is about 11 times as large in diameter as Earth.

5. **Sample answer: Both the moon and artificial satellites orbit around Earth.** (*DOK Level 2; Content Topic: ES.c.2; Practice: SP.1.b*)

6. **Sample answer: Earth has life and the moon does not, the moon has no liquid water, and the moon is smaller than Earth** (*DOK Level: 2; Content Topic: ES.c.2; Practice: SP.3.b*)

7. **Sample answer: Hypothesis: Plants can be kept alive on the moon for a year using a greenhouse. Astronauts would carry plants, soil, water, air, and materials to build a greenhouse to the moon on a spaceship. They would live on the moon and try to grow the plants in the greenhouse. If the plants lived for a year, then the hypothesis would be supported.** (*DOK Level: 2; Content Topic: ES.c.2; Practice: SP.2.b, SP.2.d*)

LESSON 16

PAGE 144

Relate to the Topic

Many answers are possible. Sample answer: near things: people, rocks, water; distant things: stars, gases, planets *(DOK Level: 3; Content Topic: ES.c.1; Practice: SP.1.a, SP.1.b, SP.7.a)*

Many answers are possible. Sample answer: new planets, stars, and forms of life *(DOK Level: 3; Content Topic: ES.c.1; Practice: SP.1.a, SP.1.b, SP.3.c)*

Reading Strategy

1. **how stars develop** *(DOK Level: 2; Content Topic: ES.c.1; Practice: SP.1.c)*

2. **nebula** *(DOK Level: 2; Content Topic: ES.c.1; Practice: SP.1.c)*

PAGE 145

A *(DOK Level: 2; Content Topic: ES.c.1; Practice: SP.1.a, SP.1.b)*

PAGE 147

1. **supernova** *(DOK Level: 2; Content Topic: ES.c.1; Practice: SP.1.a, SP.1.b, SP.1.c)*

2. **The universe is bigger in the future.** *(DOK Level: 2; Content Topic: ES.c.1; Practice: SP.1.a, SP.1.b, SP.1.c)*

PAGES 148–149

1. **constellation** *(DOK Level: 1; Content Topic: ES.c.1; Practice: SP.1.a, SP.1.b)*

2. **galaxy** *(DOK Level: 1; Content Topic: ES.c.1; Practice: SP.1.a, SP.1.b)*

3. **black dwarf** *(DOK Level: 1; Content Topic: ES.c.1; Practice: SP.1.a, SP.1.b)*

4. **universe** *(DOK Level: 1; Content Topic: ES.c.1; Practice: SP.1.a, SP.1.b)*

5. **C** *(DOK Level: 1; Content Topic: ES.c.1; Practice: SP.1.a,, SP.1.b)*

6. **D** *(DOK Level: 1; Content Topic: ES.c.1; Practice: SP.1.a, SP.1.b)*

7. **A** *(DOK Level: 1; Content Topic: ES.c.1; Practice: SP.1.a, SP.1.b)*

8. **E** *(DOK Level: 1; Content Topic: ES.c.1; Practice: SP.1.a, SP.1.b)*

9. **B** *(DOK Level: 1; Content Topic: ES.c.1; Practice: SP.1.a, SP.1.b)*

10. **13.7 billion years** *(DOK Level: 1; Content Topic: ES.c.1; Practice: SP.1.a, SP.1.b, SP.6.b)*

11. **The big bang theory is the most widely accepted idea of how the universe developed. It states that the universe began as a single hot, dense, point that violently started to expand. Over time it expanded more and cooled to start forming gas, dust, and space structures.** *(DOK Level: 2; Content Topic: ES.c.1; Practice: SP.1.a, SP.1.b, SP.7.a)*

12. **D. white dwarf** *(DOK Level: 2; Content Topic: ES.c.1; Practice: SP.1.a, SP.1.b, SP.1.c)* According to the chart, a low to average mass star goes from a red giant to a white dwarf.

13. **A. It will get bigger.** *(DOK Level: 3; Content Topic: ES.c.1; Practice: SP.1.a, SP.1.b, SP.1.c, SP.3.c)* The diagram shows that the universe is expanding.

14. **C. as a star** *(DOK Level: 1; Content Topic: ES.c.1; Practice: SP.1.a, SP.1.b, SP.7.a)* A star is a sphere of hot gases that emits its own light.

15. **Many answers are possible. Sample answer: I saw a group of stars in a pattern known as Ursa Major that includes the Big Dipper. I could use it to find my way or find north.** *(DOK Level: 3; Content Topic: ES.c.1; Practice: SP.1.a, SP.1.b, SP.7.a)*

16. **Many answers are possible. Sample answer: Understanding how the universe developed could help us understand Earth and the sun better and predict how they might change.** *(DOK Level: 3; Content Topic: ES.c.1; Practice: SP.1.a, SP.7.a)*

PAGES 150–151

1. **C. 5 billion years** *(DOK Level: 1; Content Topic: ES.c.1; Practice: SP.1.a)* Many scientists believe that the Sun is about half-way through its life cycle and will become a white dwarf star in about 5 billion years.

2. **MAXI** *(DOK Level: 1; Content Topic: ES.c.1; Practice: SP.1.a)*

3. **16** *(DOK Level: 1; Content Topic: ES.c.1; Practice: SP.1.a)*

4. Sample answer: MAXI gathered data from the explosion of a nova and a gamma-ray burst from the possible collapse of a huge star. *(DOK Level: 1; Content Topic: ES.c.1; Practice: SP.1.a)*

5. Sample answer: The ISS program is a world-wide space project and any data gathered from it should be available to scientists from all over the world, too. *(DOK Level: 2; Content Topic: ES.c.1; Practice: SP.1.a, SP.3.b)*

6. Sample answer: The exploration of space helps us to expand technology, create new industries and careers, learn about the universe we live in, and cooperate with other nations. *(DOK Level: 2; Content Topic: ES.c.1; Practice: SP.3.b, SP.6.c)*

7. Sample answer: Peer review is important in ensuring the quality and accuracy of conclusions drawn from data. *(DOK Level: 2; Content Topic: ES.c.1; Practice: SP.1.a, SP.3.b)*

8. Sample answer: I should review my own analysis first to see if I need to make any revisions. If not, I should share my analysis with the other group to try to understand why the two analyses differ. *(DOK Level: 2; Content Topic: ES.c.1; Practice: SP.1.a, SP.3.b, SP.5.a)*

SCIENCE AT WORK

PAGE 153

1. D. sand and rock dust *(DOK Level: 1; Content Topic: ES.a.3; Practice: SP.1.a)*

2. B. to make sure rain and splash water don't collect around the pool *(DOK Level: 1; Content Topic: ES.a.1; Practice: SP.1.a)*

3. Many answers are possible. Sample answer: We have a new apartment building going up in my neighborhood. There are construction workers there all the time. First they leveled the ground and then dug a hole for the foundation. Now they are nailing lumber to form the skeleton for the building. There have been many safety issues for them to consider. At the beginning of the project they used huge, noisy machines to do most of the work. They had to be careful that nobody was in the way of the machines, and they wore earmuffs. Now they must also be careful when using hammers and nail guns. *(DOK Level: 2; Content Topic: ES.a.1; Practice: SP.1.a)*

UNIT 2 REVIEW

PAGES 154–157

1. 90s *(DOK Level: 2; Content Topic: ES.b.1; Practice: SP.1.c, SP.6.b)*

2. showers *(DOK Level: 2; Content Topic: ES.b.1; Practice: SP.1.b, SP.1.c)*

3. B. hot, with showers *(DOK Level: 2; Content Topic: ES.b.3; Practice: SP.1.c)* The map shows diagonal lines along the stationary front. According to the key, these lines indicate showers. The map also shows temperatures in the 80s, which is hot.

4. About 75 Dobson Units *(DOK Level: 2; Content Topic: ES.b.1; Practice: SP.6.b)*

5. A. Thinning of the ozone layer allows more ultraviolet rays to get through to Earth's surface. *(DOK Level: 2; Content Topic: ES.b.1; Practice: SP.3.a, SP.3.c)* According to the text, ultraviolet rays can cause skin cancer. When the ozone layer is thinner, more ultraviolet rays can reach Earth and cause more cases of skin cancer.

6. D. Its thickness decreased most rapidly between 1976 and 1992. *(DOK Level: 2; Content Topic: ES.b.1; Practice: SP.3.b)* The graph shows a general decline in the thickness of the ozone layer between 1956 and 2000. To find the years when the thickness of the ozone layer decreased most rapidly, you have to find the portion of the graph with the steepest downward slope. The graph shows it was from 1978 to 1989.

7. continental shelf *(DOK Level: 1; Content Topic: ES.b.2; Practice: SP.1.a)*

8. C. waters of the continental-shelf region *(DOK Level: 2; Content Topic: ES.b.2; Practice: SP.1.a)* According to the article, these waters have the richest fishing.

9. **D. continental shelf, continental slope, ocean basin** *(DOK Level: 2; Content Topic: ES.b.2; Practice: SP.3.b)* The continental shelf is where the oceans meet the continents. The continental slope lies between the continental shelf and the ocean basin.

10. **D. Shellfish are harvested from the continental shelf.** *(DOK Level: 2; Content Topic: ES.b.2; Practice: SP.4.a)* Because we get shellfish from the continental shelf, you can conclude that polluting the water in this area will hurt the shellfish industry.

11. **The intense energy is produced by nuclear reactions in the core of the sun.** *(DOK Level: 1; Content Topic: ES.c.2; Practice: SP.6.c, SP.7.a)*

12. **C. the surface** *(DOK Level: 2; Content Topic: ES.c.1; Practice: SP.1.c, SP.3.b)* Since Altair and the sun are similar in size and age, they have a similar structure. The diagram shows that the coolest part of the sun is the surface; applying this information to Altair, you can see that the surface would be the coolest part of this star as well.

Science Extension

Many answers are possible. Sample answer for a hurricane: Bring outdoor furniture and objects indoors. Tape up windows to prevent breakage. Stock up on food and water for a few days. Stock up on flashlights, batteries, and candles in case of power outage. Follow instructions if evacuating is recommended.

Unit 2 Mini-Test

PAGES 158–159

1. **B. greater in the western half of Oregon than in the eastern half of Oregon.** *(DOK Level: 2; Content Topic: ES.b.3; Practice: SP.1.c, SP.3.b)* The map shows that most of the western half of Oregon receives more than 20 inches of precipitation in an average year. Most of the eastern half receives less.

2. **B. Desert plants are found mostly in the eastern half of Oregon.** *(DOK Level: 2; Content Topic: ES.b.3; Practice: SP.1.c, SP.3.b)* The map shows that most of the eastern half of Oregon receives less than 20 inches of rain annually, meaning that this region is relatively dry; the western half of Oregon, on the other hand, generally receives 20 or more inches of rain per year, with large portions receiving more than 60 inches of rain. Therefore, you can infer that desert plants would be found mostly in eastern Oregon. The other options are contradicted by information on the map.

3. **B. Every year Saudi Arabia removes about one-ninetieth of its petroleum reserves** *(DOK Level: 2; Content Topic: ES.a.3; Practice: SP.3.c, SP.4.a)* If Saudi Arabia removes one-ninetieth of its petroleum from the ground each year, it will take less than 100 years to deplete its known reserves.

4. **B. The first fossil is older than the second fossil.** *(DOK Level: 2; Content Topic: ES.c.3; Practice: SP.7.a)* The first fossil comes from a rock layer that is lower than the rock containing the second fossil. Based on the principle of superimposition, the first fossil is older than the second fossil.

5. **D. 32 °F at 1,000 feet, 29 °F at 2,000 feet, and 25 °F at 3,000 feet** *(DOK Level: 2; Content Topic: ES.b.1; Practice: SP.6.b)* This is the only option that shows a decrease in temperatures as altitude increases.

6. **C. Earth is the most beautiful planet.** *(DOK Level: 2; Content Topic: ES.b.1; Practice: SP.3.b)* This is a belief that cannot be proved true or false.

7. **A. Venus** *(DOK Level: 2; Content Topic: ES.c.2; Practice: SP.3.b)* It takes 243 Earth days for Venus to rotate on its axis. This means that a day-night cycle on Venus is many Earth-months long.

8. **B. 3,800 miles** *(DOK Level: 2; Content Topic: ES.c.2; Practice: SP.6.b)* $8,000 - 4,200 = 3,800$

UNIT 3: PHYSICAL SCIENCE
LESSON 17

PAGE 162

Relate to the Topic

Many answers are possible. Sample answer: We have hand soap, dish detergent, spot removers, laundry detergent, bleach, glass cleaners, tile cleaners, toilet-bowl cleaners, abrasive cleaners for the sinks, and floor polish. We dilute bleach with water because bleach is a harsh cleanser. *(DOK Level: 2; Content Topic: P.c.3, P.c.4; Practice: SP.6.c)*

Reading Strategy

1. **different forms of matter** *(DOK Level: 1; Content Topic: P.c.1; Practice: SP.6.c)*

2. **mixtures, compounds, and elements** *(DOK Level: 1; Content Topic: P.c.1; Practice: SP.6.c)*

PAGE 164

1. **nitrogen and hydrogen** *(DOK Level: 2; Content Topic: P.c.1; Practice: SP.1.b)*

2. **one nitrogen atom and three hydrogen atoms** *(DOK Level: 2; Content Topic: P.c.1; Practice: SP.1.b, SP.6.b)*

PAGE 165

1. **A, C** 2. **B, C, D**

3. **four** 4. **C**

(DOK Level: 2; Content Topic: P.c.1; Practice: SP.1.b, SP.6.b, SP.6.c)

PAGES 166–167

1. **element** *(DOK Level: 1; Content Topic: P.c.1, P.c.2, P.c.3, P.c.4; Practice: SP.1.b)*

2. **mixture** *(DOK Level: 1; Content Topic: P.c.1, P.c.2, P.c.3, P.c.4; Practice: SP.1.b)*

3. **chemical reaction** *(DOK Level: 1; Content Topic: P.c.1, P.c.2, P.c.3, P.c.4; Practice: SP.1.b)*

4. **substance** *(DOK Level: 1; Content Topic: P.c.1, P.c.2, P.c.3, P.c.4; Practice: SP.1.b)*

5. **atom** *(DOK Level: 1; Content Topic: P.c.1, P.c.2, P.c.3, P.c.4; Practice: SP.1.b)*

6. **compound** *(DOK Level: 1; Content Topic: P.c.1, P.c.2, P.c.3, P.c.4; Practice: SP.1.b)*

7. **B** 8. **A** 9. **B** 10. **A** 11. **B**
(DOK Level: 1; Content Topic: P.c.2, P.c.3; Practice: SP.1.a, SP.1.b)

12. **C. hydrogen and oxygen** *(DOK Level: 2; Content Topic: P.c.2; Practice: SP.1.a, SP.1.b)* H is the chemical symbol for the element hydrogen, and O is the chemical symbol for the element oxygen.

13. **B. magnesium sulfide** *(DOK Level: 1; Content Topic: P.c.2; Practice: SP.1.a, SP.1.b)* When a compound is made of just two elements, the suffix -*ide* is added to the root of the second element.

14. **C. oxygen** *(DOK Level: 1; Content Topic: P.c.2; Practice: SP.1.a)* The suffix -*ate* means that the compound has oxygen.

15. **Paint prevents the oxygen in the air from reacting with the iron in the steel.** *(DOK Level: 2; Content Topic: P.c.3; Practice: SP.3.b)*

16. **Many answers are possible. Sample answer: chlorine bleach (NaOCl), to brighten white fabrics; ammonia (NH$_3$), to wash floors; baking soda (NaHCO$_3$), to clean porcelain surfaces (stovetop, sink)** *(DOK Level: 3; Content Topic: P.c.3; Practice: SP.6.c)*

PAGES 168–169

1. **oxygen, carbon, hydrogen, nitrogen** *(DOK Level: 1; Content Topic: P.c.1; Practice: SP.1.c)*

2. **oxygen, silicon, calcium, potassium** *(DOK Level: 1; Content Topic: P.c.1; Practice: SP.1.c)*

3. **Sample answer: Oxygen, carbon, hydrogen, and nitrogen are the most common elements in the human body, while the four most common in Earth's crust are oxygen, silicon, calcium, and potassium. Oxygen is found in the greatest percentage in both the human body and Earth's crust. Carbon, hydrogen, and nitrogen are present in much smaller percentages in Earth's crust than in the human body. Silicon, calcium, and potassium are found in much smaller percentages in the human body than in Earth's crust.** *(DOK Level: 2; Content Topic: P.c.1; Practice: SP.3.b)*

4. **Sample answer: SiO$_2$ is most likely an inorganic compound because it does not contain any carbon. Also, most compounds in Earth's crust are inorganic.** *(DOK Level: 2; Content Topic: P.c.1; Practice: SP.1.a, SP.3.b, SP.7.a)*

5. **Sample answer: Hydrogen is usually found along with carbon in organic compounds. So if the sample has very little hydrogen, it is likely inorganic. If it contains moderate levels of hydrogen, it is likely organic.** *(DOK Level 2; Content Topic: P.c.1; Practice: SP.1.a, SP.3.b, SP.7.a)*

6. **C. 600** *(DOK Level: 2; Content Topic: P.c.1; Practice: SP.6.b, SP.8.b)* Nitrogen makes up 3 percent of the human body and 0.005 percent of Earth's crust; $3 \div 0.005 = 600$

7. **B. Calcium is found in roughly the same percentage in the human body and Earth's crust.** *(DOK Level: 2; Content Topic: P.c.1; Practice: SP.4.a)* Calcium makes up 1 percent of the human body and 4 percent of Earth's crust. The other options are not supported by the data in the table.

LESSON 18

PAGE 170

Relate to the Topic

Many answers are possible. Sample answer: My favorite cooked food is mashed potatoes. When the potatoes are raw, they are very firm solids. After you boil them, they soften and become hot. Mashing breaks them down into smaller particles and makes them even softer. *(DOK Level: 1; Content Topic: P.c.2; Practice: SP.6.c)*

Reading Strategy

1. **one shows ice cubes melting; the other shows water boiling** *(DOK Level: 1; Content Topic: P.c.2; Practice: SP.1.c)*

2. **hotdogs and hamburgers being grilled** *(DOK Level: 1; Content Topic: P.c.2; Practice: SP.1.c)*

PAGE 172

A *(DOK Level: 1; Content Topic: P.c.2; Practice: SP.1.a)*

PAGE 173

1. **chemical change** *(DOK Level: 1; Content Topic: P.c.2; Practice: SP.1.b)*

2. **physical change** *(DOK Level: 1; Content Topic: P.c.2; Practice: SP.1.b)*

PAGES 174–175

1. **solid** *(DOK Level: 1; Content Topic: P.c.2; Practice: SP.1.b)*

2. **liquid** *(DOK Level: 1; Content Topic: P.c.2; Practice: SP.1.b)*

3. **gas** *(DOK Level: 1; Content Topic: P.c.2; Practice: SP.1.b)*

4. **physical change** *(DOK Level: 1; Content Topic: P.c.2; Practice: SP.1.b)*

5. **chemical change** *(DOK Level: 1; Content Topic: P.c.2; Practice: SP.1.b)*

6. **solid—ice; liquid—water; gas—water vapor or steam** *(DOK Level: 1; Content Topic: P.c.2; Practice: SP.1.a, SP.1.b)*

7. **B**   8. **D**   9. **A**   10. **C**
(DOK Level: 1; Content Topic: P.c.2; Practice: SP.1.a, SP.1.b)

11. **physical change** *(DOK Level: 1; Content Topic: P.c.2; Practice: SP.1.a, SP.1.b)*

12. **chemical change** *(DOK Level: 1; Content Topic: P.c.2; Practice: SP.1.a, SP.1.b)*

13. **D. Chemical and Physical Changes in Cooking** *(DOK Level: 2; Content Topic: P.c.2; Practice: SP.1.a)* This title covers all the topics discussed in the article. Options 1–3 are too specific. They cover only parts of the article, so they are incorrect.

14. **D. a physical change** *(DOK Level: 2; Content Topic: P.c.2; Practice: SP.1.a)* The chocolate melted, a physical change from solid to liquid.

15. **D. baking a cake** *(DOK Level: 1; Content Topic: P.c.2; Practice: SP.1.a)* Baking a cake involves chemical changes in the liquid batter as it sets. Options 1–3 are all physical changes, so they are incorrect.

16. **Many answers are possible. Sample answers: freezing leftovers, boiling water, melting chocolate, defrosting a turkey, melting snow, dew** *(DOK Level: 1; Content Topic: P.c.2; Practice: SP.3.b)*

17. **Many answers are possible. Sample answer: I made pancake batter and cooked the pancakes on a griddle. A chemical change took place as the batter set into solid pancakes. I put butter on top and it melted, a physical change.** *(DOK Level: 3; Content Topic: P.c.2; Practice: SP.3.b)*

PAGES 176–177

1. **Sample answer: A. The ice will gradually get thicker the longer the air temperature stays below freezing; B. The more salt you add to the water, the longer it will take to boil; C. The warmer the water, the longer it will take to freeze.** *(DOK Level 2; Content Topic: P.c.2; Practice: SP.2.b)*

2. **Sample answers: A. independent variable: days below freezing; dependent variable: thickness of pond ice; B. independent variable: how much salt is in the water; dependent variable: how long the water takes to boil; C. independent variable: starting temperature of water; dependent variable: how long it takes to freeze** *(DOK Level: 2; Content Topic: P.c.2; Practice: SP.2.e)*

3. **Answers will vary. Responses should include a question related to changes in matter and briefly describe an investigation to answer the question.** *(DOK Level: 3; Content Topic: P.c.2; Practice: SP.2.d).*

4. **Answers will vary. Responses should include a prediction for the experiment designed in Question 3.** *(DOK Level: 2; Content Topic: P.c.2; Practice: SP.1.a, SP.2.b)*

5. **Answers will vary. Responses should identify the independent and dependent variables for the experiment designed for Question 3.** *(DOK Level: 2; Content Topic: P.c.2; Practice: SP.1.a, SP.2.e).*

LESSON 19

PAGE 178

Relate to the Topic
Many answers are possible. Sample answer: orange juice, hot cocoa; I think they are mixtures because I mix the ingredients together

when I make them. *(DOK Level: 1; Content Topic: P.c.4; Practice: SP.6.c)*

Reading Strategy

1. **the solubility of some solids in water** *(DOK Level: 1; Content Topic: P.c.4; Practice: SP.1.c)*

2. **solubility and temperature** *(DOK Level: 1; Content Topic: P.c.4; Practice: SP.1.c)*

PAGE 180

1. **B** 2. **B**
(DOK Level: 1; Content Topic: P.c.4; Practice: SP.1.a)

PAGE 181

1. **A** 2. **B**
(DOK Level: 2; Content Topic: P.c.4; Practice: SP.1.c)

PAGES 182–183

1. **solution** *(DOK Level: 2; Content Topic: P.c.4; Practice: SP.1.b)*

2. **Distillation** *(DOK Level: 2; Content Topic: P.c.4; Practice: SP.1.b)*

3. **solubility** *(DOK Level: 2; Content Topic: P.c.4; Practice: SP.1.b)*

4. **solute** *(DOK Level: 2; Content Topic: P.c.4; Practice: SP.1.b)*

5. **solvent** *(DOK Level: 2; Content Topic: P.c.4; Practice: SP.1.b)*

6. **hot chocolate** *(DOK Level: 2; Content Topic: P.c.4; Practice: SP.1.a)*

7. **instant coffee** *(DOK Level: 2; Content Topic: P.c.4; Practice: SP.1.a)*

8. **brass** *(DOK Level: 2; Content Topic: P.c.4; Practice: SP.1.a)*

9. **A** 10. **B**
(DOK Level: 3; Content Topic: P.c.4; Practice: SP.1.a, SP.1.c)

11. **C. A solvent is present in a greater amount in a solution, and a solute in a lesser amount.** *(DOK Level: 1; Content Topic: P.c.4; Practice: SP.1.a)* When two substances are mixed together in a solution, the solvent is the substance of which there is more.

12. **B. They are all mixtures.** *(DOK Level: 1; Content Topic: P.c.4; Practice: SP.1.a)* Even though these substances are in different states of matter, they all consist of mixtures of various substances.

13. **C. 6 ounces** *(DOK Level: 2; Content Topic: P.c.4; Practice: SP.1.c)* The answer can be found by reading the solubility curve of sucrose (sugar) on the graph on page 181.

14. **The water is the solvent, and the grape powder and sugar are the solutes. When I added water to the solutes, very little dissolved at first. Stirring for a few minutes made the grape powder and sugar mix evenly throughout the water.** *(DOK Level: 2; Content Topic: P.c.4; Practice: SP.3.c, SP.6.c)*

15. **Many answers are possible. Sample answer: I left a soft drink out on the counter and when I returned for it a few hours later, all the fizz was gone. The carbon dioxide gas that had been in solution had escaped.** *(DOK Level: 1; Content Topic: P.c.4; Practice: SP.6.c)*

PAGES 184–185

1. **solvent** *(DOK Level: 1; Content Topic: P.c.4; Practice: SP.1.b)*

2. **heterogeneous** *(DOK Level: 1; Content Topic: P.c.4; Practice: SP.1.b)*

3. **Sample answer: Clouds are mixtures of water droplets in air; ocean water is a mixture of salt, water, and minerals; mountains are made of rocks, which are mixtures of minerals and other substances.** *(DOK Level: 2; Content Topic: P.c.4; Practice: SP.6.c)*

4. **Sample answer: Rivers and streams all over the world wash over the land and dissolve every kind of mineral, then flow down and join the ocean.** *(DOK Level: 2; Content Topic: P.c.4; Practice: SP.6.c).*

5. **Sample answer: It could still be a mixture if apple juice were a solution of different substances in water.** *(DOK Level 2; Content Topic: P.c.4; Practice: SP.1.b)*

6. **Answers will vary. Students should describe homogeneous mixtures such as beverages and heterogeneous mixtures such as sandwiches or pizza.** *(DOK Level: 2; Content Topic: P.c.4; Practice: SP.1.b)*

7. **C. orange juice with pulp** *(DOK Level: 2; Content Topic: P.c.4; Practice: SP.1.b)* The bits of pulp are not dissolved in the juice, so it is a heterogeneous mixture.

LESSON 20

PAGE 186

Relate to the Topic

Many answers are possible. Sample answer: Once a potholder I was using caught fire on the stove. I put out the fire by dropping the potholder in the sink and turning on the water. *(DOK Level: 1; Content Topic: P.a.1; Practice: SP.6.c)*

Reading Strategy

1. **hydrogen and carbon** *(DOK Level: 1; Content Topic: P.a.4; Practice: SP.1.a)*

2. **the temperature needed for a substance to burn** *(DOK Level: 1; Content Topic: P.a.1; Practice: SP.1.a)*

PAGE 188

B *(DOK Level: 1; Content Topic: P.a.4; Practice: SP.3.c)*

PAGE 189

A *(DOK Level: 1; Content Topic: P.a.4; Practice: SP.1.a)*

PAGES 190–191

1. **combustion** *(DOK Level: 1; Content Topic: P.a.1; Practice: SP.1.b)*

2. **hydrocarbon** *(DOK Level: 1; Content Topic: P.a.4; Practice: SP.1.b)*

3. **activation energy** *(DOK Level: 1; Content Topic: P.a.4; Practice: SP.1.b)*

4. **kindling temperature** *(DOK Level: 1; Content Topic: P.a.4; Practice: SP.1.b)*

5. **oxygen** *(DOK Level: 1; Content Topic: P.a.4; Practice: SP.1.a)*

6. **A** *(DOK Level: 2; Content Topic: P.a.3; Practice: SP.1.a)*

7. **A, B, D** *(DOK Level: 2; Content Topic: P.a.4; Practice: SP.1.a)*

8. **A.** *(DOK Level: 2; Content Topic: P.a.4; Practice: SP.1.a)*

9. **D. More fires are caused by small heaters than by built-in heating systems.** *(DOK Level: 2; Content Topic: P.a.4; Practice: SP.3.c)* Small portable heaters are more likely to be placed near flammable objects or knocked over. In both cases, a fire is possible. Built-in heaters do not get as hot and can't be knocked over.

10. **B. The pollutants released by incomplete combustion would eventually overcome the people in the room.** *(DOK Level: 2; Content Topic: P.a.4; Practice: SP.3.c)* Combustion uses oxygen. When the oxygen in the room gets low, people will have trouble breathing. In addition, combustion will be incomplete, producing deadly carbon monoxide and other pollutants.

11. **B. Over time, people have burned fuels for many purposes.** *(DOK Level: 1; Content Topic: P.a.3; Practice: SP.3.b)* The first paragraph gives an overview of people's use of combustion over the course of history. The other options are too specific.

12. **Many answers are possible. Sample answers: Heaters should be placed out of traffic and away from anything that might catch fire. Keep a door or window open when using a combustion heater. Use high-quality kerosene in a portable heater.** *(DOK Level: 2; Content Topic: P.a.4; Practice: SP.3.b)*

13. **Many answers are possible. Sample answer: Our car has a combustion engine that uses gasoline as fuel, and it produces pollutants.** *(DOK Level: 3; Content Topic: P.a.4; Practice: SP.6.c)*

PAGES 192–193

1. **fuel** *(DOK Level: 1; Content Topic: P.c.3; Practice: SP.1.b)*

2. **the heat of combustion from the existing fire** *(DOK Level: 2; Content Topic: P.c.3; Practice: SP.1.a)*

3. **Wind carries sparks across the water, providing the activation energy for the plants on the other side of the stream to**

ignite. *(DOK Level: 2; Content Topic: P.c.3; Practice: SP.1.a)*

4. **Incomplete combustion; dark smoke in visible in the photograph** *(DOK Level: 2; Content Topic: P.c.3; Practice: SP.3.b)*

5. **Carbon dioxide and water** *(DOK Level 2; Content Topic: P.c.3; Practice: SP.3.c)*

6. **Sample answers: Use water to cool the fire below the kindling temperature, remove fuel by pulling away (or burning) plant material, cover the fire with something that prevents oxygen from reaching the fire** *(DOK Level: 3; Content Topic: P.c.3; Practice: SP.7.a)*

7. **Sample answers: Keep fuel away from the house, maintain a supply of water for fighting fires, make the house from non-combustible materials** *(DOK Level: 3; Content Topic: P.c.3; Practice: SP.7.a)*

8. **Sample answer: Both are examples of combustion and produce mostly heat, water, and carbon dioxide. Using a heater is a controlled reaction that produces little pollution. The wildfire is uncontrolled and produces smoke and ash.** *(DOK Level: 2; Content Topic: P.c.3; Practice: SP.6.c)*

LESSON 21
PAGE 194

Relate to the Topic

Many answers are possible. Sample answer: to cook food, to keep my room warm *(DOK Level: 2; Content Topic: P.a.1; Practice: SP.6.c)*

Many answers are possible. Sample answer: Because the air was very hot this morning, I wore shorts and didn't wear a jacket. *(DOK Level: 2; Content Topic: P.a.1; Practice: SP.6.c)*

Reading Strategy

1. **What is temperature?** *(DOK Level: 2; Content Topic: ES.c.3; Practice: SP.1.a, SP.1.b)*

2. **How are heat and work related?** *(DOK Level: 2; Content Topic: ES.c.3; Practice: SP.1.a, SP.1.b)*

PAGE 195

A *(DOK Level: 2; Content Topic: P.a.1; Practice: SP.1.a, SP.3.b, SP.7.a)*

PAGE 197

B *(DOK Level: 2; Content Topic: P.a.1; Practice: SP.1.a, SP.1.b)*

PAGES 198–199

1. **kinetic energy** *(DOK Level: 1; Content Topic: P.a.1; Practice: SP.1.a, SP.1.b)*
2. **Temperature** *(DOK Level: 1; Content Topic: P.a.1; Practice: SP.1.a, SP.1.b)*
3. **radiation** *(DOK Level: 1; Content Topic: P.a.1; Practice: SP.1.a, SP.1.b)*
4. **Convection** *(DOK Level: 1; Content Topic: P.a.1; Practice: SP.1.a, SP.1.b)*
5. **heat** *(DOK Level: 1; Content Topic: P.a.1; Practice: SP.1.a, SP.1.b)*
6. **conduction, convection, and radiation** *(DOK Level: 2; Content Topic: P.a.1; Practice: SP.1.a, SP.1.b)*
7. **B** *(DOK Level: 1; Content Topic: P.a.1; Practice: SP.1.a, SP.1.b)*
8. **The transfer of heat can result in work being done. For example, heat transfer in a car's engine causes a piston to move.** *(DOK Level: 1; Content Topic: P.a.1; Practice: SP.1.a, SP.1.b)*
9. **B. Your finger gets warmer when you hold it near a candle flame.** *(DOK Level: 2; Content Topic: P.a.1; Practice: SP.1.a, SP.1.b, SP.7.a)* The other options are examples of heat transfer by conduction.
10. **C. Heat will flow from the copper block to the iron block.** *(DOK Level: 2; Content Topic: P.a.1; Practice: SP.1.a, SP.1.b, SP.3.c)* Heat flows from a warmer object to a cooler object.
11. **B. convection** *(DOK Level: 2; Content Topic: P.a.1; Practice: SP.1.a, SP.1.b, SP.7.a)* The air in the balloon is a fluid, and heat is transferred among the particles in the air by convection.

12. **Many answers are possible. Sample answer: Thermal energy is the energy of the moving particles in an object. Heat, however, is the flow of this thermal energy from the particles in one object to the particles in another object.** *(DOK Level: 2; Content Topic: P.a.1; Practice: SP.1.a)*
13. **Many answers are possible. Sample answer: I burned my finger as a result of conduction when I touched a hot iron.** *(DOK Level: 2; Content Topic: P.a.1; Practice: SP.1.a, SP.1.b, SP.7.a)*

PAGES 200–201

1. **C. 1,000 calories.** *(DOK Level: 1; Content Topic: P.a.1; Practice: SP.1.a)* The prefix *kilo* means 1,000, so 1 kilocalorie equals 1,000 calories.
2. **93 Calories** *(DOK Level: 2; Content Topic: P.a.1; Practice: SP.1.a, SP.6.b, SP.7.b, SP.8.b)*
3. **Sample answer: The percentage of fat in this product is high. Since 90 of the 150 Calories contained in each serving come from fat, the fat percentage is 60%.** *(DOK Level: 2; Content Topic: P.a.1; Practice: SP.1.c, SP.3.b, SP.6.b)*
4. **Sample answer: about 375 Calories** *(DOK Level: 2; Content Topic: P.a.1; Practice: SP.1.c, SP.3.b, SP.6.b, SP.8.b)*
5. **Sample answer: This food is not a good source of dietary fiber since it contains less than 1 gram of fiber per serving.** *(DOK Level: 2; Content Topic: P.a.1; Practice: SP.1.c, SP.3.b)*
6. **Sample answer: No, because this product contains no calcium.** *(DOK Level: 2; Content Topic: P.a.1; Practice: SP.1.c, SP.3.b)*
7. **Sample answer: The process of turning raw potatoes into potato chips removes all the vitamin C.** *(DOK Level: 2; Content Topic: P.a.1; Practice: SP.1.c, SP.3.b)*

LESSON 22

PAGE 202

Relate to the Topic

Many answers are possible. Sample answer: I rode the bicycle to the store to buy groceries. The bicycle had ten speeds. *(DOK Level: 1; Content Topic: P.b.3; Practice: SP.6.c)*

Reading Strategy

1. **Many answers are possible. Sample answer: when I needed to pry something open or lift something heavy** *(DOK Level: 1; Content Topic: P.b.3; Practice: SP.6.c)*

2. **Many answers are possible. Sample answer: in a bicycle or the inside of a machine** *(DOK Level: 1; Content Topic: P.b.3; Practice: SP.6.c)*

PAGE 204

1. **B**   2. **B**
   (DOK Level: 2; Content Topic: P.b.3; Practice: SP.1.c)

PAGE 205

A *(DOK Level: 2; Content Topic: P.b.2, P.b.3; Practice: SP.1.a, SP.3.b)*

PAGES 206–207

1. **force** *(DOK Level: 1; Content Topic: P.b.2, P.b.3; Practice: SP.1.b)*

2. **simple machine** *(DOK Level: 1; Content Topic: P.b.3; Practice: SP.1.b)*

3. **compound machine** *(DOK Level: 1; Content Topic: P.b.3; Practice: SP.1.b)*

4. **mechanical advantage** *(DOK Level: 1; Content Topic: P.b.3; Practice: SP.1.b)*

5. **work** *(DOK Level: 1; Content Topic: P.b.3; Practice: SP.1.b)*

6. **A** *(DOK Level: 1; Content Topic: P.b.2; Practice: SP.1.b)*

7. **A**   8. **A**
   (DOK Level: 1; Content Topic: P.b.3; Practice: SP.1.a)

9. **B**   10. **A**   11. **C**
   (DOK Level: 1; Content Topic: P.b.3; Practice: SP.1.a)

12. **B. The wheel and the axle turn in the same direction.** *(DOK Level: 2; Content Topic: P.b.3; Practice: SP.1.c)* The arrows next to

the word *Wheel* and *Axle* both point in the counterclockwise direction.

13. **A. friction** *(DOK Level: 1; Content Topic: P.b.2; Practice: SP.1.a)* According to the article, friction is a force between surfaces that touch. To overcome friction, you must use extra effort.

14. **D. No work will be done** *(DOK Level: 1; Content Topic: P.b.2; Practice: SP.1.a)* If the resistance is larger than the effort, there will be no motion, and in physics, no motion means no work.

15. **Standing on the pedals adds to your effort force because you can use your weight—the downward pull of gravity—to help move the pedal.** *(DOK Level: 2; Content Topic: P.b.3; Practice: SP.3.b)*

16. **Many answers are possible. Sample answer: I went bike riding in the neighborhood and when I hit a bump in the street, the chain slipped off the gears. I had to stop and put it back on before I could go on.** *(DOK Level: 2; Content Topic: P.b.3; Practice: SP.6.c)*

PAGES 208–209

1. **inclined plane** *(DOK Level: 1; Content Topic: P.b.3; Practice: SP.1.a, SP.1.b)*

2. **screw** *(DOK Level: 1; Content Topic: P.b.3; Practice: SP.1.a, SP.1.b)*

3. **pulley** *(DOK Level: 1; Content Topic: P.b.3; Practice: SP.1.a, SP.1.b)*

4. **wedge** *(DOK Level: 1; Content Topic: P.b.3; Practice: SP.1.a, SP.1.b)*

5. **inclined plane** *(DOK Level: 2; Content Topic: P.b.3; Practice: SP.1.a, SP.3.b)*

6. **wedge** *(DOK Level: 2; Content Topic: P.b.3; Practice: SP.1.a, SP.3.b)*

7. **pulley** *(DOK Level: 2; Content Topic: P.b.3; Practice: SP.1.a, SP.3.b)*

8. **screw** *(DOK Level: 2; Content Topic: P.b.3; Practice: SP.1.a, SP.3.b)*

9. **Sample answer: I would disagree because the data table shows that the effort force required to move the 100-kg resistance force decreases as the ramp gets longer.** *(DOK Level: 3; Content Topic: P.b.3; Practice: SP.1.c, SP.3.b, SP.4.a)*

10. Sample answer: Mechanical Advantage = 8 and Resistance Force = 12.5 kg. The mechanical advantage is calculated by dividing length by height and 8/1 = 8. The resistance force is calculated by dividing effort force by mechanical advantage and 100/8 = 12.5 kg. *(DOK Level: 2; Content Topic: P.b.3; Practice: SP.3.c, SP.6.b, SP.7.b, SP.8.b)*

11. Sample answer: An inclined plane can be used to move a very heavy object, such as a motorcycle, to a desired height without having to lift it. *(DOK Level: 2; Content Topic: P.b.3; Practice: SP.1.c, SP.3.b)*

LESSON 23
PAGE 210

Relate to the Topic

In golf, momentum is transferred when the club hits the ball. In bowling, momentum is transferred when the ball hits the pins. *(DOK Level: 2; Content Topic: P.b.1; Practice: SP.1.a)*

Reading Strategy

1. a baseball bat *(DOK Level: 2; Content Topic: P.b.1; Practice: SP.1.c)*

2. The article is about corking bats. *(DOK Level: 2; Content Topic: P.b.1; Practice: SP.3.b)*

PAGE 212

A *(DOK Level: 2; Content Topic: P.b.1; Practice: SP.3.b)*

PAGE 213

1. fact *(DOK Level: 2; Content Topic: P.b.1; Practice: SP.3.b)*

2. opinion *(DOK Level: 2; Content Topic: P.b.1; Practice: SP.3.b)*

PAGES 214–215

1. collision   2. momentum
3. elastic   4. Energy
(DOK Level: 1; Content Topic: P.b.1, P.b.3; Practice: SP.1.b)

5. A *(DOK Level: 2; Content Topic: P.b.1; Practice: SP.1.a)*

6. A, B, C *(DOK Level: 2; Content Topic: P.b.1; Practice: SP.1.a)*

7. A *(DOK Level: 2; Content Topic: P.b.1; Practice: SP.1.a)*

8. B *(DOK Level: 2; Content Topic: P.b.1; Practice: SP.1.a)*

9. A, B, C *(DOK Level: 2; Content Topic: P.b.1; Practice: SP.1.a)*

10. D. A standing object will move if enough momentum is transferred. *(DOK Level: 2; Content Topic: P.b.1; Practice: SP.3.b)* This is the only conclusion supported by the facts in the article.

11. C. A corked bat is lighter than a solid bat. *(DOK Level: 2; Content Topic: P.b.1; Practice: SP.4.a)* This statement represents a measurement, which is a fact. The other options are statements of what people believe, think, or feel. These words indicate opinions.

12. C. Cars are not very elastic. *(DOK Level: 2; Content Topic: P.b.1; Practice: SP.3.b)* If cars were elastic, then they would spring back into shape after a collision. Instead, they remain crumpled and dented.

13. The sport utility vehicle has more momentum because it is heavier than the compact car. *(DOK Level: 2; Content Topic: P.b.1; Practice: SP.6.c)*

14. Many answers are possible. Sample answer: I was in a car on a snowy day, going very slowly around a corner, when the car in front of me braked sharply. I braked, too, but the snowplow behind me did not stop in time. The blade of the plow hit the trunk lid of my car, denting it. Luckily, we were all going so slowly that not much momentum was involved and no one was hurt. *(DOK Level: 2; Content Topic: P.b.1; Practice: SP.6.c)*

PAGES 216–217

1. Sample answer: Use the triple beam balance to measure and record the mass of each marble. Make an elevated ramp by placing the edge of a metric ruler on two textbooks. Use a piece of masking tape to mark where the ruler touches the floor. Hold the small marble on the groove at the

top of the ruler. Let go of the marble and let it travel until it stops. Measure and record the distance the marble travels. Repeat these steps two more times with the small marble. Repeat all steps with the large marble. *(DOK Level: 2; Content Topic: P.b.1; Practice: SP.2.d)*

2. Sample answer: The marble with the greatest mass will have the most momentum and will travel farthest. *(DOK Level: 2; Content Topic: P.b.1; Practice: SP.2.b)*

3. the mass of the marble *(DOK Level: 2; Content Topic: P.b.1; Practice: SP.2.e)*

4. the distance the marble traveled *(DOK Level: 2; Content Topic: P.b.1; Practice: SP.2.e)*

5. D. 45 kg × m/s *(DOK Level: 1; Content Topic: P.b.1; Practice: SP.1.a, SP.6.b, SP.8.b)* Momentum is calculated by multiplying the mass times the velocity. 15 kg × 3 m/s = 45 kg × m/s.

6. Sample answer: As mass increases, momentum increases and the marble travels farther. *(DOK Level: 2; Content Topic: P.b.1; Practice: SP.1.a, SP.3.b)*

7. Sample answer: The data support/do not support my hypothesis. *(DOK Level: 2; Content Topic: P.b.1; Practice: SP.1.a, SP.2.b)*

8. Sample answer: Completing multiple trials with each marble helps ensure that the results are more accurate. *(DOK Level: 2; Content Topic: P.b.1; Practice: SP.2.a, SP.2.c)*

9. Sample answer: The average distance traveled by a 50 g marble will be greater than 53.87 cm. *(DOK Level: 2; Content Topic: P.b.1; Practice: SP.1.a, SP.3.c)*

LESSON 24

PAGE 218

Relate to the Topic
Many answers are possible. Sample answer: I enjoy listening to rock music and R & B. The instruments are usually a guitar, a bass, and

drums. *(DOK Level: 1; Content Topic: P.a.5; Practice: SP.3.b)*

Reading Strategy

1. The sound of a foghorn is much lower than the sound of a referee's whistle. *(DOK Level: 1; Content Topic: P.a.5; Practice: SP.3.b)*

2. The sound of an exploding firecracker is much louder than the sound of a snapping twig. *(DOK Level: 1; Content Topic: P.a.5; Practice: SP.3.b)*

PAGE 220

A *(DOK Level: 2; Content Topic: P.a.5; Practice: SP.1.a, SP.7.a)*

PAGE 221

B *(DOK Level: 2; Content Topic: P.a.5; Practice: SP.1.c)*

PAGES 222–223

1. B 2. F 3. E
4. A 5. C 6. D
(DOK Level: 1; Content Topic: P.a.5; Practice: SP.1.b)

7. vibration that creates alternating regions of compression and decompression traveling through air *(DOK Level: 1; Content Topic: P.a.5; Practice: SP.1.a)*

8. B 9. A 10. B
(DOK Level: 1; Content Topic: P.a.5; Practice: SP.1.a)

11. amplitude *(DOK Level: 1; Content Topic: P.a.5; Practice: SP.1.a)*

12. B. Pitch depends on the amount of tension in the part that vibrates. *(DOK Level: 2; Content Topic: P.a.5; Practice: SP.1.a)* Stretching a rubber band increases the tension in it, raising the pitch when the rubber band vibrates.

13. A. resonance *(DOK Level: 2; Content Topic: P.a.5; Practice: SP.1.a)* When the music box is held in the air, only the box vibrates. But when it is placed on a table, it causes the table to vibrate at the same frequency through resonance. That makes the sound louder.

14. **D. rustling leaves and conversation** *(DOK Level: 2; Content Topic: P.a.5; Practice: SP.1.c)* The sound of a hair dryer has a loudness of 75 decibels. Rustling leaves (40 decibels) and conversation (60 decibels) are both quieter because those decibel levels are lower than 75.

15. **Sample answer: Most men are larger than most women, so most men have larger vocal cords than most women have. As with musical instruments, larger size correlates with the ability to produce lower-pitched sounds.** *(DOK Level: 2; Content Topic: P.a.5; Practice: SP.1.a)*

16. **No, he is not correct. An overtone frequency has to be a multiple of the note's frequency. 750 is not a multiple of 370 because $370 \times 2 = 740$.** *(DOK Level: 2; Content Topic: P.a.5; Practice: SP.4.a)*

PAGES 224–225

1. **B. SONAR** *(DOK Level: 1; Content Topic: P.a.5; Practice: SP.1.a, SP.1.b)* Volcanoes, earthquakes, and tornadoes produce infrasonic waves. SONAR produces ultrasonic waves.

2. **15 Hz** *(DOK Level: 1; Content Topic: P.a.5; Practice: SP.1.a)*

3. **ultrasonic** *(DOK Level: 1; Content Topic: P.a.5; Practice: SP.1.a, SP.1.b)*

4. **infrasonic** *(DOK Level: 1; Content Topic: P.a.5; Practice: SP.1.a, SP.1.b)*

5. **bat, beluga whale, and moth** *(DOK Level: 2; Content Topic: P.a.5; Practice: SP.1.c, SP.3.b)*

6. **Sample answer: A human can hear lower frequencies than a dolphin can, but the dolphin can hear frequencies much higher than a human can.** *(DOK Level: 2; Content Topic: P.a.5; Practice: SP.1.c, SP.3.b)*

7. **Sample answer: Theses devices could help scientists learn more about how animals use ultrasonic waves to communicate with each other.** *(DOK Level: 2; Content Topic: P.a.5; Practice: SP.1.c, SP.3.b)*

8. **Sample answer: Elephants have very good low-range hearing and may be able to detect some of the infrasonic waves produced by the tsunami.** *(DOK Level: 2; Content Topic: P.a.5; Practice: SP.1.c, SP.3.b)*

9. **Sample answer: The dog whistle can be heard by the dog but not by a human, so its use won't disturb the trainer or other people nearby.** *(DOK Level: 2; Content Topic: P.a.5; Practice: SP.1.c, SP.3.b)*

SCIENCE AT WORK
PAGE 227

1. **C. spray foam** *(DOK Level: 1; Content Topic: P.a.1; Practice: SP.1.a)*

2. **D. foil insulation** *(DOK Level: 1; Content Topic: P.a.1; Practice: SP.1.a)*

3. **Sample answer: It would be a good idea to install insulation material under the floor of the room above the garage because garages are not usually heated. So, when the outside temperature is cold and you want the room to stay warm, the insulation material would limit the amount of heated air escaping through the floor into the garage. If the room were being cooled by air conditioning, the insulation material would block the passage of warm air from the garage into the air-conditioned room.** *(DOK Level: 2; Content Topic: P.a.1; Practice: SP.3.b)*

UNIT 3 REVIEW
PAGES 228–231

1. **exothermic reaction** *(DOK Level: 1; Content Topic: P.a.2; Practice: SP.1.b)*

2. **endothermic reaction** *(DOK Level: 1; Content Topic: P.a.2; Practice: SP.1.b)*

3. **chemical reaction** *(DOK Level: 1; Content Topic: P.a.2; Practice: SP.1.b)*

4. **D. The reaction in instant cold packs is endothermic.** *(DOK Level: 1; Content Topic: P.a.2; Practice: SP.1.a)* The passage states that the pack feels cold after the chemical reaction takes place. Thus, the reaction takes in heat. A reaction that takes in heat is an endothermic reaction

5. **B. combustion** *(DOK Level: 1; Content Topic: P.a.2; Practice: SP.1.a)* A gas heater works by burning gas. The passage states that combustion is another name for burning.

6. **nuclear fusion** *(DOK Level: 1; Content Topic: P.a.4; Practice: SP.1.b)*

7. **sun** *(DOK Level: 1; Content Topic: P.a.4; Practice: SP.1.b)*

8. **helium** *(DOK Level: 1; Content Topic: P.a.4; Practice: SP.1.b)*

9. **C. Fusion reactions do not take place naturally on Earth.** *(DOK Level: 1; Content Topic: P.a.4; Practice: SP.1.a, SP.4.a)* The text states that there is nowhere on Earth as hot as the sun, where fusion can take place. Also, scientists are exploring "cold fusion" reactions in the lab, which is artificial.

10. **the force needed; the distance moved** *(DOK Level: 1; Content Topic: P.b.3; Practice: SP.1.b)*

11. **Friction** *(DOK Level: 1; Content Topic: P.b.3; Practice: SP.1.b)*

12. **C. pushing a wheeled 75-pound cart up a ramp three feet long** *(DOK Level: 2; Content Topic: P.b.3; Practice: SP.3.b)* Options 1, 2, and 5 are incorrect because they involve lifting, which takes more force than using an inclined plane. Option 3 is incorrect because friction adds resistance; thus you need more force to push a box than a wheeled cart.

13. **Sample answer: The wheels of the car and the road rub against each other and create friction.** *(DOK Level: 2; Content Topic: P.b.3; Practice: SP.1.a, SP.7.a)*

14. **A. The cue ball has more momentum before the collision than after.** *(DOK Level: 2; Content Topic: P.b.3; Practice: SP.1.c)* The arrow near the cue ball shows that the cue ball is moving before the collision but not after. Since an object that is not moving has no momentum, the cue ball has more momentum before the collision. Option 4 is incorrect because the cue ball has no speed after the collision.

Science Extension

Many answers are possible. Sample answers: Inclined plane—driveway; Wedge—door stop, ax; Lever—bottle opener, hammer, tweezers, nutcracker, crowbar, balance; Wheel and axle—screwdriver, steering wheel, car wheel, wrench, faucet; Gears—can opener, bicycle gears, salad spinner, mechanical clock, egg beater; Screw—corkscrew, screw-top lid

Mini-Test Unit 3
PAGES 232–233

1. **A. distilled water** *(DOK Level: 2; Content Topic: P.c.4; Practice: SP.1.c, SP.3.d)* The graph shows that of the four samples, distilled water contains the lowest concentration of minerals, with close to 0 ppm.

2. **C. decreases as mineral content increases** *(DOK Level: 2; Content Topic: P.c.4; Practice: SP.1.c, SP.3.b)* The line on the graph shows that as the mineral content in the water increases, the amount of water absorbed by 0.1 g of sodium polyacrylate decreases.

3. **A. absorbs 50 mL of this water** *(DOK Level: 2; Content Topic: P.c.4; Practice: SP.1.c, SP.4.a)* The graph shows the amount of water of different types that is absorbed by 0.1 gram of sodium polyacrylate. By looking at the reading for tap water, you can see that 0.1 gram of sodium polyacrylate absorbed 50 mL of tap water. So if 0.1 gram of sodium polyacrylate absorbed 50 mL of the unknown sample of water, this would be strong evidence that the unknown sample consisted of tap water.

4. **D. to soak up urine in disposable diapers** *(DOK Level: 2; Content Topic: P.c.4; Practice: SP.1.a, SP.3.b)* The paragraph states that sodium polyacrylate absorbs water; urine is mostly water. Therefore, sodium polyacrylate might function well in disposable diapers to absorb urine.

5. **C. Bowling pins do not have momentum unless they are moving.** *(DOK Level: 1; Content Topic: P.b.1; Practice: SP.1.a)* The paragraph explains that bowling pins have no momentum when they are stationary and gain momentum when they move.

6. **D. Loud sounds can kill cells in the inner ear.** *(DOK Level: 2; Content Topic: P.a.5; Practice: SP.4.a)* Earplugs reduce the volume of sounds that reach the inner ear, so wearing ear plugs in noisy places can protect the specialized cells in the inner ear and preserve hearing.

7. **B. Design B is the best choice for buildings in noisy neighborhoods.** *(DOK Level: 2; Content Topic: P.a.5; Practice: SP.1.c, SP.4.a)* According to the information in the graph, Design B transmits the lowest percentage of sound. In a building with these windows, less outside noise would be transmitted into the building.

POSTTEST

PAGES 236–244

1. **A. A male ant has wings and a worker ant does not.** *(DOK Level: 1; Content Topic: L.d.1; Practice: SP.1.a, SP.1.c)* The drawings show two main differences between male and worker ants. First, male ants have wings and workers do not. Second, male ants are larger than worker ants. The second difference is not listed among the options therefore, the correct answer is the first option.

2. **D. The queen does not mate again.** *(DOK Level: 2; Content Topic: L.d.1; Practice: SP.1.a, SP.3.b)* The males and queen mate during a flight they take outside the anthill. After that, the queen loses her wings. Since the queen can no longer fly, she cannot go on a mating flight again.

3. **B. Substance 2** *(DOK Level: 2; Content Standard: P.c.4; Practice: SP.1.c, SP.2.b, SP.3.b)* As water temperature decreases, less of Substances 1 and 3 dissolve in the water, supporting the students' hypothesis.

More of Substance 2 dissolves as the water temperature decreases, and this result weakens the students' hypothesis that decreasing water temperature always decreases the amount of a substance that will dissolve in the water.

4. **C. the water temperature** *(DOK Level: 2; Content Standard: P.c.4; Practice: SP.1.c, SP.2.e, SP.3.b)* The independent variable in an investigation is the variable that is purposely changed. The water temperature is purposely decreased by 10-degree intervals throughout the investigation. The amount of water is constant and the amount of substance that dissolves in the water is the dependent variable. The time it takes for the substances to dissolve is not a consideration in this investigation.

5. **B. planting or weeding** *(DOK Level: 2; Content Standard: P.a.4; Practice: SP.1.c, SP.3.b)* The bar graph shows the amount of energy, measured in calories, that a person uses when performing different yard chores. The task that requires the least energy (the fewest calories per hour) is planting or weeding.

6. **B. 4,100** *(DOK Level: 2; Content Standard: ES.a.2; Practice: SP.1.c, SP.6.b)* First find the years 1986–1990 on the horizontal axis. Then moving straight up from there, find the point on the trend line that represents those years. Read across to the vertical axis to see how many tornadoes occurred during that period.

7. **D. There were more tornadoes during the 1990s than during the 1980s.** *(DOK Level: 3; Content Standard: ES.a.2; Practice: SP.1.c, SP.3.b)* In general the trend line slopes upward. For the periods 1991–1995 and 1996–2000, there were far more tornadoes than during the periods 1981–1985 and 1986–1990.

8. **C. The ball travels 350 feet less in the air at Shea Stadium than it would in a vacuum.** *(DOK Level: 2; Content Standard: P.b.1; Practice: SP.4.a)* Although the other options are all true statements, only this

option provides evidence to support the conclusion that air resistance affects a baseball.

9. **A. Cereal A has less sodium and sugar than Cereal B.** *(DOK Level: 3; Content Standard: L.a.3; Practice: SP.1.c, SP.3.b, SP.4.a)* Cereal A has the same amount of potassium as Cereal B. Cereal B also has more total fat and Calories than Cereal A.

10. **B. 2** *(DOK Level: 2; Content Standard: P.c.1; Practice: SP.1.b, SP.6.b)* Elements are substances that cannot be broken down into simpler substances.

11. **D. Combustion changes some solid matter to gas and energy.** *(DOK Level: 3; Content Standard: P.c.3; Practice: SP.4.a)* The last option explains that matter changes state during combustion and is changed without being destroyed. The other options are true statements, but they do not say anything about the amount of matter involved before or after combustion.

12. **A. hypothesis** *(DOK Level: 2; Content Standard: L.a.3; Practice: SP.2.b, SP.3.b)* A hypothesis is a testable statement. An investigation can be conducted to determine whether people prefer the taste of organically grown vegetables or conventionally grown vegetables.

13. **C. data** *(DOK Level: 2; Content Standard: L.a.3; Practice: SP.1.c, SP.3.a)* When the tasters filled out the questionnaires, they provided Ruth with information about their preferences.

14. **D. conclusion** *(DOK Level: 2; Content Standard: L.a.3; Practice: SP.3.b)* Based on the questionnaire results, Ruth concluded that organically grown vegetables do taste better than conventionally grown vegetables. She had thought so before the experiment; but she had no data to support the idea. Once Ruth collected data about the preferences of a group of people, she could draw a valid conclusion.

15. **C. There are about the same number of bones in the arms and hands as in the legs and feet.** *(DOK Level: 2; Content Standard: L.a.1; Practice: SP.1.c)* The wedge that represents the percentage of bones in the arms and hands and the wedge that represents the percentage of bones in the legs and feet are about the same size, and the percentages are very close. This means that there are about the same number of bones in the arms and hands as in the legs and feet.

16. **A. Yeast cells reproduce by growing a bud that splits off the parent cell.** *(DOK Level: 2; Content Standard: L.d.1; Practice: SP.1.c, SP.6.c)* The diagram shows the budding process of a yeast cell. This process results in two cells—the original cell and the new cell. The first option summarizes the process shown in the diagram. The remaining options describe details of the budding process.

17. **D. DNA paternity tests can be done with or without cells from the alleged father.** *(DOK Level: 2; Content Standard: L.e.1; Practice: SP.3.b)* According to the information, some DNA paternity tests are done with the alleged father's cell samples. However, if the alleged father is not available, then the test can be done with the cell samples from the parents of the alleged father.

18. **B. increased pollution of the Mississippi River basin and the Great Lakes** *(DOK Level: 2; Content Standard: L.c.5; Practice: SP.1.c, SP.3.b)* The map shows eagle nesting sites along the shores of the Great Lakes and along the banks of rivers that make up the Mississippi River system. Pollution to these bodies of water could harm the bald eagles nesting in these extensive areas. The other options are incorrect because the map indicates that few bald eagles nest in these regions.

19. **D. about 8,000** *(DOK Level: 2; Content Standard: L.a.4; Practice: SP.1.c, SP.3.c)* If the current graph is extended to 325 minutes, then the first three options would be too low. The number of bacteria should be about 8,000.

20. **A. Air pollution comes from transportation and industry.** *(DOK Level: 2; Content Standard: P.a.4; Practice: SP.1.c, SP.3.b)* The chart shows five air pollutants and their sources, all from transportation (motor vehicles) or industry (smelting, manufacturing plants, power plants, refineries, etc.). The other options all provide details about particular pollutants.

21. **C. Hector should use the same amount of water in each of the four pots.** *(DOK Level: 2; Content Standard: P.a.1; Practice: SP.2.a)* To determine how the amount of salt affects water's boiling point, Hector must use the same amount of water in each pot.

22. **A. blocks the sun except for a rim of light** *(DOK Level: 2; Content Standard: ES.c.2; Practice: SP.1.c)* According to the two diagrams, the main difference between a total solar eclipse and a partial solar eclipse is the amount of sun blocked by the moon. In a total eclipse the moon almost entirely blocks the sun, but in a partial eclipse the moon blocks only a portion of the sun.

23. **C. Of the volcanic eruptions listed in the graph, Tuxtla, in Mexico, caused the most known deaths.** *(DOK Level: 2; Content Standard: ES.a.2; Practice: SP.3.b)* According to the graph, about 50,000 people died when Tuxtla erupted—the highest number of known deaths given on this graph.

24. **C. The model does not show the sizes of the different types of atoms in the molecule.** *(DOK Level: 2; Content Standard: P.c.1; Practice: SP.3.b, SP.7.a)* The model is three-dimensional, and it does show the number of atoms and chemical bonds in the molecule. Since all of the foam balls are the same size, the model will not represent the sizes of the different types of atoms in the molecule.

25. **B. 25%** *(DOK Level: 2; Content Standard: L.e.2; Practice: SP.3.c, SP.6.b, SP.8.b, SP.8.c)* A cross between two chickens with the genotype of Bb will likely result in ¼ or 25% of the offspring with the genotype BB, ½ or 50% with the genotype of Bb, and ¼ or 25% with the genotype of bb. The chickens with the genotypes BB or Bb will have black feathers (75%) and the chickens with the genotype bb will have white feathers (25%).

absolute age the number of years ago a rock formed

activation energy the energy necessary to start a chemical reaction

adaptation a trait that makes a plant or an animal better able to live in its environment

adult the stage of an organism's life cycle in which it is fully grown and developed

aerobic needing oxygen to live

air mass a large body of air with certain temperature and moisture

amniocentesis a test performed on pregnant women that detects certain birth disorders

amplitude the height of a wave

antibiotic a drug that fights bacteria

antibody a protein made by white blood cells that attacks and kills invading germs

antigen a foreign protein

aqueduct a pipe or concrete channel that carries water from a reservoir

artery a large blood vessel that carries blood away from the heart to parts of the body

asthenosphere the soft, less-rigid region of the mantle on which the plates of the lithosphere float and move around

atmosphere the air surrounding a planet

atom the smallest particle of an element

bacteria simple one-celled organisms

bar graph a type of illustration that is used to compare sets of information

basal cell skin cancer a type of slow-growing cancer that often appears on the hands or face as an open sore, reddish patch, mole, or scar

big bang theory the widely accepted model of how the universe began and developed

biome a large region with a certain climate and certain living things

black dwarf a dense body of gas formed from a white dwarf after it no longer emits light

black hole an infinite warp in space with gravity strong enough to trap light

boiling the rapid change of matter from a liquid to a gas

caption a short passage that accompanies a photograph or illustration

carbon dioxide–oxygen cycle a process in which plants use carbon dioxide given off by other living things and make oxygen, which is in turn used by the other living things

caterpillar the wormlike stage in the life cycle of a butterfly or moth

cause something that makes another thing happen

cell the smallest unit of a living thing that can carry on life processes

cell membrane a layer around the cell that controls what can enter or leave the cell

cell wall stiff outer layer around a plant cell that provides support

cellular respiration the process by which living things take in oxygen and release carbon dioxide to obtain energy

chart an organized list that gives information in a form that is easy to read

chemical change a change in the property of matter; a chemical change makes new substances

chemical equation a statement that shows the reactants and products of a reaction

chemical formula a group of symbols used to describe a compound (example: H_2O is the chemical formula for water)

chemical reaction a process in which elements or compounds are changed into other substances

chemical symbol a kind of shorthand that chemists use in which one or two letters stand for an element

chemistry the study of matter and its changes

chloroplast a structure in a plant cell that uses chlorophyll and sunlight to make food

cholesterol a fatlike substance found in all animals

chromosome a strand of genetic material, or DNA

circle graph a graph used to show parts of a whole; also known as a pie chart

classifying grouping things that are similar to help understand how they work

climate change an increase in the average surface temperature of Earth

collision the result of a moving object striking another object

combustion the chemical change also known as burning, in which oxygen reacts with fuel to create light and heat

commensalism a symbiotic relationship in which one species benefits but does not help or hurt the other species

compare to tell how things are alike

compound two or more elements combined chemically

compound machine a machine made up of two or more simple machines

conclusion a logical judgment based on facts

condensation the change from a gas to a liquid

conduction the transfer of heat from one particle of matter to another

conductor a substance that transfers heat well

conglomerate a type of sedimentary rock formed from large pebbles and stones

constellation a pattern of stars in the night sky

context surrounding material; you can often figure out the meaning of an unknown word by looking at its context—the rest of the words in the sentence

continental polar air mass a cold, dry air mass; for example, one that forms over Canada and the northern United States

continental shelf the nearly flat area of the ocean bottom where the ocean meets the continent

continental slope the sloping area that extends from the edge of the continental shelf to the ocean basin

continental tropical air mass a warm, dry air mass; for example, one that forms over the southwestern United States

contrast to tell how things are different

controlled experiment an experiment that tests only one variable

convection the transfer of heat through the movement of a fluid

convection current the circular patterns of rising and sinking fluid movement

convergence the independent evolution of similar parts of unrelated organisms as adaptations to the environment (example: wings in bats, birds, and butterflies)

core the center of something such as the sun or Earth

crust Earth's outermost and thinnest layer

cytoplasm a jellylike material that makes up most of a cell

dark energy the force driving the accelerated expansion of the universe

dependent variable the variable that changes as a result of an experiment

details small pieces of information that explain or support a main idea

diagram a picture that explains what something looks like or how it works

distillation the process for separating liquid mixtures

DNA the genetic material found in chromosomes

dominant trait a trait that can override a recessive trait

Down syndrome a disorder caused by an extra chromosome; children born with Down syndrome are mildly to severely mentally retarded and may also have other health problems

Earth and space science the study of Earth and the universe

earthquake shaking of the ground due to grinding of rock along plate boundaries

ecosystem an area in which living and nonliving things interact

effect something that happens as a result of a cause

effort the force that is being used to do work

egg in animals, the female reproductive cell

egg mass a clump of eggs

elastic able to be stretched or compressed and then returned to the original shape

electromagnetic field (EM field) the energy field surrounding and created by an electric current

electron a particle in atoms that has a negative electrical charge

element a substance that cannot be broken down into other substances by ordinary means, such as heating or crushing

embryo an organism in the early stages of development; a developing baby from the third to eighth week in the mother's womb

EM field see electromagnetic field

endothermic reaction a process in which heat is taken in (example: photosynthesis)

energy the ability of matter to do work

equator the imaginary circle around Earth halfway between the North and South Poles

erode to wear away

evaporation the slow change of a liquid to a gas

evolution the gradual change in a species over time

exothermic reaction a process in which heat is produced (example: combustion)

fact a statement about something that actually happened or actually exists

fat a substance that provides energy and building material for the body

fault a fracture in Earth's crust along which rocks slide past each other

fetal alcohol syndrome (FAS) a group of birth defects that can occur when a pregnant woman drinks alcohol

fetus a developing baby from the third to ninth month

flower in a plant, the reproductive organ that produces seeds and pollen

flu see influenza

force a push or a pull

forecast a prediction, as of the weather

fossil the remains or imprint of a long-dead organism

fossil fuel a fuel, such as coal, oil, or natural gas, that is formed from the remains of plants or animals that lived hundreds of millions of years ago

freezing the change in matter from a liquid to a solid

friction a force between surfaces that touch

front the leading edge of a moving air mass

fuel a source of energy

fusion see nuclear fusion

galaxy a massive system of gases and many stars held together by gravity

gas a state of matter that does not have a definite size or shape and expands to fill its container

gear a wheel with teeth; each gear turns on its own center

geologic time scale a chronological record of the major events in Earth's natural history, with oldest events at the bottom and newer events near the top

geologist a scientist that studies Earth and its history

geology the study of Earth and its history

genetic screening tests that can tell if certain disorders are likely to be inherited

genetics the study of how traits are inherited

glacier a mass of ice that forms when more snow falls than melts

gland a small organ that makes hormones

glossary an alphabetical listing of important words and their definitions, located at the end of a text

gravity the natural force of attraction between two objects (example: the pull of Earth on humans)

greenhouse effect the warming of Earth caused by the absorption of infrared radiation into gases in the atmosphere

groundwater water that is found underground (examples: springs and wells)

heading the name of an article section that tells the topic or main idea of the text that follows

heat the flow of thermal energy

heat engine a device that uses heat to do work

heat transfer the flow of heat through a substance or from one substance to another

hereditary capable of being passed from a parent to an offspring through a father's sperm or a mother's egg

heredity the passing of traits from parents to their young

hormone a chemical made in glands

hydrocarbon a compound made mostly of hydrogen and carbon

hypothesis a possible answer to a question

igneous rock rock formed when molten rock hardens

implied not stated

inclined plane a simple machine with a long, sloping surface that helps move an object (example: ramp)

independent variable the variable changed by a scientist in a controlled experiment

inference the use of information to figure out things that are not actually stated

influenza (flu) an illness caused by a virus

infrared radiation the energy Earth radiates back into the atmosphere

inherit to acquire a trait or disease that is passed on from one's parents (examples: hair color, Huntington's disease)

inner planets the four planets closest to the sun: Mercury, Venus, Earth, and Mars

insulator a substance that does not transfer heat well

ion an atom with a positive or negative electric charge

joint the place where two or more bones come together

key something that explains the symbols on a map or a graph

kindling temperature the temperature at which a substance will burn

kinetic energy the energy of motion

landform a feature on Earth's surface

lever a bar that turns on a pivot

life cycle the series of changes an animal goes through in its life

life science the study of living things and how they affect one another

ligament a strong band of tissue that connects bones at joints

line graph a graph that shows how one thing changes as a second thing changes

liquid a state of matter that takes up a definite amount of space but does not have a definite shape

lithosphere the fractured, rigid layer of rock formed from Earth's crust and uppermost part of the mantle

main idea the topic of a paragraph, passage, or diagram

main sequence star a star that remains relatively stable for millions or billions of years

mantle the dense hot layer of rock beneath Earth's crust

mammal an animal with a backbone, hair or fur, and milk-producing glands to feed its young

map a drawing that shows places or features on Earth

maritime polar air mass a cold, moist air mass; for example, one that forms over the northern Atlantic Ocean or the northern Pacific Ocean

maritime tropical air mass a warm, moist air mass; for example, one that forms over the Caribbean Sea, the middle of the Atlantic Ocean, or the middle of the Pacific Ocean

mechanical advantage the number of times a machine multiplies your effort to do work

meiosis the process of sperm and egg cell formation

melanoma a fast-growing skin cancer that may appear as oddly shaped blotches

melting the change in matter from a solid to a liquid

mesosphere the layer of Earth's atmosphere above the stratosphere

metamorphic rock rock formed in conditions of great heat and pressure

meteorologist a scientist who studies changes in Earth's atmosphere to forecast the weather

mitochondria the parts of a cell that give the cell the energy it needs to grow and reproduce

mitosis the process by which a cell's nucleus divides and therefore reproduces

mixture a combination of two or more kinds of matter that can be separated by physical means

molecule the smallest particle of a compound

momentum the property of a moving object that is a product of its mass and velocity

monounsaturated fat a type of fat found in some vegetable products

mutation a change in a gene

mutualism a relationship in which two species help each other

natural selection the survival of organisms best suited to their environment

nebula a giant cloud of gas and dust in space

neutron a particle with no electrical charge that is found in the nucleus of an atom

neutron star a super-dense sphere formed after a supernova

nitrate a substance made by soil-dwelling bacteria using nitrogen from the air

nuclear reaction changes in the nucleus of an atom

nuclear fusion the reaction in which two nuclei combine, forming a larger atom

nucleus in life science, a cell's control center, which contains genetic material; in chemistry and physics, the protons and neutrons forming the core of an atom (plural: nuclei)

ocean basin the bottom of the sea

opinion a statement that expresses what a person or group of people think, feel, or believe about a fact

organ a group of tissues working together to perform a specific function

organ system a group of two or more organs

osteoporosis a condition of brittle bones common to older people, especially women

outer planets the four planets farthest from the sun: Jupiter, Saturn, Uranus, and Neptune.

oxidation the process in which a substance reacts with oxygen, causing the formation of a new compound called an oxide

overtone a frequency of sound that is an exact multiple of another frequency produced at the same time

ozone a form of oxygen

paleontologist a scientist who studies ancient forms of life

paraphrase to restate information in a different way that keeps the original meaning

parasite an organism that lives on or in another organism and harms it

parasitism a symbiotic relationship in which one partner is helped and the other is hurt

pedigree chart a diagram that shows family relationships and the occurrence of particular genetic traits

photosynthesis the process by which plants use carbon dioxide, energy from sunlight, and water to make food

pH scale a measurement from 0 to 14 of the strength of an acid or a base

physical change a change in the appearance of matter without a change in its properties (example: the dissolving of sugar in water)

physics the study of energy and forces and their effect on matter

pitch the perceived frequency of a sound

pivot the point around which an object turns

placenta a structure that attaches the embryo/fetus to the uterus and allows substances to pass between the embryo/fetus and the mother

plaque deposits of cholesterol on the inside walls of arteries

plate a large piece of Earth's lithosphere

plate boundaries the edges of plates of the lithosphere where two plates meet

plate tectonics the theory that Earth's lithosphere consists of plates that slowly move as result of currents in the mantle

pneumonia an infection of the lungs caused by viruses or bacteria

polyunsaturated fat a type of fat found in some vegetable foods and fish

precipitation water falling from the atmosphere in the form of rain, snow, or sleet

process diagram a type of drawing that shows steps in a process, often with arrows showing how one step leads to another

product a substance that forms in a chemical reaction

proton a positively charged particle in the nucleus of an atom

protostar a hot, dense, fast-spinning cloud in space in the process of becoming a star

Punnett square a diagram used to show all possible combinations of a trait among offspring of two parents

pupa the nonfeeding stage in the life cycle of some insects when their adult tissues are formed

pure tone a sound made up of a single frequency

radiant energy energy that exists in the form of waves, such as light waves or radio waves

radiation the transfer of heat by electromagnetic waves

radioactive decay the natural process by which unstable radioactive elements change to more stable elements

radiometric dating a process that determines the absolute age of rocks by measuring the decay of radioactive materials within them

reactant a substance that reacts in a chemical reaction

recessive trait a trait that will not appear if it is paired with a dominant trait

red giant a large, cool star that glows red

relative age the age of one rock in comparison to another rock

renewable resource a resource that does not get used up (example: water)

reservoir a lake created by a dam

resistance a force that must be overcome to do work

resonance the process in which a vibrating object causes another object to vibrate at the same frequency

resource a material that people need from Earth

respiration the process by which living things take in oxygen and release carbon dioxide to obtain energy

rhinovirus a virus that causes certain types of colds

ribosome a part of a cell that makes the proteins the cell needs in order to grow

saturated fat a type of fat that is solid at room temperature

scan to look over something quickly to find details

sedimentary rock rock formed when particles are deposited and then harden over time

sequence the order in which things happen

silicon the most common element in Earth's crust

simple machine a device to do work (example: lever)

skim to look over something quickly to get the main ideas

solar system a sun and the objects that revolve around it, such as planets and their moons

solid a state of matter that has a definite shape and takes up a definite amount of space

solubility the amount of a solute that will dissolve in a given amount of solvent at a given temperature and pressure

solute the substance in a solution that is present in the smaller amount

solution a type of mixture in which the ingredients are distributed evenly throughout

solvent the substance in a solution that is present in the greater amount

sound a sensation caused by vibrations and perceived by hearing

sound wave alternating regions of compressed and less compressed air

space probe unmanned spacecraft used for the exploration of space

spectrometer a device used to analyze what things are made of

species a group of organisms with similar characteristics that can interbreed to produce fertile offspring

sprain a joint injury in which the ligaments are stretched or torn

squamous cell skin cancer a type of cancer that looks like raised, pink spots or growths that may be open in the center

star a sphere of extremely hot, glowing gases that emits its own light due to nuclear reactions in its core

stationary front the zone between two air masses, caused when the masses stop moving

stratosphere the dry layer of Earth's atmosphere above the troposphere

substance matter that is of one particular type

summarize to condense or shorten a larger amount of information into a few sentences

supernova the powerful explosion of a large, massive star

symbiosis the interaction between two different species that have evolved a close relationship

table a type of chart that organizes information in rows and columns

temperature the measure of the average kinetic energy of particles in a substance

theory a well-supported explanation for observations made in the natural world

thermal energy the total energy of moving particles that make up matter

thermosphere the uppermost layer of the atmosphere

timbre the quality of a sound, which depends on the number and strength of overtones

timeline an illustration that shows when a series of events took place and the order in which they occurred

tissue a group of similar cells that perform the same function

topic sentence the sentence that contains the main idea in a paragraph

trait an inherited characteristic such as hair color or blood type

trench a deep canyon formed along a plate boundary

tropical rain forest dense forest found near the equator where the climate is hot and wet

troposphere the layer of Earth's atmosphere closest to the surface

ultraviolet light a type of light with wavelengths too short to be visible to the human eye; also known as black light

ultraviolet rays a type of harmful energy in sunlight

universe everything that exists, including all planets, stars, solar systems, and galaxies

uterus a woman's womb, in which an unborn baby develops

vaccination an injected dose of dead or weakened disease-causing agent; the body reacts to a vaccination by forming antibodies to fight the disease

vacuole a storage space for water and minerals in a cell

variable a factor tested in an experiment

virus a tiny particle of genetic material with a protein covering

volcano an opening in Earth's crust from which melted rock erupts

water cycle the circulation of water on Earth through evaporation from the surface into the atmosphere and back to the surface as precipitation

weather map a map showing where cold, warm, and stationary fronts are, as well as areas of high and low pressure

wheel and axle a simple machine composed of two objects that turn in a circular motion on the same center, multiplying both force and speed

white dwarf a very small, dense star formed from a star of low to average mass as it ages

work the process of using force to cause an object to move

zygote a fertilized egg resulting when the sperm from the father joins with the egg produced by the mother